W0010015

Exam Ref 70-767
Implementing a SQL
Data Warehouse

Jose Chinchilla
Raj Uchhana

Exam Ref 70-767 Implementing a SQL Data Warehouse

Published with the authorization of Microsoft Corporation by:
Pearson Education, Inc.

Copyright © 2018 by Pearson Education

ISBN-13: 978-1-5093-0647-3
ISBN-10: 1-5093-0647-1

Library of Congress Control Number: 2017953180
1 17

Trademarks

Microsoft and the trademarks listed at https://www.microsoft.com on the "Trademarks" webpage are trademarks of the Microsoft group of companies. All other marks are property of their respective owners.

Warning and Disclaimer

Special Sales

For information about buying this title in bulk quantities, or for special sales opportunities (which may include electronic versions; custom cover designs; and content particular to your business, training goals, marketing focus, or branding interests), please contact our corporate sales department at corpsales@pearsoned.com or (800) 382-3419.

For government sales inquiries, please contact governmentsales@pearsoned.com.

For questions about sales outside the U.S., please contact intlcs@pearson.com.

Editor-in-Chief	Greg Wiegand
Acquisitions Editor	Trina MacDonald
Development Editor	Troy Mott
Managing Editor	Sandra Schroeder
Senior Project Editor	Tracey Croom
Editorial Production	Backstop Media
Copy Editor	Christina Rudloff
Indexer	Julie Grady
Proofreader	Christina Rudloff
Technical Editor	Martin 'MC' Brown
Cover Designer	Twist Creative, Seattle

To my wife, Dolly, for creating a dream world where every day is a beautiful adventure and anything is possible. To our daughters, Ashia and Aria, who ignite passion into the world. And being a parent, I am humbled by all that my parents, Saubhagya and Usha, have done for us. For all the love and support you have all given me, you have my undying love and admiration.

—RAJ UCHHANA

Contents at a glance

Contents

What do you think of this book? We want to hear from you!

Microsoft is interested in hearing your feedback so we can continually improve our
books and learning resources for you. To participate in a brief online survey, please visit:

https://aka.ms/tellpress

chapter 3   Build data quality solutions   203

What do you think of this book? We want to hear from you!

Microsoft is interested in hearing your feedback so we can continually improve our books and learning resources for you. To participate in a brief online survey, please visit:

https://aka.ms/tellpress

Introduction

This Exam Ref is the official study guide for the new Microsoft 70-767 Implementing a SQL Data Warehouse certification exam. It offers professional-level preparation that helps candidates maximize their exam performance and sharpen their skills on the job. It focuses on the specific areas of expertise modern IT professionals need to successfully build modern data warehouses to support advanced business intelligence solutions.

The 70-767 exam focuses on the key elements of Data Warehousing using SQL Server 2016. It covers fundamental data modeling concepts, logical and physical database design and implementation. SQL Server Integration Services (SSIS) is covered in detail to provide IT professionals with a strong understanding of the SSIS control flow tasks and data flow transformations to support a ETL solution to load a data warehouse.

Master Data Services (MDS) and Data Quality Services (DQS) installation, configuration and development are also covered with step-by-step instructions to maintain master data and data quality solutions.

This book covers every major topic area found on the exam, but it does not cover every exam question. Only the Microsoft exam team has access to the exam questions, and Microsoft regularly adds new questions to the exam, making it impossible to cover specific questions. You should consider this book a supplement to your relevant real-world experience and other study materials. If you encounter a topic in this book that you do not feel completely comfortable with, use the "Need more review?" links you'll find in the text to find more information and take the time to research and study the topic. Great information is available on MSDN, TechNet, and in blogs and forums.

Organization of this book

This book is organized by the "Skills measured" list published for the exam. The "Skills measured" list is available for each exam on the Microsoft Learning website: *https://aka.ms/examlist*. Each chapter in this book corresponds to a major topic area in the list, and the technical tasks in each topic area determine a chapter's organization. If an exam covers six major topic areas, for example, the book will contain six chapters.

Microsoft certifications

Microsoft certifications distinguish you by proving your command of a broad set of skills and experience with current Microsoft products and technologies. The exams and corresponding certifications are developed to validate your mastery of critical competencies as you design and develop, or implement and support, solutions with Microsoft products and technologies both on-premises and in the cloud. Certification brings a variety of benefits to the individual and to employers and organizations.

> *MORE INFO* **ALL MICROSOFT CERTIFICATIONS**
>
> For information about Microsoft certifications, including a full list of available certifications, go to *https://www.microsoft.com/learning*.

Acknowledgments

Jose Chinchilla This book couldn't have been possible without the support and understanding from the entire editorial and production team, with special thanks to Trina MacDonald (Pearson) and Troy Mott (Backstop Media). It has been a long journey together.

Special thanks to my wife, Madeline, for providing me with the warmth, love and support that fueled the light in my life that allowed me to keep writing through many nights. To my children, Sofia, Stephanie and Sebastian, for filling my life with love and happiness and for reminding me everyday that there is so much out there to enjoy together.

Raj Uchhana My genuine appreciation for the dedication and patience of our publisher and editorial staff. Our editor, Trina MacDonald, a true professional and a friend all wrapped up in one, who orchestrated this book into existence. To Troy Mott, the Development Editor, for his tireless reviews and valuable suggestions. And to the Pearson Publishing house for giving us the privilege of spreading knowledge and learning. Finally, my gratitude to Jose Chinchilla, co-author, for all his assistance. He has genuine care and generosity for everyone.

Microsoft Virtual Academy

Build your knowledge of Microsoft technologies with free expert-led online training from Microsoft Virtual Academy (MVA). MVA offers a comprehensive library of videos, live events, and more to help you learn the latest technologies and prepare for certification exams. You'll find what you need here:

https://www.microsoftvirtualacademy.com

Quick access to online references

Throughout this book are addresses to webpages that the author has recommended you visit for more information. Some of these addresses (also known as URLs) can be painstaking to type into a web browser, so we've compiled all of them into a single list that readers of the print edition can refer to while they read.

Download the list at *https://aka.ms/examref767/downloads*.

The URLs are organized by chapter and heading. Every time you come across a URL in the book, find the hyperlink in the list to go directly to the webpage.

Errata, updates, & book support

We've made every effort to ensure the accuracy of this book and its companion content. You can access updates to this book—in the form of a list of submitted errata and their related corrections—at:

https://aka.ms/examref767/errata

If you discover an error that is not already listed, please submit it to us at the same page.

If you need additional support, email Microsoft Press Book Support at *mspinput@microsoft.com*.

Please note that product support for Microsoft software and hardware is not offered through the previous addresses. For help with Microsoft software or hardware, go to *https://support.microsoft.com*.

We want to hear from you

At Microsoft Press, your satisfaction is our top priority, and your feedback our most valuable asset. Please tell us what you think of this book at:

https://aka.ms/tellpress

We know you're busy, so we've kept it short with just a few questions. Your answers go directly to the editors at Microsoft Press. (No personal information will be requested.) Thanks in advance for your input!

Stay in touch

Let's keep the conversation going! We're on Twitter: *http://twitter.com/MicrosoftPress*.

Important: How to use this book to study for the exam

Certification exams validate your on-the-job experience and product knowledge. To gauge your readiness to take an exam, use this Exam Ref to help you check your understanding of the skills tested by the exam. Determine the topics you know well and the areas in which you need more experience. To help you refresh your skills in specific areas, we have also provided "Need more review?" pointers, which direct you to more in-depth information outside the book.

The Exam Ref is not a substitute for hands-on experience. This book is not designed to teach you new skills.

We recommend that you round out your exam preparation by using a combination of available study materials and courses. Learn more about available classroom training at *https://www.microsoft.com/learning*. Microsoft Official Practice Tests are available for many exams at *https://aka.ms/practicetests*. You can also find free online courses and live events from Microsoft Virtual Academy at *https://www.microsoftvirtualacademy.com*.

This book is organized by the "Skills measured" list published for the exam. The "Skills measured" list for each exam is available on the Microsoft Learning website: *https://aka.ms/examlist*.

Note that this Exam Ref is based on publicly available information and the author's experience. To safeguard the integrity of the exam, authors do not have access to the exam questions.

CHAPTER 1

Design and implement a data warehouse

Designing and implementing a data warehouse with SQL Server requires an understanding of both the business processes that users want to report, analyze, and derive insights from and the structures that make up the logical and physical design of a data warehouse. The combination of these skills results in the design of a practical data model that can be used by business users to quickly answer business questions that most transactional systems cannot address efficiently.

IMPORTANT

Have you read page xvii?

It contains valuable information regarding the skills you need to pass the exam.

This chapter covers how to create a logical and physical model of common business processes in a data warehouse by using dimension and fact tables. It also covers how to optimize and scale your data warehouse using SQL Server.

Skill 1.1 covers the design and implementation of dimension tables. In this section, you look at how to create logical and physical designs for dimension tables in star and snowflake schemas. It also covers how to create shared and conformed dimensions that can be used across multiple fact tables.

Skill 1.2 covers design and implementation of fact tables. In this section, you look at how to define additive and semi-additive measures and how to create physical relationships between dimensions and other fact tables.

Skills 1.3 through 1.5 cover the features available in SQL Server to architect a data warehouse database capable of scaling the read and write performance to support data loads and data analysis and reporting.

Skills in this chapter:

- Skill 1.1: Design and implement dimension tables
- Skill 1.2: Design and implement fact tables
- Skill 1.3: Design and implement indexes for a data warehouse workload
- Skill 1.4: Design storage for a data warehouse
- Skill 1.5: Design and implement partitioned tables and views

Skill 1.1 Design and implement dimension tables

This section goes over, in detail, the logical and physical design of dimension tables in star and snowflake schemas. To provide a better understanding of the process of designing and implementing dimension tables, this section uses examples of simple and common business processes found in everyday life. These examples can help you identify related attributes that can be grouped together in a dimension table to give you a better understanding of the business process.

Next you cover how to relate these dimensions to other dimensions and fact tables to create a data model that allows efficient and intuitive reporting and analysis.

This section covers how to:

- Determine attributes
- Implement dimensions
- Design shared and conformed dimensions
- Design hierarchies
- Determine support requirements for slowly changing dimensions
- Determine keys and key relationships for a data warehouse
- Determine star or snowflake schema requirements
- Determine the granularity of relationship by using fact tables
- Determine auditing or lineage requirements
- Implement data lineage of a dimension table

Determine attributes

Dimension tables group related attributes that provide context to business processes. Attributes can be used to describe the "what," "when," "where," "who," and "how" for any given business process. They are commonly used in reports and dashboards as filters and slicers.

As mentioned in the chapter's introduction, it is important to understand the business processes that you are trying to model in the data warehouse to determine the dimensions and attributes that are required. In general, you can do this by analyzing the entity relationship model (ERM) of line of business (LOB) applications and by carrying out discovery sessions with business users and subject matter experts from different areas of the business. A good point of reference for structuring these discussions efficiently is to review existing reports and dashboards from the LOB applications.

As part of the discovery sessions, it is also important to review manual processes that require you to manipulate data to produce a specific analysis. This data manipulation is typically done in spreadsheets and often combines data from external sources or data that is manually maintained by certain business users.

Another way to determine attributes and dimensions is to analyze forms and instruments that are used to track certain business processes, such as the sale of goods and services. Typically, this is tracked in a sales receipt or invoice. The invoice can record information that describes what was sold, when was it sold, where was it shipped, who sold it, and who it was sold to, as seen in the invoice example from Wide World Importers in Figure 1-1.

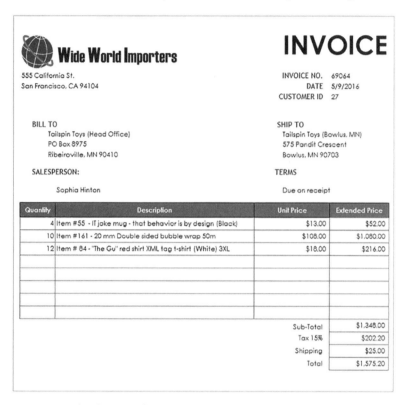

FIGURE 1-1 An invoice example

From this invoice shown in Figure 1-1, you can quickly decompose the "what," "when," "where," and "who" as shown in Table 1-1.

TABLE 1-1 Decomposition of the invoice example

Description	Value
What	Item #55, Item #161, Item #84
When	5/9/2016
Where (Ship To)	Bowlus, MN
Where (Bill To)	Ribeiroville, MN
Who (Ship To Client)	Tailspin Toys (Bowlus, MN)
Who (Bill To Client)	Tailspin Toys (Head Office)
Who (Salesperson)	Sophia Hinton

Next, you can proceed to determine attributes by using the decomposition of the "what," "when," "where," and "who" of this invoice example, as shown in Table 1-2.

TABLE 1-2 List of attributes from the invoice example

Attribute	Value
Item ID	Item #55, Item #161, Item #84
Item Name	IT joke mug - that behavior is by design (Black), 20 mm Double sided bubble wrap 50m, "The Gu" red shirt XML tag t-shirt (White) 3XL
Day	9
Month	5
Year	2016
City Name	Bowlus, Ribeiroville
State Code	MN
Customer Name	Tailspin Toys (Bowlus, MN), Tailspin Toys (Head Office)
Sales Person Name	Sophia Hinton

The next step is to group related attributes into dimension tables. Grouping related attributes into dimensions facilitates data filtering, slicing, and dicing. The proposed dimensions from the example invoice are shown in Table 1-3.

TABLE 1-3 List of dimensions and related attributes from the invoice example

Attribute	Dimension
Item ID, Item Name	Item
Day, Month, Year	Date
City Name, State Code	Geography
Customer Name	Customer
Sales Person Name	Employee

Implement dimensions

After you determine attributes and group them into dimensions, you can define the dimension tables in your data warehouse. Each attribute becomes a column in the dimension table and holds specific data type values. It is important to choose data types correctly and to plan for future needs, such as the need to integrate data from additional data sources with varying data types.

It is also a good idea to familiarize yourself with the different data types, constraints, and properties supported by the database platform you use to develop your data warehouse, in this case SQL Server 2016. In addition, you should also understand how certain table design patterns improve or affect a data warehouse workload.

Documentation of all data types supported in SQL Server 2016 is available at: https://docs.microsoft.com/en-us/sql/t-sql/data-types/data-types-transact-sql

Documentation on table properties, constraints, and other options for SQL Server 2016 is available at: *https://docs.microsoft.com/en-us/sql/t-sql/statements/create-table-transact-sql.*

In most cases, you define attribute columns in dimension tables as strings, Booleans, and dates, such as [CustomerName], [ActiveFlag], and [DateofBirth]. In special cases, certain attributes might be defined as numeric, but these are typically non-additive in nature, for example [ProductSize] and [HouseholdIncome]. Additive and semi-additive numeric values belong in fact tables.

In general, most dimension tables contain four types of columns as described in Table 1-4. These four types of dimension columns are the building blocks of proper dimensional data warehouse design.

TABLE 1-4 Four main types of dimension columns

Column Type	Description
Surrogate key	Columns with a value that uniquely identifies a dimension member in the data warehouse.
Alternate key	Columns with a value that uniquely identifies a dimension member in the LOB application.
Attributes	Columns that can be used as filters, slicers, row, and column headers in reports to provide context to measures.
Metadata	Columns that track data lineage, auditing, and other data warehouse processes.

The surrogate key value in a dimension table acts as the table's primary key and is typically auto-generated when the table is loaded. In SQL Server, this column is commonly defined as an integer with the IDENTITY property for an automatically incrementing value. Each new record in the dimension table, also known as a dimension member, is guaranteed a unique key value because of the unique constraint imposed by the primary key definition and the incremental sequential identity value.

Surrogate key values have no meaning to business users and are usually hidden from them. Surrogate keys are used in the data warehouse to create table relationships with fact tables and in some cases with other dimension tables.

Alternate keys are the unique identifiers of the dimension members in the LOB application database system. Typically, they are the primary key in the LOB source system tables and are also referred to as the *business key* or *candidate key.* Alternate keys are needed for data lineage tracking and for slowly changing dimension processes. Examples of alternate keys include the EmployeeID or Social Security number in the Employee dimension.

So, you might ask yourself, why not use alternate keys as the data warehouse primary keys? There are several reasons, such as:

1. Some LOB database systems use data types in their primary key columns that generate inefficient query plans that require table joins. Some of these data types include GUIDs and strings. Integer-based primary keys use less space, making them more efficient as fewer data pages need to be read.

2. Some LOB database systems use composite primary keys. This practice can lead to inefficient query plans and multiple columns need to be used in table joins as well, potentially increasing the amount of data pages that need to be read.

3. Certain data warehouses require you to integrate data from multiple source systems. In many cases, primary key values collide when combinig data between different source systems.

4. Requirements might dictate the need to track changes of dimension member attributes over time, which is also known as a Type 2 Slowly Changing Dimension (SCD). This requires you to uniquely identify a specific instance of a dimension member and all its corresponding transactions.

In addition to key columns, dimension tables also include other attribute columns that are typically used for filtering and as rows or columns in reports. These are the columns that provide the context in business analysis. For example, the attribute columns of the Stock Item (Product) dimension in the Wide World Importers data warehouse database include columns that provide context for the name of the stock item, its color, size, and weight. These attribute columns can be used to filter results in a report that lists stock items above a certain size and weight.

The fourth type of dimension columns are metadata columns. These columns are used internally in data warehouse ETL (or ELT) operations and processes. For example, important metadata columns include data lineage and auditing columns. These columns tag each row in a dimension with values that help data warehouse operators track the results of each ETL (or ELT) execution. Some of these columns include [BatchID] to track inserted or updated rows as part of a particular ETL batch execution and also include timestamp columns to track when a row was inserted or modified.

Another set of common metadata columns includes columns used to track Type 2 Slowly Changing Dimensions. These columns include two date columns to track the start and end dates of a particular version of a dimension member. These start and end date columns are used to accurately report historical data.

Design shared and conformed dimensions

Dimensions can be shared across many analysis in the data warehouse. For example, the Product dimension can be used in a report to show Sales by Product as well as Purchases by Product. These reports are based on two different fact tables that model two different business processes, the sale of goods and services, and the purchase of products to replenish stock.

You could create and load two separate product tables, one based on a distinct selection of products purchased from suppliers and another based on the products sold to customers. A better solution is to conform the product dimension as a single dimension based on the complete list of products and use it to create relationships with fact tables that have a product reference, as shown in Figure 1-2.

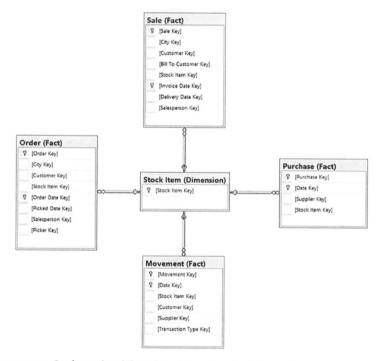

FIGURE 1-2 Conformed and shared Stock Item (Product) dimension

Design hierarchies

A common design approach to improve user experience is to define user hierarchies. Hierarchies allow business users to perform drill-down analysis by using a predefined object that contains levels arranged in a logical order. The calendar hierarchy in the date dimension is a common and simple hierarchy to understand. Figure 1-3 shows the calendar hierarchy in an Excel pivot table analysis. The calendar hierarchy in this example has four member levels consisting of Year, Quarter, Month, and Date. Notice that as you expand the levels of the calendar hierarchy, the [SalesAmount] measure gets broken down to quarterly, monthly, and daily aggregate amounts.

Calendar Drilldown	Sales Amount
⊕2013	$52,563,273
⊕2014	$57,418,917
⊕2015	$62,090,221
⊖2016	$25,971,029
⊖Q1	$15,030,734
⊕January	$5,103,948
⊕February	$4,596,535
⊖March	$5,330,251
2016-03-01	$274,394
2016-03-02	$309,374
2016-03-03	$223,804
2016-03-04	$195,295
2016-03-05	$101,176
2016-03-07	$146,005
2016-03-08	$225,703

FIGURE 1-3 Calendar hierarchy example

Date dimension tables are populated with a record for every day of the year. It is a common practice to generate the date dimension by using a script that populates the dimension table with dates spanning several decades into the past and into the future. In addition to the date column, additional date part columns are populated corresponding to the month, quarter, and year. Table 1-5 shows a typical date dimension with the date parts used in the calendar hierarchy.

TABLE 1-5 Date parts in the Date dimension

Date	Month	Quarter	Year
...			
2016-03-01	March	Q1	2016
2016-03-02	March	Q1	2016
2016-03-03	March	Q1	2016
2016-03-04	March	Q1	2016
2016-03-05	March	Q1	2016
2016-03-06	March	Q1	2016
2016-03-07	March	Q1	2016
2016-03-08	March	Q1	2016
...			

The calendar hierarchy is an example of a natural hierarchy because each attribute can be related to another in a natural order. For example, you can relate dates to a month, months to a quarter, and quarters to a year. This is considered a one-to-many relationship.

Another example of a natural hierarchy is the City-State-Country hierarchy in the Geography dimension. In this case, many cities can be related to a single state and many states can be related to a single country.

Hierarchies that do not follow a natural order are considered unnatural hierarchies. For example, you might find a relationship between attributes such as Gender, Race, and Title in an Employee dimension. There is no natural or logical way of relating one attribute to another because there can be many Gender and Race values for a Title and many Title values for Gender and Race. This is considered a many-to-many relationship. Although you can create a hierarchy by using these attributes, you are "forcing" a relationship rule that is not naturally occurring. You could potentially end up with six different hierarchies, as shown in Table 1-6.

TABLE 1-6 Examples of unnatural Employee dimension hierarchies

Gender->Race->Title Gender->Title->Race	Title->Gender->Race Title->Race->Gender	Race->Title->Gender Race->Gender->Title

Determine support requirements for slowly changing dimensions

A common business requirement is the ability to report historical data. Most LOB applications do not implement mechanisms to keep track of changed values of dimensional data over time. For example, if an existing customer moves to a different city and state at the beginning of the current year, the original address, city, state, and postal code is simply overwritten with the new address information. If a report showing sales by city and state for the last two years is generated after the customer moves, all sales data for this customer now shows under the new city and state.

Ideally, sales data for this customer should show under the corresponding city and state at the time of the sale. Because of this LOB application limitation, the requirement of keeping track of changes of dimension values over time for historical reporting is commonly delegated to the data warehouse and is known as the *Slowly Changing Dimension (SCD)* concept.

There are several ways of handling changes to dimension values. The three most common ways are known as Type 0, Type 1, and Type 2 SCD. Each of these SCD types handle changes differently.

Type 0 SCD is a misnomer because this type of SCD ignores changes to attribute values. In other words, the original dimension values that were initially inserted persist regardless of changes over time. This type of SCD is commonly used for attributes that you do not expect to change, for example, a customer's date of birth or Social Security number. Typically, if a change is detected in these attributes, the system raises an alert to someone in charge (data steward) to validate the unexpected value change.

Type 1 SCD tracks changes by overwriting the current attribute value. This type of SCD simply replicates the change from the source system in the data warehouse. Type 1 SCD is commonly used for those attributes that are not relevant for historical reporting, such as a customer's phone number.

Type 2 SCD tracks changes by inserting a new record with the changed values and keeping the old record with the original attribute values. This type of SCD typically requires two meta-data columns to store the start and end dates that the record is valid for. These dates are used as lookup values during fact table loads to determine the corresponding dimension member key that was valid at the time the transaction took place. A NULL value in a record's end date is often used to indicate that it is the current record, but some choose to use a standard end date of "12/31/9999" instead of a NULL value. In addition, a third metadata column can be used as a flag to indicate that it is the current record.

Keep in mind that you can define all attributes to be handled the same way or you can define certain attributes to be handled as one type of SCD and other attributes as a different type of SCD.

Let's look at how attribute value changes are handled by each type of SCD in specific scenarios.

- **Scenario 1**   Assume that a new customer, John Smith, places an order on 12/10/2015. Later that day, a scheduled data warehouse job kicks-off and inserts John Smith as a new customer into the Customer dimension. As shown in Figure 1-4, the [StartDate] value of the record corresponds to the date the customer is initially loaded into the data warehouse. Because this is the latest record for this customer, the [EndDate] value is set to a default value in the future, 12/31/9999. The [IsCurrent] flag is set to "TRUE" because it is the latest record in the database.

CustomerKey	CustomerID	FullName	Phone	City	State	StartDate	EndDate	IsCurrent
101	1230001	John Smith	305-555-0100	Miami	FL	12/10/2015	12/31/9999	TRUE

FIGURE 1-4 New customer added to the Customer dimension

- **Scenario 2**   The same customer places a second order on 3/15/2016, but provides a new phone number as his main contact information. Because the [Phone] attribute is defined as a Type 1 SCD, the existing customer's record is overwritten with the new phone number as shown in Figure 1-5.

CustomerKey	CustomerID	FullName	Phone	City	State	StartDate	EndDate	IsCurrent
101	1230001	John Smith	813-555-0100	Miami	FL	12/10/2015	12/31/9999	TRUE

FIGURE 1-5 Handling of a Type 1 SCD attribute

Notice that the [StartDate] and [EndDate] values remain the same and that only the value for the [Phone] attribute has changed.

- **Scenario 3**   Assume that the customer in the example moves to a different city and provides an updated address when he places a third order on 10/5/2016. Because the City attribute is defined as a Type 2 SCD attribute, we expire the customer's current record and insert a new record with the changed values as shown in Figure 1-6.

CustomerKey	CustomerID	FullName	Phone	City	State	StartDate	EndDate	IsCurrent
101	1230001	John Smith	813-555-0100	Miami	FL	12/10/2015	10/4/2016	FALSE
102	1230001	John Smith	813-555-0100	Tampa	FL	10/5/2016	12/31/9999	TRUE

FIGURE 1-6 Handling of a Type 2 SCD attribute

Notice the following in the newly inserted record:

- The inserted record has a new [CustomerKey] value
- The [IsCurrent] value is set to "TRUE"
- The [StartDate] value corresponds to the date that the City value changed in the source system
- The [EndDate] value is now the default "12/31/9999" value
- The [City] value reflects the new value updated in the source system
- All other attribute values are the same

Notice the following in the expired record:

- The [EndDate] value is updated with the date corresponding to the previous day when the City value changed the source system
- The [IsCurrent] value is changed to "FALSE"

Determine dimension keys and key relationships for a data warehouse

Dimension keys are required to create table relationships in a data warehouse. These relationships are used to enforce referential integrity and to provide a connection between tables to satisfy logical joins, such as inner, outer, and cross joins. Table relationships are created between primary keys and foreign keys through foreign key constraints in SQL Server. Figure 1-7 shows a foreign key constraint relationship between Fact.Purchase and Dimension.Supplier tables in the Wide World Importers data warehouse database. The [Supplier Key] is the primary key of the Supplier dimension. The [Supplier Key] in the Purchase fact table references the Supplier dimension's primary key through a foreign key constraint.

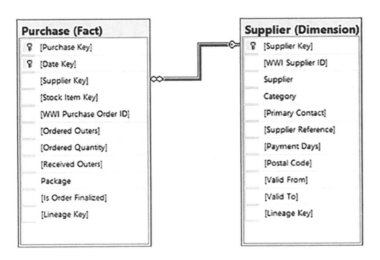

FIGURE 1-7 One-to-Many relationship example

In star and snowflake schemas, fact tables reference dimension tables' primary key column values. In snowflake schemas, certain dimensions might also reference other dimension tables' primary key column values. These table relationships can be classified according to the cardinality between tables. Cardinality refers to the number of occurrences of a dimension member in one table compared to the number of occurrences in the other table. In other words, cardinality tells you how many times a column value is referenced in each side of the table relationship. The degree of relationship between tables in a data warehouse can be classified into five main types:

- Zero-to-One (0:1)
- One-to-One (1:1)
- One-to-Many (1:M)
- Many-to-Many (M:M)
- Self-referencing

In a Zero-to-One (0:1) relationship, no occurrence of a dimension member may exist in a fact table. For example, there might be no sales records for a particular city or state. Although, a city may exist in the City dimension, there might be no corresponding sales transactions in a Sales fact table for that particular city.

In One-to-One (1:1) relationships, only one occurrence of a dimension member relates to exactly one occurrence in the other table. For example, a country and capital city relationship is considered a 1:1 relationship because a capital city belongs to only one country and a country only has one capital city.

The most common relationship in a data warehouse is the One-to-Many (1:M) relationship. This is the relationship that exists between the Supplier dimension and the Purchase fact table in Figure 1-6. It is considered 1:M because a dimension member in the Supplier dimension can be referenced by many rows in the Purchase fact table. For example, every month a purchase order is created to re-stock certain items sold by Litware, Inc. In this case, there are 12 records per year in the Purchase fact table, each referencing Litware, Inc.'s [Supplier Key] from the Supplier dimension.

In some modeling tools and entity-relationship diagrams (ERD) notations, One-to-Many and Zero-to-Many relationships are expressed as Zero-or-One-to-Many (0|1:M) relationships. This notation is particularly important to use when values on one side of the table can be NULL values.

Another type of relationship is the Many-to-Many (M:M) relationship. This type of relationship exists when a dimension member can be referenced multiple times by each side of the relationship. M:M relationships are typically modeled by using an intermediate table that serves as a bridge between the two tables. An example of an M:M relationship can be found between the Customer and Product dimension in the Wide World Importers data warehouse database as shown in Figure 1-8.

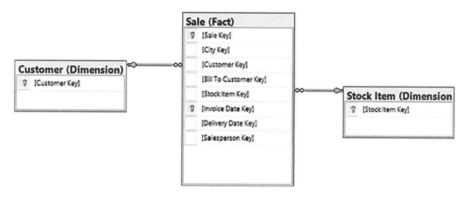

FIGURE 1-8 M:M relationship example

Notice that the Sales fact table acts as the intermediate table between the two dimensions. The Customer dimension is considered to have a Many-to-Many relationship to the Stock Item (Product) dimension because, as you read the relationship from left-to-right in Figure 1-7, there is a One-to-Many (1:M) relationship between the Customer dimension and the Sales fact table and there is a Many-to-One (M:1) relationship between the Sales fact table and the Stock Item dimension. In other words, it is the combination of the 1:M and relationships that create the M:M logical relationship.

The fifth type of relationship sometimes used in data warehouse design is the self-referencing relationship. This type of relationship involves a single table and, as the name implies, references itself as part of the foreign key constraint. An example of this type of relationship can be found in the Sales.Customer table of the Wide World Importers online transactional processing (OLTP) database. Every customer record in the Customer dimension has a *BillTo* customer specified by the [BillToCustomerID] column. This *BillTo* customer is also a customer record with its own unique key. The foreign key constraint of the [BillToCustomerID] column references the table's primary key column, creating the self-reference. This type of relationship is also referred to as a self-referencing parent-child relationship because each customer record becomes a child of the referenced customer parent record.

Determine star or snowflake schema requirements

After you determine your dimensions and attributes, you can create a logical model to represent the relationships to the business process you are trying to model. In the sales business process example, we determined the need for at least five dimensions, as shown in Figure 1-9.

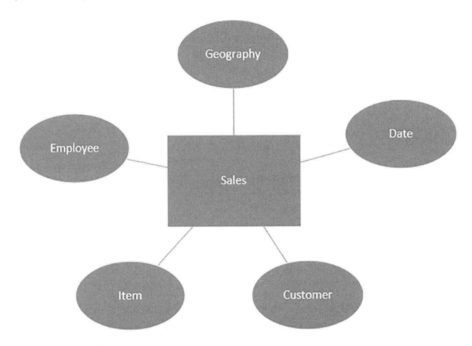

FIGURE 1-9 Logical data model from the Wide World Importers sales business process example

As you might have noticed, at the center of the data model is the business process measure we are trying to model. Business process measures are tracked in their own table structures known as fact tables. The transaction amounts and item quantities from the invoice example in

Figure 1-1 are stored in a fact table. Fact tables are covered in more detail in *Skill 1.2 Design and implement fact tables*. You might have also noticed that the dimensions identified only have a direct relationship with the central fact table. This relationship model is known as a star schema because it closely resembles a central core (fact table) with rays of light (dimension tables) emanating from its center as shown in Figure 1-10.

FIGURE 1-10 Star schema representation from the Wide World Importers invoice example

You can model things differently if business scenarios and requirements call for it. For example, notice in the star schema in Figure 1-10 that it has a single Geography dimension where City and State attributes are grouped together. You could create two separate dimensions instead, one to hold cities and another to hold states. Each record in the City dimension would have a direct relationship to the central Sales fact table and also to the State dimension table. The State dimension would only have a relationship to the City dimension. As you continue to normalize the dimensions, the logical model looks more like a snowflake as shown in Figure 1-11.

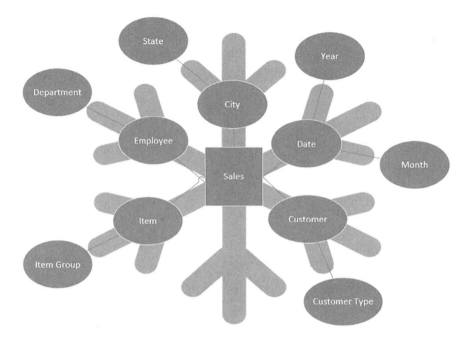

FIGURE 1-11 Snowflake schema from the Wide World Importers sales business process

In the snowflake model approach, the State dimension has "snowflaked" off the City dimension. This means that to get to the State dimension attributes, you now have to use City as an intermediate joined table. The more intermediate tables that are added, the more tables need to be joined to get to a particular attribute in the leaf level tables.

So, which schema is better? Both star schema and snowflake schema offer advantages over one another for different scenarios. There is no right or wrong choice, it all depends on business requirements, use cases, and other factors, which include volume and cardinality of the source data. In most cases, star schemas offer a better starting point because they are simpler to design, load, and maintain. In certain data warehouse designs you end up with what you can call "starflake" schemas, where you keep the structure a star schema as long as possible and only snowflake if absolutely necessary.

Determine auditing or lineage requirements

One important criteria for success for any data warehouse project is to deliver data that is trustworthy. Data can be trusted if you understand where it originates and what happens to it as it goes through the extract, transform, and load (ETL) process. Data lineage provides an audit trail of the data from its origin to its destination.

Data lineage involves maintaining metadata repositories and auditing interactions with the data as it flows from its origin to its destination. A metadata repository can include information about the source and target systems, data types, data mappings, filters, business rules, transformations, and aggregations applied to the data in the different data flows.

Auditing provides information about what happens to the data in the data flows. Auditing can capture data flow batch start and end timestamps, errors and warnings, variable and parameter values, row counts, and other execution and performance metrics.

Some ETL tools like SQL Server Integration Services (SSIS), provide a graphical representation of data flows and keep track of the data lineage between source and destinations through its internal metadata discovery and tracking mechanisms. SSIS allows you to implement your own auditing framework and provides native logging capabilities as well.

Implement data lineage of a dimension table

A common approach for auditing framework can be observed in the Wide World Importers sample SSIS ETL packages that load the data warehouse database. As part of every data flow, a "Get Lineage Key" step is executed to update the [Data Load Started], the beginning of the batch execution of the City dimension load. In the last step of the City dimension data flow task, the [Data Load Completed] column is updated for the corresponding [Lineage Key] row. Figure 1-12 shows the City dimension table load SSIS data flow task.

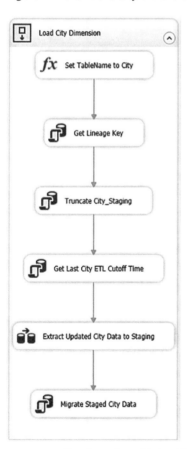

FIGURE 1-12 City dimension table load SSIS data flow task

Skill 1.2 Design and implement fact tables

Fact tables are another set of important data warehouse structures that store the measures that keep track of business processes. They bring dimension keys and measures together to facilitate business process analysis at a specific grain. The grain or granularity of a fact table determines the highest or lowest level of detail stored for a specific business metric.

> **This section covers how to:**
> - Identify measures
> - Design and implement fact tables
> - Create composite keys
> - Implement additive, semi-additive, and non-additive measures
> - Identify dimension table relationships
> - Design a data warehouse that supports many-to-many relationships

Identify measures

As discussed previously, fact tables are modeled around a specific business process. The measures in a fact table, or *facts*, are the numeric representations of the events that occur in the business process. Examples of measures in the Sales business process include the *Quantity of Items Sold* and the *Sales Amount*.

Measures can be identified by analyzing what a business wants to track about a specific business process. For example, a business might be interested in how many units of a specific product are sold and how much revenue it represents. In the invoice example in Figure 1-1, you can quickly source these measures from the Quantity and Extended Price columns within the invoice.

In addition, measures can be identified from strategic organizational goals and indicators known as key business metrics and key performance indicators (KPIs). Some of the metrics or KPIs related to the Sales business process include Sales Growth, Profit Margin, and Sales Actual vs Target. Measures are the foundation of business metrics and KPIs. Fact tables provide the ability to track these metrics and KPIs over time and across multiple other dimensions.

So, are all numeric values measures? Not quite. A rule of thumb to identify a value as a measure is to test if the value can be summed up by one or more dimensions or aggregated over time. For example, the *Extended Price* column in the invoice example in Figure 1-1 can be summed up by the Product, Date, Customer, and Geography to arrive to an aggregate *Extended Price* by any of these dimensions. *Invoice No.* and *Customer ID* are numeric fields that cannot be summed up, therefore they cannot be considered as measure candidates.

There are some numeric fields that can be considered measures although they don't make sense if you add them up. An example of this is *Unit Price*. Some data modelers define this as a numeric attribute of a product while others consider it a measure. It depends on how it is used, but in most cases, it can be considered a special type of measure with limitations on how it can be aggregated. It doesn't make sense to add up the *Unit Price* column by itself in an invoice, but it makes sense to use it to calculate a *Unit Price Average*. It is mostly there to derive the Extended Price or Total Price by multiplying the Unit Price by the Quantity column. The behavior of this measure can be considered semi-additive or non-additive. The different types of measures are described in the section titled *Implement additive, semi-additive, and non-additive measures.*

Design and implement fact tables

Fact table design starts with the definition of the business process it should model, followed by the declaration of the table's granularity. For example, you can start by defining the business process to be modeled as the sales of items in a *FactSales* fact table. You can then declare the table's grain as daily sales by customer.

In the section titled "Design and implement dimension tables," you discovered that dimensions attributes describe the "what," "when," "where," "who," and "how" about any given business process. Fact table measures on the other hand, describe the "how many" or "how much" about any given business process. In the invoice example in Figure 1-1, the Quantity and Extended Price columns provide the answer to: "How many items were sold?" and "How much was sold?" respectively.

Fact tables usually contain four types of columns, as described in Table 1-7.

TABLE 1-7 Column types in fact table

Column Type	Description
Primary key	Column or columns that determine the uniqueness of the table.
Foreign keys	Columns with a value that references a primary key column of a dimension.
Measures	Columns with a value that contains quantifiable data, usually numeric, that can be aggregated.
Metadata	Columns that track data lineage, auditing and other data warehouse processes.

Create composite keys

The primary key of a fact table is usually a composite key made up of all or a subset of its foreign keys. The primary key in a fact table determines the uniqueness of each row. In some cases, a surrogate key can also act as the fact table's primary key. This fact table's surrogate key is typically an auto-incremental numeric field, commonly defined as an identity column. The main purpose of the fact table's surrogate key is to ensure row uniqueness in situations where it is a business requirement to allow duplicate rows in your fact table. It is necessary to reduce the size of the table's clustered index when the primary key is based on many foreign keys.

When using a surrogate key as the fact table's primary key, uniqueness is enforced during the ETL process.

Foreign keys in a fact table determine what dimensions have a direct relationship with the fact table. This is also referred to as the dimensionality of the table. The table's dimensionality reflects the grain or granularity of the fact table. The relationship between a fact table's foreign key and the corresponding dimension primary key is usually a one-to-many relationship. Figure 1-13 shows a one-to-many relationship example between the [Fact].[Sale] fact table and the [Dimension].[Stock Item] dimension table.

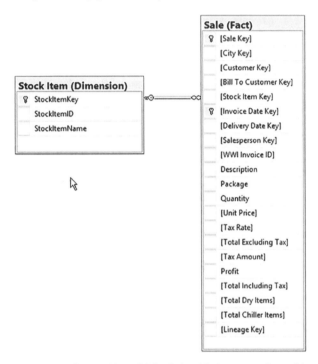

FIGURE 1-13 One-to-Many (1:M) relationship between a fact table and a dimension

Measure columns in a fact table are the numeric fields that can be aggregated, filtered, and sliced by any of the dimensions in the table. They are usually defined as data types that support aggregation, such as numeric, decimal, money, and int.

Like dimension tables, metadata columns in fact tables are used internally in data warehouse ETL/ELT operations and processes. For example, important metadata columns include data lineage and auditing columns. These columns tag each row in a fact table with values that help data warehouse operators track the results of each ETL (or ELT) execution. Some of these columns include [BatchID] to track the rows that were inserted or updated as part of a particular ETL/ELT batch execution and also include timestamp columns to track when a row was inserted or modified.

Implement additive, semi-additive, and non-additive measures

There are three types of measures: additive, semi-additive, and non-additive. They are also referred to as fully-aggregatable, semi-aggregatable and non-aggregatable facts.

Additive measures are numeric values that can be summed up by all the dimensions in the fact table, for example the Sales Amount. These are the most common measures and they are the easiest to understand and implement. They are typically used in drill-down analysis and often serve as building blocks for other measures and calculations.

Semi-additive measures are numeric values that can be summed up by some dimensions in the fact table, but not all. In most cases, they can be aggregated by any other dimension except time. An example of a semi-additive measure is Account Balance. You can determine the ending balance of an account at the end of a month, but adding up these monthly account balances do not make sense. Semi-additive measures are usually found in fact tables that store periodic snapshots of data.

Non-additive measures, as the name implies, are measures that cannot be summed up. These measures include percentages such as Discount Percent, ratios such as Profit Margin, and averages such as Average Unit Cost.

Identify dimension table relationships

Table relationships are important in relational databases to enforce data integrity. A relationship exists between two tables when one or more columns from one table match one or more columns on another table, or in some cases within the same table. In SQL Server, table relationships are defined using foreign key constraints.

A foreign key constraint is typically defined between a column in a table to a primary key column in another table. For example, in the Wide World Importers DW database we can observe several foreign key constraints between `[Fact].[Sale]` and several dimension tables including `[Dimension].[City]`, `[Dimension].[Customer]` and `[Dimension].[Stock Item]`. These type of relationships can be considered zero-to-many (0:M), one-to-one (1:1) or one-to-many (1:M) relationships depending on their cardinality. The `[Fact].[Sale]` table in any of these cases is considered a child table and the dimension tables are considered the parent tables.

Tables can also relate to other tables in a many-to-many (M:M) relationship. For example, a customer and stock item (product) can be considered to have a many-to-many relationship because many customers can purchase many stock items and many stock items can be purchased by many customers. Many-to-many relationships often involve a third intermediate table that relate to the other two tables. These intermediate tables are often fact tables or relationship tables often referred to as *fact-less* fact tables.

Tables can also reference themselves in what is known as a self-referencing table. In this case a column in a table references another column within the same table. An example of common self-referencing table found in some data warehouses is the Employee dimension table. An approach to model the Employee dimension table is to relate an employee record to its manager's or supervisor employee record using a column such as [ManagerEmployeeKey] or [ReportsToEmployeeKey] for example. With this approach an organization's hierarchical structure can be derived by traversing the table recursively.

During a data warehouse modeling exercise, it is important to identify how dimension tables realate to each other. To effectively identify these relationships, during the modeling exercise the business processes need to be identified and modeled along with the dimensions that directly relate to them. An Enterprise Business Matrix (EBM), is valuable tool that can be used to identify and document how dimension tables and business processes relate to each other. An important outcome of building an EBM is the documentation of shared and conformed dimensions to categorize, describe, slice and dice different facts and measures the same way for consistent and accurate reporting and analysis. Table 1-8 shows an example of a Enterprise Business Matrix for the Wide World Importers fictitious company based on the DW database model.

TABLE 1-8 Enterprise Business Matrix for the Wide World Importers company

Business process	shared and conformed dimensions				
	Date	Customer	City	supplier	stock tiem
Sales of Items	√	√	√		√
Supplier Purchases	√		√	√	√
Order Processing	√	√	√		√
Inventory Movements	√	√	√	√	√

Design a data warehouse that supports many-to-many relationships

There are several business scenarios that require modeling many-to-many relationships such as Customers-to-Products and Products-to-Customers. Some of these many-to-many relationship requirements arise from the need to support:

- Different perspectives for reporting and analysis
- Complex business processes
- Relational source system limitations

Some divisions and business units within an organization may be interested in reporting and analyzing data slightly different than others. For example the Sales managers may be interested in identifying customers who live in a particular sales territory to mail them store discounts and promotions to boost sales in the stores of that region. Product managers may be interested in analyzing products with high inventory to promote them to customers who have purchased them in the past. These two analyses require many-to-many relationships between dimension tables using fact tables as shown in Figure 1-14.

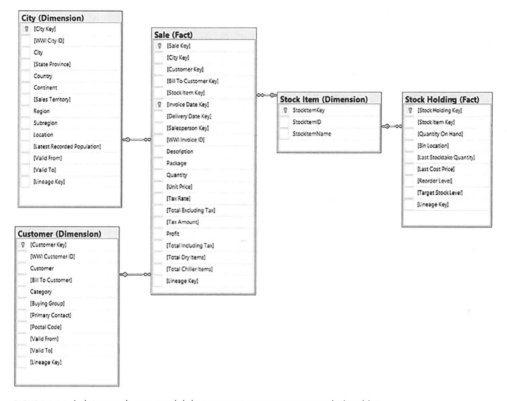

FIGURE 1-14 A data warehouse model that supports many-to-many relationships.

To satisfy the Sales manager's requirement a SQL query as shown below can be executed to select customers from the Southeast region for example:

```
SELECT distinct
dcust.Customer
FROM [Fact].[Sale] fs
inner join [Dimension].[Customer] dcust on dcust.[Customer Key] = fs.[Customer Key]
inner join [Dimension].City dc on dc.[City Key] = fs.[City Key]
WHERE dc.[Sales Territory] = 'Southeast'
```

In the query above, notice that three tables needed to be joined, [Fact].[Sales], [Dimension].[Customer] and [Dimension].[City]. The [Fact].[Sales] table in this query acts as a relationship table between the two dimension tables, thus creating a many-to-many relationship.

To satisfy the Product manager's analysis requirement, a SQL query as shown below can be executed to select the Top 10 products with high inventory that can be promoted to customers who have bought them in the past.

```
SELECT distinct
dcust.Customer, fs.[Stock Item Key]
FROM [Fact].[Sale] fs
inner join [Dimension].[Customer] dcust on dcust.[Customer Key] = fs.[Customer Key]
```

```
inner join [Dimension].[Stock Item] dsi on dsi.[StockItemKey] = fs.[Stock Item Key]
WHERE fs.[Stock Item Key] in
(
SELECT TOP 10 fsh.[Stock Item Key]
FROM [Fact].[Stock Holding] fsh
order by [Quantity On Hand] DESC
)
```

Skill 1.3 Design and implement indexes for a data warehouse workload

An important requirement in data warehouse design is the ability to support a mix of work-loads, including loading data and reporting on the data within acceptable performance thresholds. A good data warehouse architecture, along with an appropriate index design, can always ensure acceptable workload performance.

Designing an indexing solution for a data warehouse is a complex topic because you need a good understanding of the structure and workload for a data warehouse, as well as an under-standing of the several types of indexes available in SQL Server. This section discusses how to improve the performance of a data warehouse workload by designing and implementing the several types of SQL Server indexes.

> **This section covers how to:**
> - Design an indexing solution
> - Implement clustered, nonclustered, filtered, and columnstore indexes
> - Select appropriate indexes

Design an indexing solution

Designing an indexing solution requires the right number of indexes in the data warehouse. Insufficient indexing causes queries to run slow, while too many indexes cause data loads to run slower and the database size to increase. Finding the right balance between index per-formance and index storage requirements is not an easy task. A good understanding of the data warehouse workload, its structure, and index types are all very important for designing a proper indexing solution.

A traditional data warehouse workload typically consists of scheduled data loads via extract, transform, and load (ETL) process executions, followed by SQL Server Analysis Services (SSAS) OLAP cube processing. In some organizations, all reporting and analysis is sourced through the

OLAP cube and is commonly known as OLAP reporting. In other organizations, data reporting and analysis is sourced directly from the dimension and fact tables of the data warehouse database. This type of reporting is commonly referred to as relational reporting and uses SQL queries.

First, you need to understand the main types of indexes that SQL Server supports to improve these types of workloads. A complete list and full description of the types of indexes is provided in the Microsoft Docs technical documentation located at *https://docs.microsoft.com/ en-us/sql/relational-databases/indexes/indexes*.

The two main types of indexes that are part of almost every data warehouse index solution are rowstore and columnstore indexes. Rowstore indexes store table or view data horizontally based on rows of data. Columnstore indexes store table or view data vertically based on column values. Rowstore indexes are the traditional indexes that have been present since the early versions of SQL Server. Columnstore indexes are a newer type of in-memory index that provide increased performance benefits over traditional rowstore indexes in data warehousing workloads.

Row store indexes are structures stored on the storage system that allow quick retrieval of row data stored in a table or view. Rowstore indexes are based on a Balanced Tree (B-Tree) structure to find rows of data in a quick and efficient manner. In a B-tree index structure, index rows are stored in index pages in the root and intermediate nodes. Data pages are stored in the leaf nodes.

SQL Server uses the index pages in the root and intermediate nodes in a way that is similar to how you use the index in the back of a book. For example, to find a page in a book that has a reference to the word "database," you skip to the page in the index that contain words beginning with the letter "d," then scan alphabetically through the list of words until you find the entry (index row) with the word "database." After you find the entry, you look up the page number and turn to the page with the actual content.

Rowstore indexes can be defined as *clustered* or *nonclustered* row indexes. A clustered rowstore index sorts and stores table or view data in rows in the order of the clustered index key. The clustered index key is usually the table's primary key, although you can also define a clustered index on tables with no primary key. A table with a clustered index is commonly known as a clustered table. A clustered table can have one and only one clustered index.

Nonclustered rowstore indexes store the nonclustered index key values with a pointer, known as the *row locator*, to the data row in a heap table or to the clustered index key in a clustered table.

Figure 1-15 illustrates the B-Tree structure of rowstore indexes consisting of a root node, intermediate nodes, and leaf nodes.

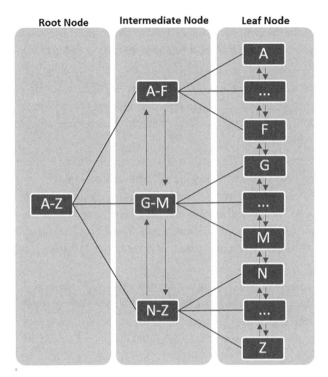

FIGURE 1-15 An illustration of a B-tree index structure

A columnstore index is an in-memory technology that stores and manages data by using a column-based format. Columnstore indexes store data in rowgroups as opposed to rowstores. The rowgroups contain compressed column values, known as column segments. This columnar storage format greatly improves query performance because only the specific column segments for the query requested values need to be decompressed. The compression algorithm behind a columnstore index can greatly reduce the storage footprint when compared to a traditional rowstore index. A columnstore index is the recommended index for large data warehouse fact tables.

To illustrate the difference between rowstore and columnstore indexes, look at the subset of columns and rows for the `[Dimension].[City]` table in the Wide World Importers DW database, as shown in Figure 1-16.

City	State Province	Country
Unknown	N/A	N/A
Carrollton	New York	United States
Carrollton	Illinois	United States
Carrollton	Texas	United States
Carrollton Manor	Maryland	United States
Carrolltown	Pennsylvania	United States
Carrothers	Ohio	United States
Carrsville	Virginia	United States
Carrsville	Kentucky	United States
Carsins	Maryland	United States
Carson	New Mexico	United States
Carson	California	United States

FIGURE 1-16 Sample rows of a subset of columns from the [Dimension].[City] table

In Figure 1-16, you can see that in the subset of columns for the `[Dimension].[City]` table there are three columns and 12 rows of data. A rowstore index applied to this table structure would store data in 22 rows across one or more row-based data pages. In contrast, a column-store index applied to this table structure would store data in three column segments across one or more column-based data pages (rowgroups), as shown in Figure 1-17.

Rowstore (data page): 1			Rowstore (data page): 2			Rowstore (data page): 3		
City	**State Province**	**Country**	**City**	**State Province**	**Country**	**City**	**State Province**	**Country**
Unknown	N/A	N/A	Carrollton Manor	Maryland	United States	Carrollton	Texas	United States
Carrollton	New York	United States	Carrolltown	Pennsylvania	United States	Carsins	Maryland	United States
Carrothers	Ohio	United States	Carrollton	Illinois	United States	Carson	New Mexico	United States
Carrsville	Kentucky	United States	Carrsville	Virginia	United States	Carson	California	United States

FIGURE 1-17 Rowstore index illustration of the sample rows of a subset of columns for the Dimension.City table

Notice how different the data pages look for each index. In Figure 1-17, the rowstore index data pages contain all the values for each column stored in row format. A query with a WHERE clause of [City] = 'Carrollton' would require a read operation on three data pages as rows matching this clause are found in each of the three data pages above. In Figure 1-18 below, the columnstore index data pages are organized differently in columnar format. The same query filtering on [City] = ' Carrollton' only needs to decompress and read the City column segment from two rowgroups. Columnstore indexes use the mechanism where only the columns required by the query are uncompressed and read from disk to significantly reduce disk Input/Output (I/O) operations. In addition, columnstore indexes use dictionaries to replace duplicate values to make the index smaller.

Segment: City	Segment: State Province	Segment: Country
Row Group 1		
Unknown	N/A	N/A
Carrollton	New York	United States
Carrollton	Illinois	United States
Carrollton	Texas	United States
Carrollton Manor	Maryland	United States
Carrolltown	Pennsylvania	United States
Row Group 2		
Carrothers	Ohio	United States
Carrsville	Virginia	United States
Carrsville	Kentucky	United States
Carsins	Maryland	United States
Carson	New Mexico	United States
Carson	California	United States

FIGURE 1-18 Columnstore index illustration of the sample rows and columns for the [Dimension].[City] table

Implement clustered, nonclustered, filtered, and columnstore indexes

So why are indexes so important? Imagine how time consuming it would be if you had to scan every page in a book to find all the references to a specific word. This is exactly what SQL Server would have to do if there were no indexes. SQL Server would resort to do a table scan operation, which is essentially a full read of all rows in a table. A table scan is typical on tables with no clustered indexes, also known as heap tables. A table scan is the most inefficient read operation that SQL Server performs while all data pages in the table are read. Table scans increase memory, disk, and CPU resource utilization and cause queries to perform slow.

To illustrate the performance impact of table scans, compare the execution plans of a query executed against a table with a clustered index and a table without a clustered index (heap table). For this comparison, use the [Dimension].[City] table in the Wide World Importers DW database. Notice that this table has been defined with a primary key on the [City Key] column along with a clustered index as shown in Figure 1-19.

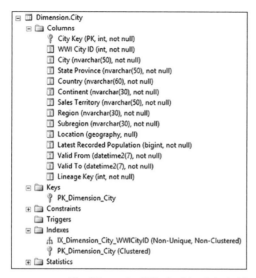

FIGURE 1-19 The [Dimension].[City] table of the Wide World Importers DW database

Execute the following query to return all cities in the state of Florida from the [Dimension].[City] table:

```
SELECT [City]
FROM [WideWorldImportersDW].[Dimension].[City]
WHERE [State Province] = 'Florida'
```

This query's result returns 4,024 rows. The corresponding execution plan and read operation information for this query is shown in Figure 1-20.

SELECT	Clustered Index Scan (Clustered)
Cost: 0 %	[City].[PK_Dimension_City]
	Cost: 100 %

Clustered Index Scan (Clustered)
Scanning a clustered index, entirely or only a range.

Physical Operation	Clustered Index Scan
Logical Operation	Clustered Index Scan
Actual Execution Mode	Row
Estimated Execution Mode	Row
Storage	RowStore
Number of Rows Read	116295
Actual Number of Rows	4024
Actual Number of Batches	0
Estimated I/O Cost	2.57127
Estimated Operator Cost	2.69935 (100%)
Estimated CPU Cost	0.128081
Estimated Subtree Cost	2.69935
Number of Executions	1
Estimated Number of Executions	1
Estimated Number of Rows	3554.47
Estimated Number of Rows to be Read	116295
Estimated Row Size	79 B
Actual Rebinds	0
Actual Rewinds	0
Ordered	False
Node ID	0

FIGURE 1-20 The execution plan and read operation tooltip with a clustered index

You can observe from Figure 1-20 that the read operation performed is a clustered index scan. The [Dimension].[City] table's clustered index [PK_Dimension_City] was read entirely to return the data selected in the query. Notice that 116,295 rows were read (*Number of Rows Read*) to retrieve 4,024 rows (*Actual Numbers of Rows*).

Compare the execution plan and read operation by executing the same query on a copy of the [Dimension].[City] table with no clustered index (heap). Figure 1-21 shows the corresponding execution plan and read operation information.

Physical Operation	Table Scan
Logical Operation	Table Scan
Actual Execution Mode	Row
Estimated Execution Mode	Row
Storage	RowStore
Number of Rows Read	116295
Actual Number of Rows	4024
Actual Number of Batches	0
Estimated I/O Cost	2.5795
Estimated Operator Cost	2.7075 (100%)
Estimated CPU Cost	0.128003
Estimated Subtree Cost	2.7075
Number of Executions	1
Estimated Number of Executions	1
Estimated Number of Rows	3132.85
Estimated Number of Rows to be Read	116295
Estimated Row Size	79 B
Actual Rebinds	0
Actual Rewinds	0
Ordered	False
Node ID	0

FIGURE 1-21 The execution plan and read operation tooltip for the query without a clustered index

Figure 1-21 shows that the type of read operation is now a table scan. The rest of the information displayed in this tooltip is very similar to the information displayed in the tooltip in Figure 1-20. As in the previous execution, all 116,295 rows were read to retrieve the same 4,024 rows.

Table scans and index scans perform similar full read operations on the underlying rows. In large tables, these unnecessary reads lead to poor query performance. Therefore, a proper index solution should eliminate as many table and index scans as possible, especially on highly selective queries, like the query in the previous example. Query performance vastly improves when only the necessary rows are read.

Query performance can be improved by utilizing another type of rowstore index called a nonclustered index. Similar to a clustered index, a nonclustered index also stores data in a B-tree structure. There are several differences between a clustered and nonclustered index however, including how data is sorted and stored in the underlying table and the content that is stored in the leaf nodes. In a nonclustered index, the data rows in the table are not sorted and stored in order based on the nonclustered keys. Nonclustered index leaf nodes contain index pages instead of data pages as a clustered index does.

One of the key features of nonclustered indexes is the ability to include non-key columns to cover more queries. Query performance can improve significantly when a nonclustered index includes all columns in the query. This type of index is known as a covering index. The following script provides an example of a nonclustered index that can be defined to cover the query in the previous example in the [Dimension].[City] table:

```
CREATE NONCLUSTERED INDEX NC_IX_StateProvince
ON [Dimension].[City] ([State Province])
INCLUDE ([City])
```

Notice that the key column is [State Province] and the included column is [City]. The key column is used in the WHERE clause and the included column for the SELECT portion. Figure 1-22 shows the corresponding execution plan and read operation information after applying the covering index to the [Dimension].[City] table.

SELECT	Index Seek (NonClustered)
Cost: 0 %	[City].[NC_IX_StateProvince]
	Cost: 100 %

Index Seek (NonClustered)
Scan a particular range of rows from a nonclustered index.

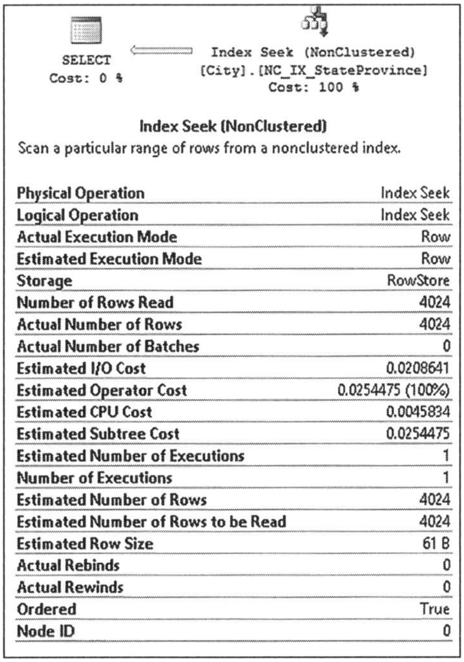

Physical Operation	Index Seek
Logical Operation	Index Seek
Actual Execution Mode	Row
Estimated Execution Mode	Row
Storage	RowStore
Number of Rows Read	4024
Actual Number of Rows	4024
Actual Number of Batches	0
Estimated I/O Cost	0.0208641
Estimated Operator Cost	0.0254475 (100%)
Estimated CPU Cost	0.0045834
Estimated Subtree Cost	0.0254475
Estimated Number of Executions	1
Number of Executions	1
Estimated Number of Rows	4024
Estimated Number of Rows to be Read	4024
Estimated Row Size	61 B
Actual Rebinds	0
Actual Rewinds	0
Ordered	True
Node ID	0

FIGURE 1-22 The execution plan and read operation tooltip for the query with a covering index

Notice in Figure 1-22 that the *Number of Rows Read* equals the *Actual Number of Rows*. This is an improvement over the previous two query execution plans shown in Figure 1-20 and

Figure 1-21 where table and index scans were performed. After the covering nonclustered index was added, SQL Server performed an index seek instead. This is a much more efficient operation because only the rows that are needed in the query are read. In this covering index example, the read overhead was reduced by almost 97 percent.

Another feature of nonclustered indexes is the ability to add a filter to include or exclude rows based on a column filter predicate. These types of nonclustered indexes are referred to as filtered indexes. For example, assume that you are only interested in cities in Florida where you have the latest recorded population. The column `[Latest Recorded Population]` stores this value in the `[Dimension].[City]` column. The query in this example looks as follows:

```
SELECT [City]
FROM [WideWorldImportersDW].[Dimension].[City]
where [State Province] = 'Florida'
and [Latest Recorded Population] > 0
```

The definition of the filtered nonclustered index to cover the query is as follows:

```
CREATE NONCLUSTERED INDEX [NC_IX_StateProvince2] ON [Dimension].[City]
([State Province])
INCLUDE ([City])
WHERE [Latest Recorded Population]>0
```

Notice the last line in the index definition. A `WHERE` clause predicate has been defined matching the predicate of the query. Figure 1-23 shows the execution plan and read operation information after the query is executed with the filtered nonclustered index in place.

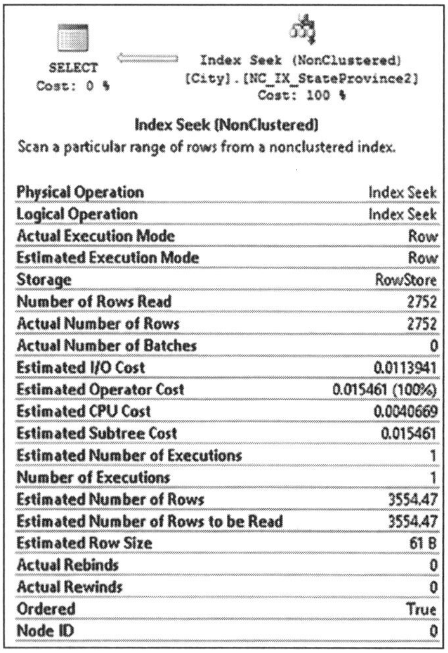
SELECT
Cost: 0 %
Index Seek (NonClustered)
[City].[NC_IX_StateProvince2]
Cost: 100 %
Index Seek (NonClustered)
Scan a particular range of rows from a nonclustered index.
Physical Operation Index Seek
Logical Operation Index Seek
Actual Execution Mode Row
Estimated Execution Mode Row
Storage RowStore
Number of Rows Read 2752
Actual Number of Rows 2752
Actual Number of Batches 0
Estimated I/O Cost 0.0113941
Estimated Operator Cost 0.015461 (100%)
Estimated CPU Cost 0.0040669
Estimated Subtree Cost 0.015461
Estimated Number of Executions 1
Number of Executions 1
Estimated Number of Rows 3554.47
Estimated Number of Rows to be Read 3554.47
Estimated Row Size 61 B
Actual Rebinds 0
Actual Rewinds 0
Ordered True
Node ID 0

FIGURE 1-23 The execution plan and read operation tooltip for the query with a filtered nonclustered index

Notice in Figure 1-23 that the *Number of Rows Read* and *Actual Number of Rows* values have been reduced because only the rows that had a value matching the query's WHERE clause predicate were read.

From this simple query and indexing example, you can see the performance benefits of having the proper indexing to improve the performance of a query. As a general rule, query performance is improved by reducing the number of rows that SQL Server has to read. Table and index scans should be avoided during query execution for selective queries.

Select appropriate indexes

A highly selective query is a query that returns a subset of the rows in a table or combination of tables. Higher selectivity is typically achieved by queries with a WHERE clause predicate or by joining to a smaller table with a reduced number of matching rows. High selectivity usually indicates a high number of unique values or a small number of matching values. Low selectivity usually indicates a small number of unique values or a high number of matching values.

An example of a highly selective query would be query that looks up an Employee by Social Security Number (SSN). Only a single record is expected to match a given SSN. As a contrast, an example of a low selectivity query would be a query that looks up an Employee by the State or Province Name of their home address. This query would return many employees.

A query is considered selective if the execution plan utilizes a more efficient operation such as an index seek rather than a table or index scan. SQL Server uses an internal cost-based optimizer known as the SQL Query Optimizer to determine the execution plan with the lowest cost while also taking in consideration the cost of finding candidate plans. The execution plan operation chosen by the SQL Query Optimizer depends not just on its WHERE clause predicate but also on other factors such indexes and column statistics.

In many cases, table and index scans are inevitable, such as in the case of queries with low selectivity. Examples of low selectivity queries include queries that aggregate sales data by year or queries that average profit across products. Performance tuning of these non-selective queries can be challenging using traditional rowstore indexes. For this matter, a columnstore index is best suited because they are in-memory structures and outperform disk-based rowstore index scans.

For data warehouse workloads, a common index design approach is to implement a mix of rowstore and columnstore indexes. A mixed index implementation is recommended for fact tables because their data access patterns can vary the most. Dimension tables can also benefit from a mixed index design approach, but rowstore indexes typically provide good query coverage.

Rowstore indexes in fact tables are used to cover highly selective queries. Their goal is to ensure query plans use index seek operations. Columnstore indexes in fact tables are used to improve query performance for non-selective queries that result in an index scan operation. Their goal is to speed up scan operations by providing an in-memory structure to traverse through the data.

In addition to relational reporting, other workloads, such as ETL executions and OLAP cube processing, also benefit from a mixed rowstore and columnstore index design approach. For example, ETL executions are improved by optimizing dimension key lookups in data flows. OLAP cube processing also benefits from improved performance while selecting distinct values from dimension attributes and during cube aggregation processing. A mixed rowstore and columnstore index design solution is the recommended approach for all SQL Server data warehouse workloads.

Index selection is performed before and after data is loaded in the data warehouse tables. Before data can be loaded, dimensions, fact tables, and table relationships need to be designed. During the design phase, certain indexes can be identified and designed to provide a best effort query performance. This initial effort is considered *best effort* because it is purely based on observations from the table relationships and business rule enforcements in the database. There might be little or no understanding of user data access patterns up to this point.

The three main types of database rules that are usually designed in a database before data is loaded include uniqueness constraints, primary key relationships, and foreign key relationships. A UNIQUE constraint automatically creates a nonclustered index on the table, while a PRIMARY KEY constraint automatically creates a clustered index on the table. A FOREIGN KEY constraint does not automatically create an index on the table. Typically, columns that reference a FOREIGN KEY constraint are good candidates for an index.

To illustrate the results of defining UNIQUE and PRIMARY KEY constraints on a table, define a table as follows:

```
CREATE TABLE dbo.Test
(
 Column1 int NOT NULL,
 Column2 int NULL
);
```

Then, define a PRIMARY KEY constraint:

```
ALTER TABLE Test
ADD CONSTRAINT PK_Column1 PRIMARY KEY (Column1);
```

And finally, define a UNIQUE constraint:

```
ALTER TABLE Test
ADD CONSTRAINT UC_Column2 UNIQUE (Column2);
```

Figure 1-24 shows the result of the previous scripts in SQL Server Management Studio (SSMS).

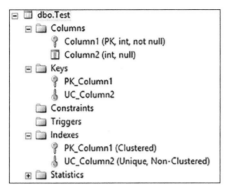

FIGURE 1-24 Test table with PRIMARY KEY and UNIQUE constraint definition

Notice that the PRIMARY KEY definition on [Column1] resulted in the automatic creation of a clustered index and the UNIQUE constraint on [Column2] resulted in the automatic creation of a nonclustered index.

PRIMARY KEY and UNIQUE constraints are common constraints defined for both dimension and fact tables. In dimension tables, the surrogate key is usually defined with a PRIMARY KEY constraint. A dimension surrogate key is typically an auto-incremental numeric field that has no meaning to the business, as described in Section 1.1. Fact tables can also be defined with a PRIMARY KEY based on either a surrogate key or a composite key. Typically, when a surrogate key is defined as the PRIMARY KEY in a fact table, uniqueness is enforced through a UNIQUE constraint by using some or all the fact table's foreign keys.

In addition to PRIMARY KEY and UNIQUE constraints, FOREIGN KEY constraints are typically defined before data is loaded. An index is not automatically generated when you define a FOREIGN KEY constraint, but it is always recommended to manually create a nonclustered index on all foreign keys.

You can observe the benefits of an index on a foreign key column when executing a query that joins a fact table with one or more dimensions. This type of query is the most typical query in a data warehouse. Consider a query that sums up all sales by sales person. The query joins the [Fact].[Sales] table with the [Dimension].[Employee] table as shown in the following query:

```
SELECT
[Employee]
,sum([Total Excluding Tax]) as TotalSales
FROM [Fact].[Sale]
INNER JOIN [Dimension].[Employee] ON [Employee].[Salesperson Key] = [Sale].[SalesPerson
Key]
GROUP BY [Employee]
```

The FOREIGN KEY constraint definition for the column [Sale].[EmployeeKey] referencing the [Dimension].[Employee] table is as follows:

```
ALTER TABLE [Fact].[Sale]  WITH CHECK ADD  CONSTRAINT [FK_Fact_Sale_Salesperson_Key_
Dimension_Employee]
FOREIGN KEY([Salesperson Key])
REFERENCES [Dimension].[Employee] ([Employee Key])
```

Table 1-9 lists some general guidelines you can use to implement the different types of indexes.

TABLE 1-9 General guidelines for index selection

Guideline	Columnstore	Rowstore	No index
Large and wide table	Y	N	N
Highly selective queries	N	Y	N
More inserts than updates	N	Y	N
Analytical queries	Y	N	N
Small table	N	N	Y

The Wide World Importers DW database is a denormalized data warehouse database modeled after the OLTP database for the same fictitious company. It models several business processes including Sales, Transactions, Orders, Purchasing, and Inventory Movements. You can use some of the tables included in the Wide World Importers DW database to implement the different type of indexes covered so far.

The first type of index that is most commonly implemented in a table is the clustered index. A table can only have a single clustered index. A clustered index can be defined either as a rowstore or as a columnstore index. A clustered rowstore index is created by default as a PRIMARY KEY constraint is defined when a table is initially created as follows:

```
CREATE TABLE [Dimension].[Employee]
(
    [Employee Key] [int] NOT NULL,
    [WWI Employee ID] [int] NOT NULL,
    [Employee] [nvarchar](50) NOT NULL,
    [Preferred Name] [nvarchar](50) NOT NULL,
    [Is Salesperson] [bit] NOT NULL,
    [Photo] [varbinary](max) NULL,
    [Valid From] [datetime2](7) NOT NULL,
    [Valid To] [datetime2](7) NOT NULL,
    [Lineage Key] [int] NOT NULL,
 CONSTRAINT [PK_Dimension_Employee] PRIMARY KEY ([Employee Key] ASC)
)
```

The CREATE TABLE code creates a new table with both a PRIMARY KEY constraint based on the [Employee Key] column and a clustered rowstore index named [PK_Dimension_Employee]. Notice that as part of the CONSTRAINT argument, you can explicitly define a primary key index either as a CLUSTERED or NONCLUSTERED index. By default, if no index type is specified, SQL Server creates a CLUSTERED index for the primary key.

A clustered index can also be defined on a table with no primary key by omitting the PRI-MARY KEY constraint argument and instead defining an INDEX argument as follows:

```
CREATE TABLE [Dimension].[Employee]

(
    [Employee Key] [int] NOT NULL,
    [WWI Employee ID] [int] NOT NULL,
    [Employee] [nvarchar](50) NOT NULL,
    [Preferred Name] [nvarchar](50) NOT NULL,
    [Is Salesperson] [bit] NOT NULL,
    [Photo] [varbinary](max) NULL,
    [Valid From] [datetime2](7) NOT NULL,
    [Valid To] [datetime2](7) NOT NULL,
    [Lineage Key] [int] NOT NULL,
INDEX CX_ProductKey CLUSTERED (ProductKey)
)
```

In this case, a table with no primary key is created along with a clustered index named [CX_ProductKey]. Notice that other types of indexes can also be defined by using the syntax above, including additional nonclustered rowstore indexes, a single clustered columnstore index, or a single nonclustered columnstore indexes. The general syntax of the INDEX argument for each type of index is shown in Table 1-10 as follows.

TABLE 1-10 INDEX argument syntax for rowstore and columnstore index definition in the CREATE TABLE statement

Index Type	INDEX argument syntax
Clustered rowstore	INDEX {index_name} CLUSTERED ({column1_name},{...})
Nonclustered rowstore	INDEX {index_name} NONCLUSTERED ({column1_name},{...})
Clustered columnstore	INDEX {index_name} CLUSTERED COLUMNSTORE
Nonclustered columnstore	INDEX {index_name} COLUMNSTORE ({column1_name},{...}) or INDEX {index_name} NONCLUSTERED COLUMNSTORE {{column1_name},{...})

In addition to defining indexes when you initially create a table, you can also add indexes to existing tables by using one of the CREATE INDEX statements shown in Table 1-11.

TABLE 1-11 CREATE INDEX statement syntax for rowstore and columnstore index definition

Index Type	CREATE INDEX syntax
Clustered rowstore	CREATE CLUSTERED INDEX {index_name} ON {table_name} ({column1_name},{...})
Nonclustered rowstore	CREATE NONCLUSTERED INDEX {index_name} ON {table_name} ({column1_name},{,,,})
Clustered columnstore	CREATE CLUSTERED COLUMNSTORE INDEX {index_name} ON {table_name}
Nonclustered columnstore	INDEX {index_name} NONCLUSTERED COLUMNSTORE ({column1_name},{...})

Any attempt to create a clustered columnstore index on the `[Dimension].[Employee]` table however, fails with the following message:

```
The statement failed. Column 'Photo' has a data type that cannot participate in a
 columnstore index. Omit column 'Photo'.
```

This error points out one of the several data types not supported by clustered columnstore indexes at the time of this writing. The unsupported clustered columnstore index data types include:

- ntext, text, and image
- nvarchar(max), varchar(max), and varbinary(max) (Applies to SQL Server 2016 and prior versions, and nonclustered columnstore indexes)
- rowversion (and timestamp)
- sql_variant
- CLR types (hierarchyid and spatial types)
- Xml

Newer versions and releases of SQL Server however, might support some of these data types. For the most up to date documentation of data types supported by clustered columnstore indexes, please refer to the Limitations and Restrictions section of the CREATE COLUMNSTORE INDEX (Transact-SQL) Microsoft Doc, located at *https://docs.microsoft.com/en-us/sql/t-sql/statements/create-columnstore-index-transact-sql*.

A clustered rowstore index can be converted to a clustered columnstore index by following these steps in SQL Server Management Studio (SSMS):

1. Drop the `PRIMARY KEY` constraint, if one exists.
2. Drop the clustered rowstore index
3. Define the clustered index as a columnstore index.

   This can also be accomplished by using the `DROP_EXISTING = ON` argument of the `CREATE INDEX` statement as follows:

```
CREATE CLUSTERED COLUMNSTORE INDEX [PK_Dimension_Employee]
ON [Dimension].[Employee] WITH (DROP_EXISTING = ON)
```

As previously discussed, nonclustered indexes offer additional features to improve query performance. A nonclustered rowstore index can be defined with included columns by using the `INCLUDE` syntax. This can greatly improve query performance because a single nonclustered rowstore index can cover all the columns a query returns and can be defined to filter on specific rows. Nonclustered columnstore indexes cannot be defined with included columns, but they can be filtered.

A filtered nonclustered index can be extremely powerful when queries are typically executed with a `WHERE` clause predicate. For example, a common filter to use when querying dimension columns is to filter out null values or values where a certain flag is set to TRUE. This is particularly helpful for slowly-changing dimensions.

You might have noticed that almost all dimension tables in the Wide World Importers DW database are implemented as slowly-changing dimensions by using the [Valid From] and [Valid To] columns. The latest version of a dimension member is identified by having a [Valid To] default value of '9999-12-31 23:59:59.9999999'. A common query executed by operational reports in the data warehouse might require to report data using the latest dimension member's attribute values. In this case, a query is expected to join to the dimension table where [Valid To] = '9999-12-31 23:59:59.9999999'. A filtered index would be a perfect candidate index on dimension tables for the data warehouse indexing solution in this scenario.

Also, as mentioned earlier, a common approach for an indexing solution design and implementation plan is to mix rowstore and columnstore indexes on data warehouse tables. The combination of these two types of indexes can improve performance significantly for both read and write operations. Large fact tables can benefit from this indexing solution. For example, examine the [Fact].[Sale] table in the Wide World Importers DW database. The primary key is defined with a nonclustered rowstore index on the key columns, [Sale Key] and [Invoice Date Key]. A clustered columnstore index is defined along with additional nonclustered rowstore indexes for the foreign key columns. The definition of this table is as follows:

```
CREATE TABLE [Fact].[Sale](
    [Sale Key] [bigint] IDENTITY(1,1) NOT NULL,
    [City Key] [int] NOT NULL,
    [Customer Key] [int] NOT NULL,
    [Bill To Customer Key] [int] NOT NULL,
    [Stock Item Key] [int] NOT NULL,
    [Invoice Date Key] [date] NOT NULL,
    [Delivery Date Key] [date] NULL,
    [Salesperson Key] [int] NOT NULL,
    [WWI Invoice ID] [int] NOT NULL,
    [Description] [nvarchar](100) NOT NULL,
    [Package] [nvarchar](50) NOT NULL,
    [Quantity] [int] NOT NULL,
    [Unit Price] [decimal](18, 2) NOT NULL,
    [Tax Rate] [decimal](18, 3) NOT NULL,
    [Total Excluding Tax] [decimal](18, 2) NOT NULL,
    [Tax Amount] [decimal](18, 2) NOT NULL,
    [Profit] [decimal](18, 2) NOT NULL,
    [Total Including Tax] [decimal](18, 2) NOT NULL,
    [Total Dry Items] [int] NOT NULL,
    [Total Chiller Items] [int] NOT NULL,
    [Lineage Key] [int] NOT NULL,
    INDEX CCIX_FactSale CLUSTERED COLUMNSTORE,
 CONSTRAINT [PK_Fact_Sale] PRIMARY KEY NONCLUSTERED ([Sale Key] ASC,[Invoice Date Key]
ASC)
```

The table is a columnar format table because it is defined with a clustered columnstore index. Notice that a nonclustered primary key has been defined. A primary key constraint is permissible in a table along with a clustered columnstore index as long as the primary key contraint is defined as nonclustered.

A columnstore clustered index is possible to be defined as the PRIMARY KEY constraint has been defined a nonclustered rowstore index. This approach allows for uniqueness enforcement while providing the benefit of quicker index scans through its columnstore clustered index. Figure 1-25 shows the [Fact].[Sale] table in SSMS with keys and indexes defined.

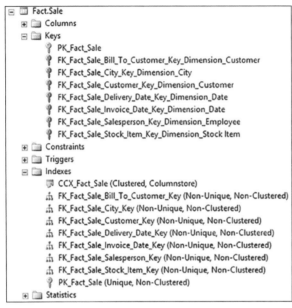

FIGURE 1-25 Foreign key constraints and indexes defined in the [Fact].[Sale] table of the Wide World Importers DW database

It is important to understand that this is not a set and forget solution. You need to constantly evaluate the need for new indexes, eliminate unused indexes, and find opportunities to consolidate indexes. The goal of the indexing solution is to improve performance while maintaining a balance of the number of indexes and corresponding storage space required.

Skill 1.4 Design storage for a data warehouse

One of the most critical resources for every SQL Server implementation is the underlying storage. The storage infrastructure in a data warehouse solution can be the source of slow query performance and data loads. The data warehouse storage's performance can be measured by analyzing the time it takes for read and write operations to complete, known as latency, and by analyzing how much data volume it can read or write in each time frame, known as throughput. High latency and low throughput can be an indication of an improper selection for the storage infrastructure or incorrect hardware and software configurations.

Design an appropriate storage solution, including hardware, disk, and file layout

The selection of an appropriate storage solution can be somewhat difficult to determine during the initial design phase of a data warehouse solution because no real-world workloads can be used as a benchmark. In most cases, the expected performance of a storage subsystem can be estimated based on several criteria:

■ Volume of data

■ Rate of change and growth of the data

■ Data retention policy

■ Number of concurrent users

■ Typical workloads expected

The volume of data is one of the most important criteria because it determines how much storage is required initially. In addition, the expected rate of growth and data retention policy has an impact on how much space is required in the long run. Understanding how much data is added, maintained, and removed during a period is important when determining proper storage size.

The data retention policy imposes special storage solution requirements. The amount of historical data that needs to be loaded and persisted in the data warehouse can create an unnecessary maintenance burden and performance bottleneck if most reporting and analysis is centered around more recent data. Data that is less frequently accessed might need to be stored in lower-tier storage such as SATA drives. More frequently accessed data might need to be stored in higher-tier storage, such as solid-state drives.

It is also important to understand how much and how often data changes in the source systems because this has a direct impact on the amount of data that needs to be inserted, updated, and perhaps deleted in the data warehouse. A high number of inserts, updates, and deletions can create concurrency issues while users try to read this data. Update operations for example, can create locks on an entire table or just a subset of rows. In the meantime, users trying to read from this table or subset of rows might experience extended wait times or even time-outs.

Two important metrics associated with storage are throughput and Input/Output Per Second (IOPS). Throughput is a measure of the amount of data that can be transferred in a period. This is typically measured in megabytes or gigabytes per second. IOPS is the number of I/O read or write operations that can complete in a second. It is important to distinguish IOPS metrics for random and sequential read and write operations to get a more precise picture. For instance, a storage subsystem with high throughput might not have high IOPS. A high throughput only determines how much data comes through, but not how rapidly it can be read or written.

The number of concurrent users executing queries and reports is also a key factor when choosing a storage subsystem. A proper storage solution should be able to support a typical user workload and be able to scale when demand for increased throughput and IOPS is required. A data warehouse where queries are subjected to extensive wait periods might be an indication of insufficient CPU and memory resources, or more importantly, a poorly designed storage solution.

Hardware

In most organizations, the storage subsystem SQL Server uses is based on either Direct-Attached Storage (DAS) or on Storage-Area Network (SAN). Direct attached storage, as the name implies, consists of storage devices that are connected directly to the server and can only be accessed by the server it is attached to. DAS storage initially referred to disk drives inside the server enclosure, but later evolved to storage appliances that connect physically to the server via one or more cables and controllers. Figure 1-26 shows a logical illustration of DAS storage.

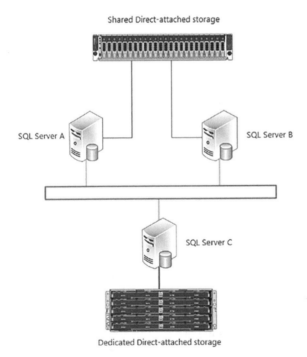

FIGURE 1-26 Illustration of direct-attached storage in a local area network

Notice that in Figure 1-26 two servers share a DAS storage device while a third server has a dedicated DAS storage device. Typically, the servers connect directly to the DAS storage device through a host bus adapter (HBA) using SCSI, Fibre Channel, or SATA connectivity. Internal disks within the same server enclosure can also be considered DAS storage.

In contrast, a Storage-Area Network connects to a server via Fibre Channel (FC) or Internet Protocol (IP) via SAN switches and allows multiple servers to access shared pools of block storage across one or more storage devices. A SAN presents a pool of block storage as a drive to the server that can be accessed and managed just like a direct attached drive would. Figure 1-27 shows a logical illustration of SAN storage.

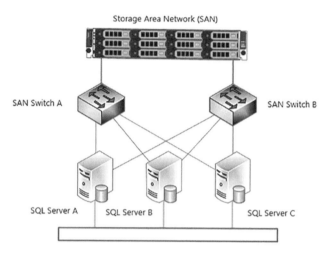

FIGURE 1-27 Illustration of storage-area network

Notice in Figure 1-27, that the servers do not connect directly to the storage device itself. Instead, it connects via a SAN switch. One or more SAN switches provide multiple paths to transfer data between the servers and the storage device. Multipathing provides a resilient storage architecture by allowing automatic failover to another path to get to and from the storage device in case an adapter or switch fails. In Figure 1-27 you can observe that there are at least two paths for each server to reach the storage device. Additional SAN switches can provide more paths in case of failure. This multipathing provided by multiple SAN switches is often referred to as a storage fabric because the crisscrossing paths resemble a piece of woven fabric.

Typically, DAS is considered as a more economical storage subsystem because it does not require additional equipment like SAN switches do. It is also considered simpler to configure because it does not require network and path configurations like SAN storage does. SAN is considered a more scalable storage solution however, because it can manage larger pools of disks and can provide higher availability through its storage fabric.

Disk

Disk storage technology has evolved tremendously in the last couple of decades. The word *disk* was used to refer to the disk-shaped magnetic media that was used in early computers. Nowadays, a disk is considered simply a device that stores data either magnetically (hard disk drives), optically (CD and DVD drives), or through integrated circuits (solid state drives).

Solid state drives (SSD) offer the most throughput and IOPS compared to any other disk type. SSDs have no mechanical components, unlike hard disk drives (HDD) that use rotating platters and a moving arm to read data from the platter surfaces. SSDs have low read and write latency because data can be read directly from any location on the drive. Another important characteristic of SSDs is that read and write performance is not affected by fragmentation as HDDs are because there are no fragment seek times.

Newer storage subsystems incorporate a mix of hard disk drives and solid state drives to implement tiered storage. Data-tiering refers to the process of assigning a certain type of storage media to distinct categories of data. For example, data that is considered historical and that is accessed less frequently is usually stored in low-tier storage. This lower-tier storage usually consists of slow spinning HDDs. Data that is accessed more frequently is usually stored in higher-tier storage such SSDs.

More and more, SSDs are becoming the norm for SQL Server storage subsystems because the increased throughput and reduced latency of SSDs improve read and write performance. SQL Server data files benefit from the increased random read and write operation speed of SSDs because there are no delays due to moving mechanical parts or data fragmentation as with HDD drives. Sequential writes performed on log files are much faster on SSDs because they support greater data transfer rates.

Read and write throughput and IOPS can be scaled to a large degree by striping the read and write operations across many disks. This is also known as a Redundant Array of Independent Disks (RAID). A RAID combines multiple disks as a single logical disk for increased performance and fault tolerance. Different RAID levels provide better performance and fault tolerance benefits.

The RAID levels most commonly recommended for SQL Server are RAID 5 and RAID 10 (or 1+0). RAID 5 provides fault tolerance and more usable storage, but at a cost for each write operation. RAID 5 is commonly used in databases that experience more reads than writes, such as read-only reporting databases. RAID 5 can be performed with as little as three disks. Usable space is reduced to two-thirds of the total raw capacity of the drives and can sustain a single drive failure.

RAID 10 provides more fault tolerance and better read and write performance than RAID 5, but sacrifices more usable storage. Usable storage is reduced to half of the total raw capacity of the drives, but can sustain up to two drive failures as long as the drives are not in the same mirrored pair. RAID 10 provides a good balance of performance and redundancy.

A common approach to storage allocation is the use of storage pools from storage-area networks. In this approach, dedicated groups of disks from the SAN device are allocated to a single server for its exclusive use. The disks in this pool are then configured as RAID 5 or 10 depending on its use. For example, out of a total of 24 disks, 4 pools of 6 disks each are grouped together in a RAID level and a logical unit number (LUN) is assigned from each of the pools of 6 disks. The LUN is presented to the server as a logical disk.

This approach has some benefits and drawbacks. It is a good approach to physically segregate server workloads. Each server has exclusive use of the physical pool of drives and no other server workload interferes with them. This is a great approach when you need to guarantee a minimum I/O performance and reduce latency from mixed workloads.

One of the major drawbacks to a segregated pool of disks is that I/O performance potential is reduced because read and write operations are spread on a smaller number of disks. Read and write operations performed over many disks pooled together perform much better because I/O is distributed across all the disks. Each disk in the large pool of disks stores only a small chunk of the data.

For example, a 240 MB file is distributed across 24 disks, broken into 24 chunks of 10 MB each. Each disk stores a 10 MB chunk of the file. This is also known as data striping. In this case, the 240 MB file is segmented and striped across each drive. When the file is requested from disk, all 24 disks provide their 10 MB segment of data concurrently, increasing throughput.

A more popular approach in recent years is the use of a single pool made up of the entire set of disks in the SAN device. Logical disks are carved out from the entire pool and presented to each server connected to the SAN device. This approach has the advantage of providing each server with the full throughput potential of the combined array of disks. Servers that experience a sudden demand for I/O throughput can take advantage of this shared throughput capacity. The effect of this higher utilization in most cases is negligible and most of the time does not affect other servers.

One advantage of a shared single pool of many disks is the ability to expand or reduce the size of the LUN as needed. If a server requires more storage capacity, a new LUN can be provided or an existing LUN can be expanded. If no space is available, the SAN device can be expanded with more physical disks if it has empty disk slots or it can be expanded by adding an expansion enclosure to hold more disks. The existing disk pool can be expanded to include the new disks added to the SAN device.

In addition to providing the ability to scale up as storage capacity requirements increase, most SAN devices provide tiered storage as well. Some SAN device manufacturers offer a hybrid storage solution that includes a mix of flash arrays, SSDs, and HDDs. Data that is accessed more frequently or is considered mission critical is moved to faster storage within the SAN device. Data that is accessed less frequently or considered less important is moved to slower performing drives. Data tiering can be done manually by the SAN administrator, but in most cases is done automatically by the SAN device itself by using internal data access statistics and algorithms.

File Layout

SQL Server file access patterns vary depending on the type of file. Data files are accessed using random read and write operations. Transaction log files are accessed using sequential operations. It is typically recommended to separate data and transaction log files into separate volumes to improve performance. The performance benefit comes from the segregation of workload patterns on the physical drives. In addition, SQL Server uses the tempdb system database for sorting, storing temporary objects, and many other activities. It is also recommended to place tempdb in a dedicated volume to support its unique workload.

Data files (.mdf and .ndf) are usually placed on one or more dedicated volumes with plenty of room for file growth. Disk drives allocated for data files need to support a high number of random write operations. Random write operations often cause heavy disk fragmentation and thus produce seek delays due to the constant repositioning of the disk head in the HDD. SSDs can reduce the read and write latency of random access operations because there are no moving disk read heads.

Log files are usually placed on a volume with dedicated drives that support high sequential write operations. Sequential write operations do not introduce as much fragmentation as random write operations. Both HDDs and SSDs can be used to place log files, although SSDs provide faster throughput and IOPS than HDDs.

Tempdb is considered a special type of database that is usually placed on a dedicated volume. Although tempdb is not considered a mission critical database, it plays a key role in SQL Server query performance. Some SQL Server environments rely heavily on tempdb and might experience sustained read and write operation demands. It is considered a best practice to place tempdb files in a dedicated volume to separate some of these unpredictably heavy I/O patterns from physical drives assigned to data and transaction log files.

Database backup file placement is often overlooked and sometimes placed in the same volume as data, transaction log, and tempdb files. A database backup and restore is an asynchronous operation that places a high I/O demand on the storage subsystem. A typical approach is to run backup jobs in volumes with faster drives so that the backup jobs can complete as quickly as possible and then move to a slower storage volume for longer term archival. It is important to emphasize that when the need arises to restore a database from a backup file, the restore operation needs to run as quickly as possible too. In this case for example, the most recent full backup file and all corresponding differential backup files might need to remain in the faster volume to be able to quickly restore the database and avoid the cost of copying the files over from the slower storage. Table 1-12 shows a common file layout for SQL Server files and tempdb.

TABLE 1-12 Common file layout of SQL Server files and tempdb

Disk	File(s)
Disk 1	Operating System & SQL Server binaries
Disk 2	System databases (master, model, msdb)
Disk 3	User database data files (.mdf & .ndf)
Disk 4	User database transaction log files (.ldf)
Disk 5	tempdb data and transaction log files
Disk 6	Database backup files

As can be observed from Table 1-12 an operating system and SQL Server binaries are often combined on a single disk. They can be separated but is not required. Disks 2 and 3 are often used for system and user databases files. It is important to separate system database files from user database files as some environments may experience high disk utilization by the msdb system database. The msdb system database is used to store SQL Agent jobs, backup history and by some features including Servive Broker and Database Mail.

Disk 4 is dedicated for user database transaction log files. SQL Server environments that experience a high volume of transactions typically write heavily to transaction logs. If more than one database uses its transaction log heavily, then it is recommended to place transaction log files in separate dedicated disks.

Disk 5 stores tempdb files. More than one tempdb data file is recommended for multi-processor SQL Server instances in which tempdb allocation contention is observed. For more details on how to optimize the performance of tempd, visit: *https://technet.microsoft.com/en-us/library/ms175527.*

Disk 6 is optional but is often used to store database backup files. Only recent backup files are store in this disk for fast retrieval in case a database restored is required. Older backup files are moved to more permanent storage or simply purged according to the organization's retention policies.

Skill 1.5 Design and implement partitioned tables and views

Table partitioning is a SQL Server feature that can greatly improve the performance of queries and data loads while simplifying the management of tables with large volumes of data. A partitioned table is essentially a combination of several groups of rows, known as partitions, that are physically stored together across one or more filegroups. Query performance can be improved through partition elimination. Data load performance and management of large tables can be improved through partition switching.

Table partitioning is generally recommended in a data warehouse with large fact tables. There is no specific recommendation as to how many rows a table must contain to consider it as a partitioning candidate. The decision to partition a table can be based on a combination of factors, including data growth, data access patterns, data retention policies, and maintenance overhead.

> **This section covers how to:**
> - Design a partition structure to support a data warehouse
> - Implement sliding windows
> - Implement partition elimination
> - Design a partition structure that supports the quick loading and scale-out of data

Design a partition structure to support a data warehouse

Table partitioning is a design consideration that is typically not included as part of the initial architecture during the data warehouse's design phase. This is in part because there might be little or no information provided to the data warehouse architect on how large a table might grow within a certain period or the types of queries that might be frequently executed against the data warehouse tables.

In most cases, table partitioning needs arise from one or more technical problems preventing the data warehouse's performance from scaling-up alongside data volume growth and increased utilization. These technical problems usually manifest after the data warehouse has been implemented in a production environment with real-world workloads. Some of these technical problems can manifest from slow queries or queries timing-out, extended high resource utilization, long-running or even failed data loads, and backups and index maintenance jobs for example. In general, most data warehouse workloads can be scaled-up by using a combination of proper partitioning and partition aligned indexes.

A table partition consists of a partition column, a partition function, and a partition scheme. The partition column is the column in the table that holds the values that are used as boundary values to group rows of data in a corresponding partition. Only one column can be defined as the partition column. A computed column is allowed as long as it is explicitly defined as PERSISTED. SQL Server uses the partition column to determine which partition to store new and existing rows in. SQL Server also uses it for partition elimination to determine which partitions need to be read based on the WHERE clause or JOIN condition of a query.

The partition function specifies a set of range boundaries based on the values of the partition column. The boundaries can be defined as a RANGE LEFT or RANGE RIGHT. A boundary defined as RANGE LEFT means that the boundary value belongs to its left partition. The boundary value is the last value in the left partition. A boundary defined as RANGE RIGHT means that the boundary value belongs to its right partition. The boundary value in this case is the first value in the right partition.

For example, assume that you want to create monthly partitions based on the [Invoice-DateKey] column from a modified version of the [Fact].[Sale] table in the Wide World Importers DW database. The [InvoiceDateKey] partition column needs to be added to the PRIMARY KEY constraint. You can define a partition function either as RANGE LEFT by using the last day of each month as the boundary value or as RANGE RIGHT by using the first day of each month. The code below shows the syntax for each boundary range option for partitions corresponding to January through April 2016.

The syntax for the range left partition function is as follows:

```
CREATE PARTITION FUNCTION MonthlyRangeLeft_pf (DATE)
AS RANGE LEFT FOR VALUES
('2016-01-31', '2016-02-29', '2016-03-31');
```

The syntax for the range right partition function is as follows:

```
CREATE PARTITION FUNCTION MonthlyRangeRight_pf (DATE)
AS RANGE RIGHT FOR VALUES
('2016-01-01', '2016-02-01', '2016-03-01');
```

Notice the difference in the boundary values defined for each range option. Figure 1-28 shows the four partitions created by both the RANGE LEFT and RANGE RIGHT boundaries.

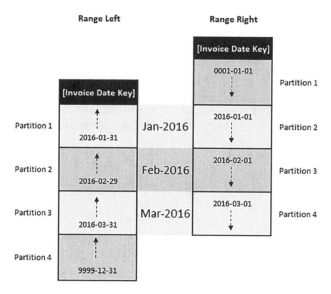

FIGURE 1-28 Partitions created using Range Left and Range Right boundaries in the partition function

Notice that in Figure 1-28 the RANGE LEFT boundary value for the Feb-2016 partition is the date 2016-02-29 because the year 2016 was a leap year. This is an important consideration when defining date boundaries. If you use the last day of the month as your boundary value, it is recommended that you create these values programmatically, for example by using the

EOMONTH() SQL function, to ensure that the leap day is assigned to the corresponding February partition. To avoid adding the leap day complexity, it might easier to define a date based partition function as a RANGE RIGHT by using the first day of the month.

Also notice that only three boundary values were specified in the partition function but four partitions were created. The total number of partitions created is equal to N+1, where N is the number of boundary values provided in the partition function. The additional partition is an automatic "catch-all" partition to group values outside the left or right range boundary value.

In a more real-world scenario, you need to list the date corresponding to every first day of the month for the periods you want to partition. This can easily be done with a dynamic SQL query that generates the partition function for you. Depending on how much data grows in a period, you can choose to generate daily, weekly, monthly, quarterly, or yearly partitions instead.

The partitions created by the partition function shown in Figure 1-28 are expressed in Table 1-13 as follows.

TABLE 1-13 Partitions from the partition function example expressed with comparison operators

Partition	Range Left	Range Right
0001-01-01		>=0001-01-01 & <2016-01-01
Jan-2016	<= 2016-01-31	>=2016-01-01 & <2016-02-01
Feb-2016	>2016-01-31 & <= 2016-02-29	>=2016-02-01 & <2016-03-01
Mar-2016	>2016-02-29 & <=2016-03-31	>=2016-03-01
9999-12-31	>2016-03-31 & <=9999-12-31	

The logical partitions created by the partition function need to be mapped to one or more filegroups by the partition scheme. A partition can only be mapped to a single filegroup. A filegroup, on the other hand, can contain one or more partitions.

A partition scheme can be defined by using the RANGE RIGHT partition function from the previous example as follows:

Map all four partitions to a single filegroup

```
CREATE PARTITION SCHEME SingleFilegroup_PS
AS PARTITION MonthlyRangeRight_PF
ALL TO ([PRIMARY]);
```

Figure 1-29 shows a representation of all the partitions mapped to a single filegroup.

Filegroup: Primary

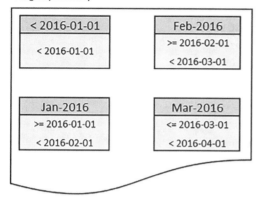

FIGURE 1-29 Partitions mapped to a single filegroup by the partition scheme

Notice that all partitions are mapped to a single filegroup named PRIMARY. When a database is created using default settings, a default filegroup named PRIMARY is created along with a primary data file. In this case, all system and user objects that are created in the database, such as tables and indexes, are assigned to the default filegroup containing the primary data file.

Additional filegroups and files can be created for a database. A filegroup can span across one or more files, but a file can only belong to a single filegroup. The primary data file's name extension is typically .mdf. Secondary data file name extensions are typically .ndf.

In the following partition scheme examples, assume that four additional filegroups (FG1, FG2, FG3, FG4) have been created in the [Fact].[Sale] table by using the ALTER DATABASE statement.

Map two partitions per filegroup (even partition distribution)

```
CREATE PARTITION SCHEME TwoFilegroups_PS
AS PARTITION MonthlyRangeRight_PF
TO (FG1, FG1, FG2, FG2)
```

Figure 1-30 shows the partitions mapped evenly across two filegroups.

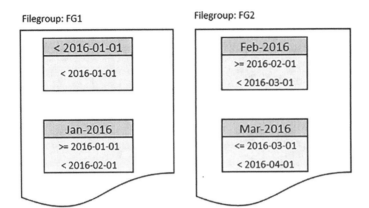

FIGURE 1-30 Partitions mapped to a single filegroup by the partition scheme

Map one partition per filegroup

```
CREATE PARTITION SCHEME PartitiontoFilegroups_PS
AS PARTITION MonthlyRangeRight_PF
TO (FG1, FG2, FG3, FG4)
```

Figure 1-31 shows a representation of the partitions mapped to individual filegroups.

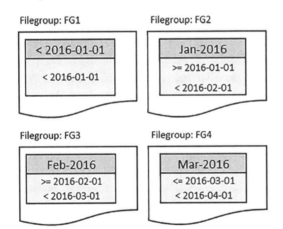

FIGURE 1-31 Partitions mapped to an individual filegroup by the partition scheme

Now that the partition function and partition scheme are defined, you can create the partitioned fact table by using one of the partition schemes on the modified version of the [Fact].[Sale] table as follows:

```
CREATE TABLE [Fact].[SaleModified](
    [Sale Key] [bigint] NOT NULL,
    [Customer Key] [int] NOT NULL,
    [Stock Item Key] [int] NOT NULL,
    [Invoice Date Key] [date] NOT NULL,
[WWI Invoice ID] [int] NOT NULL,
    [Quantity] [int] NOT NULL,
    [Unit Price] [decimal](18, 2) NOT NULL,
    [Lineage Key] [int] NOT NULL,
CONSTRAINT [PK_FactSaleModified] PRIMARY KEY ([Sale Key],[Invoice Date Key])
) ON [SingleFilegroup_PS([Invoice Date Key])
```

Notice that the table definition for the [Fact].[Sale] table has been modified considerably from the original table version in the Wide World Importers DW database for simplicity and learning purposes. This example defines a PRIMARY KEY constraint that includes the partition column, which is a requirement when partitioning a table with a unique clustered index. Remember that a PRIMARY KEY constraint generates a unique clustered index by default.

In addition, a partition scheme named [SingleFilegroup_PS] has been supplied instead of a filegroup. By executing the CREATE TABLE statement, a partitioned table is created with four partitions stored in filegroup FG1.

One of the benefits of partition functions and partition schemes is that they can be used in more than one table. You can create several fact tables with the same partition scheme if the fact table's partition column matches the data type of the partition column used in the partition function. For example, you can create the [Fact].[Order] table with the same partition scheme [SingleFilegroup_PS] used in the [Fact].[Sale] table by using the [Order Date Key] as the partition column.

So far, this section has discussed how to partition tables. Now, let's look at how partitioning works with indexes. Indexes are partitioned using the same steps that are required to partition tables. When an index is created on a partitioned table, the index is partitioned by default using the same partition schema of the table, unless a partition schema is explicitly defined for the index. If the index inherits the base table's partition schema, it is considered to be aligned with the table and is often referred to as a *partition aligned index*.

An index can also be considered aligned with the table even if the index is implemented with a different named partition function but is equivalent to the table's partition function. To be considered an equivalent partition function, the data type of the partition column must be the same on both partition functions, and the number of partitions and boundary values must also match.

One of the major benefits of aligning a table and its indexes is the ability for SQL Server to switch partitions faster and more efficiently. Partition switching refers to the process of reassigning a partition from one partitioned table to another. The switching of partitions can occur in a matter of seconds because it is a metadata change and no data is physically moved. A typical use case for partition switching can be found in the incremental loading of the data warehouse.

During the ETL process, new data is inserted into a partition in a staging table with the exact table definition as the target table. The loaded partition of the staging table is then switched over to the target table. After the partition switch completes, the new data is now available in the target table to be queried. The switch in of the new partition makes the data available almost immediately. To users querying the table, the switch is seamless.

Indexes can also be partitioned independently from their base tables by using a partition function that does not match that of the base table. Although, aligned indexes are preferred and generally recommended as best practice, nonaligned indexes can be useful in certain cases where the base table is not partitioned, the unique index of the table cannot contain the partition column, or the table is expected to join to several tables using different join columns. Partition switching does not work with nonaligned indexes.

There are several guidelines to partition the distinct types of indexes as summarized in the Table 1-14.

TABLE 1-14 Guidelines to partition different types of indexes

Unique type	Cluster Type	Guideline
Unique	Clustered & Nonclustered	Partition column must be explicitly added to the clustering key column list.
Non-unique	Clustered	Partition column does not have to be explicitly added to the clustering key column list. If omitted, SQL Server automatically adds it.
Non-unique	Nonclustered	Partition column can be part of the key column list or of the included nonkey column list

In addition to these guidelines, there are special memory requirements for partitioned indexes. Nonaligned indexes require more memory to handle concurrent sorts during an index build. The more partitions there are in a nonaligned index, the more memory is required. The total amount of memory required is a factor of the number of partitions times the minimum size for each sort table, which is equal to 40 pages with 8 kilobytes per page. This can increase if SQL Server applies degrees of parallelism to the build operation.

There is a maximum limit of 15,000 partitions that can be created for a table or index. If you were to create a partition for each day of the year, you can potentially partition data spanning more than 41 years (15,000 partitions / 365 days)!

You should use partitioning with care because the increase in the number of partitions can have performance implications due to higher demand on server resources, including memory, processor, and disk resources. Frequent and sustained high resource utilization might be observed due to higher degrees of parallelization for read and write operations on partitioned tables and indexes during data loads, query executions, and index maintenance.

In addition, there are certain partition management operations, such as partition splitting and partition merging, that can degrade performance when moving large volumes of data in and out of non-empty partitions.

Another way of partitioning data in a data warehouse is by implementing partitioned views. This was the method of choice before table partitioning was made available in SQL Server 2005. This method allows you to split a large table into smaller tables and still lets you query across them as a single object. The partitioned view is essentially a view that combines many small tables by using a UNION ALL operator.

Like table partitioning, a partitioning column is required with a CHECK constraint defined for each table. The CHECK constraint limits the data that each table stores and is used by SQL Server during query execution to read only from the corresponding tables that satisfy the query. This mechanism is like the concept of table partition functions and is how partitioned views also provide the benefits of partition elimination.

As opposed to table partitioning, partitioned views don't require a partition function or partition scheme to be defined. There is no need to specify boundary values and there is no need to satisfy a thorough list of requirements to be able to switch data in or out of a partition. One key differentiator between partitioned views and table partitioning is that partitioned views allow you to bring together tables from the same database and from different databases on the same server. These types of partitioned views are known as *local* partitioned views. In addition, you can bring together tables from databases in other servers as well. This type of partitioned view is known as a *distributed* partitioned view.

For example, assume that you decided to implement the [Fact].[SaleModified] table as a partitioned view. In this case, multiple tables holding specific years of data need to be created along with a corresponding CHECK constraint.

The following code shows a create table statement with a check constraint for 2014 sales data:

```
CREATE TABLE [Fact].[SaleModified2014](
    [Sale Key] [bigint] NOT NULL,
    [Customer Key] [int] NOT NULL,
    [Stock Item Key] [int] NOT NULL,
    [Invoice Date Key] [date] NOT NULL
CONSTRAINT CKC_2014 CHECK ([Invoice Date Key] between '2014-01-01' and '2014-12-31'),
    [WWI Invoice ID] [int] NOT NULL,
    [Quantity] [int] NOT NULL,
    [Unit Price] [decimal](18, 2) NOT NULL,
    [Lineage Key] [int] NOT NULL,
 CONSTRAINT [PK_FactSaleModified2014] PRIMARY KEY ([Sale Key],[Invoice Date Key])
 )
```

The following code shows a create table statement with a check constraint for 2015 sales data:

```
CREATE TABLE [Fact].[SaleModified2015](
    [Sale Key] [bigint] NOT NULL,
    [Customer Key] [int] NOT NULL,
    [Stock Item Key] [int] NOT NULL,
    [Invoice Date Key] [date] NOT NULL
CONSTRAINT CKC_2015 CHECK ([Invoice Date Key] between '2015-01-01' and '2015-12-31'),
    [WWI Invoice ID] [int] NOT NULL,
```

```
      [Quantity] [int] NOT NULL,
      [Unit Price] [decimal](18, 2) NOT NULL,
      [Lineage Key] [int] NOT NULL,
    CONSTRAINT [PK_FactSaleModified2015] PRIMARY KEY ([Sale Key],[Invoice Date Key])

)
```

The following code shows a create table statement with a check constraint for 2016 sales data:

```
  CREATE TABLE [Fact].[SaleModified2016]
(
      [Sale Key] [bigint] NOT NULL,
      [Customer Key] [int] NOT NULL,
      [Stock Item Key] [int] NOT NULL,
      [Invoice Date Key] [date] NOT NULL
CONSTRAINT CKC_2016 CHECK ([Invoice Date Key] between '2016-01-01' and '2016-12-31'),
      [WWI Invoice ID] [int] NOT NULL,
      [Quantity] [int] NOT NULL,
      [Unit Price] [decimal](18, 2) NOT NULL,
      [Lineage Key] [int] NOT NULL,
  CONSTRAINT [PK_FactSaleModified2016] PRIMARY KEY ([Sale Key],[Invoice Date Key])
  )
```

Now, insert some values into each table as follows:

```
INSERT INTO [Fact].[SaleModified2014]
 VALUES(60969,122,16,'2014-01-01',18768,40,32.00,11)
 INSERT INTO [Fact].[SaleModified2015]
 VALUES(126913,289,142,'2015-01-01',39074,48,18.00,11)
  INSERT INTO [Fact].[SaleModified2016]
 VALUES(198858,300,75,'2016-01-01',61340,120,18.00,11)
```

You can now define the partitioned view by doing a UNION ALL of the three tables you created.

```
CREATE VIEW [Fact].[SaleModifiedLast3Years]
 AS
SELECT [Sale Key], [Customer Key], [Stock Item Key], [Invoice Date Key],
[WWI Invoice ID], [Quantity], [Unit Price]
  FROM [WideWorldImportersDW].[Fact].[SaleModified2014]
  UNION ALL
SELECT [Sale Key], [Customer Key], [Stock Item Key], [Invoice Date Key],
[WWI Invoice ID], [Quantity], [Unit Price]
  FROM [WideWorldImportersDW].[Fact].[SaleModified2015]
  UNION ALL
SELECT [Sale Key], [Customer Key], [Stock Item Key], [Invoice Date Key],
[WWI Invoice ID], [Quantity], [Unit Price]
  FROM [WideWorldImportersDW].[Fact].[SaleModified2016]
```

Now that you have defined the partitioned view, you can query the view by executing a regular select statement.

Select data from partitioned view

```
SELECT * FROM [Fact].[SaleModifiedLast3Years]
```

The query returns the three rows you previously inserted. The execution plan of the select query shows data being selected from each table, as shown in Figure 1-32.

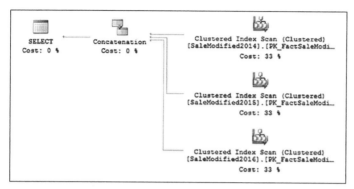

FIGURE 1-32 Execution plan of a non-selective query of the [Fact].[SaleModifiedLast3Years] partitioned view

The benefits of a partitioned view can be observed for more selective queries that use the partition column as part of the WHERE clause. For example, consider a query that only selects data for 2015.

Selective query for the month of January, 2015

```
SELECT * FROM [Fact].[SaleModifiedLast3Years]
  WHERE [Invoice Date Key] between '2015-01-01' and '2015-01-31'
```

The execution plan of the query is shown in Figure 1-33.

FIGURE 1-33 Execution plan of a selective query on the [Fact].[SaleModifiedLast3Years] partitioned view

As you can see from the execution plan in Figure 1-33, only the [Fact].[SaleModified2015] table was read. The other two tables in the partition view were eliminated from the execution plan. This is like the concept of partition elimination for table partitioning.

Partitioned views can be a way to improve performance when implementing table partitioning is not possible. In addition, partitioned views offer more flexibility than table partitioning because swapping data in and out is as simple as modifying the partitioned view. For example, to add data for the year 2017, add a new table in the UNION ALL statement of the partitioned view. This change is a metadata only change and does not require data to be moved.

Implement sliding windows

A sliding window partitioning strategy is a common data management practice in most data warehouse environments with a data retention policy that establishes how long data is retained in operational database tables. The retention policy can establish how often data is purged or archived and how far back data should be retained in the operational database.

Highly regulated industries, such as healthcare and finance, have legal requirements to retain data for a certain period before it can be deleted. Organizations in these regulated industries with high volumes of data often put a data archival and deletion strategy in place that allows them to maintain compliance while keeping their operational databases streamlined with data that is actively accessed. A sliding window partition strategy provides a mechanism to move large volumes of data in and out of a table quickly and with minimal or zero disruption.

A sliding window partition strategy allows for the same number of partitions to be maintained on a table by adding new partitions for future data and by removing partitions for data outside the retention period. The net effect of adding new partitions and removing old partitions is always being able to maintain a constant number of partitions. The old partitions are either deleted or archived.

For example, consider a sliding window partition strategy where only data for the past three years (current year + previous two years) should be maintained in the [Fact].[Sale] table. This is considered the *active* data. Data older than three years should be moved into an archive table. On January 1st, 2016, the sliding window partition process kicks-off and performs the following three main tasks:

1. Move the 2013 year data from the table partition into an archive table by using the SWITCH function.

2. Merge the 2013 and 2014 year ranges in the partition function by using the MERGE function.

3. Add a new empty 2016 year partition by modifying the partition function by using the SPLIT function.

Figure 1-34 shows an illustration of the two main tasks performed during a sliding window partition process execution.

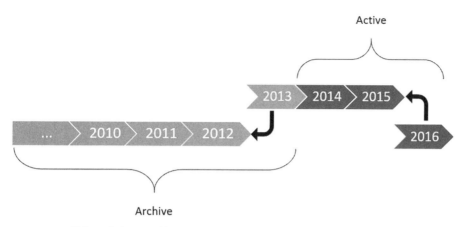

FIGURE 1-34 Sliding window partition process illustration

As illustrated in Figure 1-34, at the start of each year the oldest partition is archived and a new empty partition is added for the new year. As expected from the requirement in the example, only active data for the three most recent years remains on the table partitions. Data older than three years is moved to the archive table partitions.

Take a look at how to implement this sliding window partition strategy by using a modified version of the [Fact].[Sale] table from the Wide World Importers DW database. First, define the partition function, partition scheme, and table that would be present until midnight on December 31, 2015.

Partition function

```
CREATE PARTITION FUNCTION [MostRecent3Years_PF](date) AS RANGE RIGHT
FOR VALUES (N'2013-01-01', N'2014-01-01', N'2015-01-01');
```

Partition scheme

```
CREATE PARTITION SCHEME [MostRecent3Years_PS] AS PARTITION [MostRecent3Years_PF]
ALL TO ([USERDATA]);
```

Create table [Fact].[SaleModified]

```
CREATE TABLE [Fact].[SaleModified](
    [Sale Key] [bigint] NOT NULL,
    [Customer Key] [int] NOT NULL,
    [Stock Item Key] [int] NOT NULL,
    [Invoice Date Key] [date] NOT NULL,
[WWI Invoice ID] [int] NOT NULL,
    [Quantity] [int] NOT NULL,
    [Unit Price] [decimal](18, 2) NOT NULL,
    [Lineage Key] [int] NOT NULL,
CONSTRAINT [PK_FactSaleModified] PRIMARY KEY ([Sale Key],[Invoice Date Key])
) ON [MostRecent3Years_PF]([Invoice Date Key])
```

The partition function in this example creates four partitions. Remember that the number of partitions is equal to the number of boundary values plus 1 (n+1). Because the partition is defined as a RANGE RIGHT, the first partition (PARTITION 1) stores rows with [Invoice Date Key] values less than the first boundary value, in this case 2012 and earlier year data. The assumption is that this partition is empty because 2012 year data was archived on January 1st, 2015. The second partition (PARTITION 2) includes 2013 year data, the third partition (PARTITION 3) includes 2014 year data, and the fourth partition (PARTITION 4) contains 2015 year data.

The next step is to move the 2013 year data currently stored in PARTITION 2 out of the [Fact].[SaleModified] table and into an archive table by using the SPLIT function as follows:

Switch partition

```
ALTER TABLE [Fact].[Sale]
SWITCH PARTITION 2 TO [Fact].[SaleModified_Archive]
```

Notice that there are certain requirements that need to be met for partition switching to work. For a complete list of requirements, visit *https://technet.microsoft.com/en-us/library/ms191160*. The following list shows a subset of these requirements:

- Source and target tables must share the same filegroup.
- Source and target tables must have the same column structure, order, and nullability.
- Source and target tables must have the same FOREIGN KEY constraints.
- Source and target tables must not be replicated.
- Partitions must be on the same column.
- The receiving nonpartitioned table or receiving partition of a partitioned table must exist and it must be empty.
- Boundary values of the source partition must be within the boundary of the target partition.
- Tables must have the same clustered indexes and nonclustered indexes.
- Indexes must be aligned with table partitions.
- Triggers must not activate while moving partitions.

In addition, when using the SWITCH function, you might need to specify a partition number depending on if the source and target tables are partitioned or not. Table 1-15 summarizes the partition number requirements.

TABLE 1-15 Partition number specification based on table partitioning

Source	Target	Restriction
Partitioned	Non-partitioned	Partition number of the source table must be specified.
Non-partitioned	Partitioned	Partition number of the target table must be specified.
Partitioned	Partitioned	Partition number of both the source table and target table must be specified.
Non-partitioned	Non-partitioned	No partition number needs to be specified.

PARTITION 2 of [Fact].[SaleModified] is empty now that the data has been switched out. PARTITION 1 was already empty because the partition function created this empty partition automatically. Now, you can proceed to merge PARTITION 2 with PARTITION 1. Because both partitions being merged are empty, there is no data movement and it is a metadata only change. Execute the MERGE function as follows:

Merge range in partition function

```
ALTER PARTITION FUNCTION MostRecent3Years_PF()
MERGE RANGE ('2013-01-01')
```

The boundary '2013-01-01' is now removed from the partition function. The first boundary is now the '2014-01-01'. PARTITION 1 now stores rows with [Invoice Date Key] values for 2013 and prior year data. In this case, this first partition is empty again because all the 2013 year data was switched out. The second partition (PARTITION 2) now stores 2014 year data, and the third partition (PARTITION 3) now stores 2015 year data.

At this point, there is no partition to store 2016 year data. Next, you need to create a new empty partition by using the SPLIT function as follows:

Split function

```
ALTER PARTITION FUNCTION MostRecent3Years_PF()
SPLIT RANGE ('2016-01-01')
```

The split function creates a new boundary value of '2016-01-01' in the partition function. A new empty fourth partition (PARTITION 4) is added and is now available to store rows with [Invoice Date Key] values for 2016 and future year data.

A sliding window partition strategy can also allow you to quickly make new data available in a large partitioned table. This is done by creating an empty staging table with the exact table and index structure as the target table. The data load process inserts all new data into the staging table and the data is then switched into a new empty partition in the target table. This pattern is typically implemented for daily incremental loads of large fact tables.

For example, to load the entire 2016 year data into the PARTITION 4 of the [Fact].[SaleModified] table, you first need to create a staging table with an exact table structure as follows:

Create staging table [Fact].[SaleModified_Staging]

```
CREATE TABLE [Fact].[SaleModified_Staging](
    [Sale Key] [bigint] NOT NULL,
    [Customer Key] [int] NOT NULL,
    [Stock Item Key] [int] NOT NULL,
    [Invoice Date Key] [date] NOT NULL,
[WWI Invoice ID] [int] NOT NULL,
    [Quantity] [int] NOT NULL,
    [Unit Price] [decimal](18, 2) NOT NULL,
    [Lineage Key] [int] NOT NULL,
 CONSTRAINT [PK_FactSaleModified_Staging] PRIMARY KEY ([Sale Key],[Invoice Date Key])
) ON [MostRecent3Years_PS] ([Invoice Date Key])
```

You can now proceed to load 2016 year data into the staging table. Both staging and target tables have been created identically and contain the same number of partitions. Notice that the same partition scheme as the target table has been defined for the staging table. The staging table's 2016 year data is stored in PARTITION 4, similar to the target table. The partition switch syntax is as follows:

Partition switch from the staging table to [Fact].[SaleModified] target table

```
ALTER TABLE [Fact].[SaleModified_Staging]
SWITCH PARTITION 4 TO [Fact].[SaleModified] PARTITION 4
```

Notice that, as per Table 1-15, both partition numbers from the source to target table need to be specified in the SWITCH statement. The 2016 year data is now available to be queried from the [Fact].[SaleModified] table.

An important T-SQL function that can be useful when reloading an existing partition is the TRUNCATE TABLE function using the WITH (Partitions()) argument. In some cases, a previously loaded partition in a large table might need to be emptied and switched in with updated data. For example, suppose that updated 2016 year data has been loaded into the staging table. Before data can be switched in from the staging table, you need to have an empty partition available in the target table. You can use the TRUNCATE TABLE statement to truncate the specific partition in [Fact].[SaleModified], in this case PARTITION 4, as follows:

Truncate table with partitions argument

```
TRUNCATE TABLE [Fact].[SaleModified] WITH (PARTITIONS (4))
```

The TRUNCATE TABLE function, along with the WITH (PARTITIONS()) argument, provides a mechanism to empty the contents of a partition. This can be very useful in situations where you want to reutilize an existing partition and avoid creating a new partition.

The partition merge and partition split process can be a fast metadata change process as long as the partitions being merged and split are empty. A partition merge or split on a non-empty partition requires data movement that can place extended locks and cause extensive waits. For this reason, it is always recommended to have empty partitions on both ends of the partition range.

In some cases, the TRUNCATE TABLE function, along with the WITH (PARTITIONS()) argument, can be very useful when performing a partition split on a non-empty partition. For example, you can copy the data out of a partition into a temporary table, truncate the partition, and then perform a partition split.

A sliding window partition strategy allows you to manage a finite number of partitions in large data warehouse tables by switching new data in and switching historical data out with minimal overhead. A sliding window partition can be managed automatically by creating an automatic sliding window partition that dynamically creates the necessary steps, such as a partition switches, partition merges, and partition splits. You can read more about how to implement an automatic sliding window in a partitioned table at *https://technet.microsoft.com/en-us/library/aa964122*. Although, this article was written for SQL Server 2005, most of the concepts still apply for SQL Server 2016.

A sliding window strategy can also be implemented for partitioned views. A sliding window strategy for partitioned views is much simpler than in table partitioning because there is no partition function to SPLIT or MERGE. The only tasks that are required for partitioned views are to remove the table to be archived from the UNION ALL list and to add the table with the new year data in the view definition. From this point of view, partitioned views are simpler to implement and maintain.

SQL Server provides catalog views that can be queried to gather information about partitions, including information about their structure and statistics. For example, sys.partitions provides information about each partition, such as the partition number, object id, and index id for the object it belongs to, the compression state, and the approximate number of rows that the partition stores.

In addition, you can query catalog views for partition functions, partition schemes, and filegroups including:

- sys.partition_functions
- sys.partition_range_values
- sys.partition_parameters
- sys.data_spaces
- sys.filegroups
- sys.destination_data_spaces
- sys.partition_schemes

For example, you can query the sys.partition_functions and sys.partition_range_values to get the boundary values of the [MostRecent3Years_PF] partition function as follows:

```
SELECT f.name as PartitionFunctionName,  r.value as BoundaryValue
FROM sys.partition_functions f
inner join sys.partition_range_values  r on r.function_id = f.function_id
where name = 'MostRecent3Years_PF'
```

You can also query the sys.partitions and sys.indexes catalog views to gather the number of rows per partition for the clustered index of the [Fact].[SaleModifed] table as follows:

```
SELECT   i.name as IndexName,  p.partition_number as PartitionNumber,   p.rows as
CountofRows
FROM sys.partitions As p
INNER JOIN sys.indexes As I ON p.object_id = i.object_id AND p.index_id = i.index_id
WHERE p.object_id = object_id('Fact.SaleModified') and i.index_id > 0
ORDER BY i.index_id, p.partition_number
```

Implement partition elimination

As previously described, partition aligned indexes used in queries that execute frequently can have tremendous performance gains due to partition elimination. During partition elimination, entire partitions are skipped from being read, and therefore the query plan becomes much more efficient because only rows needed by the query are read.

The previous section discussed how to implement yearly partitions based on the [Invoice Date Key] of the [Fact].[SaleModified] table. You can verify that this partitioning strategy provides performance gains by executing a query that aligns with the partition function as follows:

Top 10 Customers by Revenue for 2015

```
SELECT TOP 10 [Customer Key], sum([Quantity] * [Unit Price]) as Revenue
FROM  [Fact].[SaleModified]
WHERE  [Invoice Date Key] between '2015-01-01' and '2015-12-31'
and [Customer Key] <> 0
GROUP BY [Customer Key]
ORDER BY Revenue DESC
```

The query lists the Top 10 Customers by Revenue for the year 2015. Notice that the WHERE clause aligns perfectly with the partition column and one of the boundary ranges of the partition function. Only the 2015 partition should be read and the partitions for 2014 and 2016 should be eliminated from the query plan. The execution plan and index seek information box is shown in Figure 1-35 below.

Clustered Index Scan (Clustered)
Scanning a clustered index, entirely or only a range.

Physical Operation	Clustered Index Scan
Logical Operation	Clustered Index Scan
Actual Execution Mode	Row
Estimated Execution Mode	Row
Storage	RowStore
Number of Rows Read	71898
Actual Number of Rows	44364
Actual Number of Batches	0
Estimated Operator Cost	0.381419 (47%)
Estimated I/O Cost	0.301792
Estimated Subtree Cost	0.381419
Estimated CPU Cost	0.0796267
Estimated Number of Executions	1
Number of Executions	1
Estimated Number of Rows to be Read	72245.2
Estimated Number of Rows	56737.6
Estimated Row Size	27 B
Actual Rebinds	0
Actual Rewinds	0
Partitioned	True
Actual Partition Count	1
Ordered	True
Node ID	3

FIGURE 1-35 Execution plan showing partition elimination

As expected, the Actual Partition Count is equal to 1. This means that a single partition corresponding to 2015 was read and the other two partitions for 2014 and 2016 were eliminated from the execution plan. Although, a clustered index scan was performed, partition elimination still provided a performance benefit for this query because only the required 2015 year data partition was scanned.

Next, look at how the execution query looks when joining a partitioned table to a non-partitioned table. This example shows how to join to the [Dimension].[Customer] dimension table.

Query joining a partitioned table to a non-partitioned table

```
SELECT c.[Customer Key], c.[Customer], f.[WWI Invoice ID], f.[Quantity], f.[Unit Price]
FROM  [Fact].[SaleModified] f
INNER JOIN [Dimension].[Customer] c ON c.[Customer Key] = f.[Customer Key]
WHERE f.[Customer Key] = 110
AND f.[Invoice Date Key] between '2015-06-01' and '2015-06-30'
```

In this query, invoice details for a particular customer are requested for the month of June in 2015. The execution plan and index scan information box is shown in Figure 1-36.

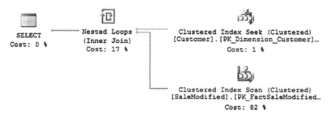

Clustered Index Scan (Clustered)
Scanning a clustered index, entirely or only a range.

Physical Operation	Clustered Index Scan
Logical Operation	Clustered Index Scan
Actual Execution Mode	Row
Estimated Execution Mode	Row
Storage	RowStore
Number of Rows Read	71898
Actual Number of Rows	14
Actual Number of Batches	0
Estimated Operator Cost	0.406689 (82%)
Estimated I/O Cost	0.327063
Estimated Subtree Cost	0.406689
Estimated CPU Cost	0.0796267
Estimated Number of Executions	1
Number of Executions	1
Estimated Number of Rows to be Read	72245.2
Estimated Number of Rows	55.0844
Estimated Row Size	31 B
Actual Rebinds	0
Actual Rewinds	0
Partitioned	True
Actual Partition Count	1
Ordered	True
Node ID	2

FIGURE 1-36 Execution plan and information box showing partition elimination between a partitioned table and a non-partitioned table

Notice in Figure 1-35 that partition elimination still occurs for the clustered index scan in the partitioned [Fact].[SaleModified] table. In this case, a nonclustered index can be added to improve query performance. Remember that all nonclustered indexes need to include the partition column as part of the index key columns or as an included column. The nonclustered index definition to improve performance for this query is as follows:

Nonclustered index

```
CREATE NONCLUSTERED INDEX NCIX_Customer_InvoiceDate
ON [Fact].[SaleModified] ([Customer Key],[Invoice Date Key])
INCLUDE ([WWI Invoice ID],[Quantity],[Unit Price])
```

The execution plan after adding the nonclustered index is shown in Figure 1-37.

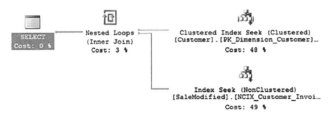

Index Seek (NonClustered)

Scan a particular range of rows from a nonclustered index.

Physical Operation	Index Seek
Logical Operation	Index Seek
Actual Execution Mode	Row
Estimated Execution Mode	Row
Storage	RowStore
Number of Rows Read	14
Actual Number of Rows	14
Actual Number of Batches	0
Estimated Operator Cost	0.0033426 (49%)
Estimated I/O Cost	0.003125
Estimated Subtree Cost	0.0033426
Estimated CPU Cost	0.0002176
Estimated Number of Executions	1
Number of Executions	1
Estimated Number of Rows	55.0844
Estimated Number of Rows to be Read	55.0844
Estimated Row Size	24 B
Actual Rebinds	0
Actual Rewinds	0
Partitioned	True
Actual Partition Count	1
Ordered	True
Node ID	2

FIGURE 1-37 Execution plan and information plan after adding the nonclustered index

In this latest execution plan, the nonclustered index provided additional performance gains because the index operator changed to an index seek instead of an index scan. Partition elimination still occurred because only a single partition was read as noted in the Actual Partition Count value of 1.

Design a partition structure that supports the quick loading and scale-out of data

Scaling-out the data refers to the mechanism put in place to spread the processing of data across as many servers as necessary to improve querying and data loading performance. It should not be confused with scaling-up, which refers to increasing the resources of a server, such as CPU and memory resources. Scaling-up is usually the initial step towards scaling a database. As resource utilization demand increases, additional hardware, such as processing power and memory, can satisfy this need.

Scaling-up can be quicker and less complex than scaling-out because no changes are required to the database architecture. Additional hardware can be installed on an existing server or you can purchase a completely new, bigger, and more powerful server to migrate the data over to. Conversely, scaling-out means adding additional servers instead of making a single server more powerful.

There are several factors that can dictate what data scale-out solution can be implemented. The first factor depends on how often data changes. If data changes frequently certain scale-out solutions that require data replication might not work because data contention might increase. Data that is inserted or updated frequently needs to be constantly replicated across multiple databases. The cost of replicating changes might be too high and degrade performance instead.

A second factor to consider is the ability to implement a scale-out solution that is transparent to the user or reporting applications. Some scale-out solutions might require changes to table relationships, stored procedures, and the way user queries are written. Certain reporting applications might not be able to support a scale-out solution that requires executing distributed queries or querying linked servers.

A third factor is the ability to partition the data in a way that aligns to typical query patterns. An effective scale-out solution involves partitioning data across several databases located on separate servers to handle queries that require a portion of the data. For example, data that is partitioned by customer geography, where each database on each server contains only customers from a region such as North America or European regions, works if all queries filter on region. If the queries typically select customers and their transactions across regions, this partition strategy does not work because it requires that all databases across all servers be queried.

In this last case, no performance benefits can be observed from partition elimination because no databases are eliminated from the query execution plan. There might still be a performance benefit from this scale-out solution if the combined processing power of all servers exceeds the added processing overhead of assembling the results.

A fourth and last factor in the type of scale-out solution that can be implemented is the interdependence of the data. In this scale-out solution, data is split based on how data is typically related and used within areas of the database. For example, fact tables use foreign key relationship constraints to enforce referential integrity. A partition strategy that involves splitting dimension and fact tables on different databases does not work in this case because referential integrity enforcement across databases is not supported. A better partition approach is to group related tables together that only relate to each other and don't have relationships to the rest of the data model. This group of related tables that are isolated from the rest are often referred to as data marts.

There are many options to scale-out the data, but the six more frequently implemented scale-out solutions involve the following mechanisms:

1. Allowing multiple database engines to access a single copy of the database.

2. Replicating the database to multiple database servers.

3. Implementing linked servers and executing distributed queries.

4. Implementing distributed partitioned views.

5. Routing queries to the correct database using some middleware service.

6. Implementing a stretch database with Azure.

One of the easiest scale-out solutions is to share a single copy of a database on a SAN storage device. This scale-out solution is often referred to as a shared disk scale-out solution, where processing power is scaled-out to many servers using a single disk image of the data. In this case, the database is attached as a read-only database to each of the database servers. This scale-out solution is only suitable for scenarios where read-only operations are required, such as reporting solutions. This scale-out solution does not work in scenarios where data is constantly updated and reports need to reflect the most recent data loaded in the database.

A shared database scale-out solution works great for data warehouses that are only updated after business hours or during scheduled maintenance windows. In this case, the database is placed in read-write mode in one of the servers and data is loaded. After the data loads complete, the database is placed in read-only mode again. If reporting is expected to continue after business hours or during the scheduled maintenance window, a separate copy of the database is used for data loads and the read-only database image is replaced with the newly loaded database image. Figure 1-38 shows an illustration of a shared database scale-out solution.

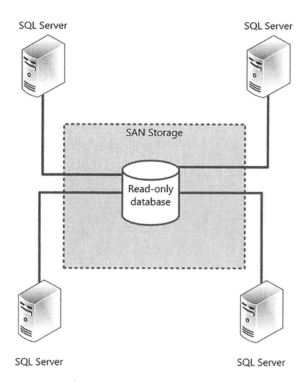

FIGURE 1-38 Illustration of a shared database scale-out solution

A second approach to scale-out is to replicate the data to multiple servers, each containing its own copy of the database. This scale-out solution has additional storage implications because multiple copies of the database are needed. Data updates are replicated by using peer-to-peer transactional replication. The main advantage of this scale-out solution is the ability to replicate data updated in any SQL Server to all other copies of the database. A peer-to-peer replication scale-out solution works great for environments where data is updated with moderate frequency and where no data update conflicts are expected. If data update conflicts are expected, merge replication might be more appropriate. The drawback of merge replication is that it imposes more overhead than peer-to-peer replication. Figure 1-38 shows an illustration of peer-to-peer replication.

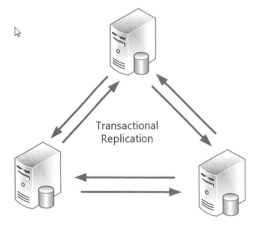

FIGURE 1-39 Illustration of peer-to-peer replication scale-out solution

A third scale-out solution involves the configuration of linked servers. Databases from linked-servers can be queried as if they were local databases. A scaled-out database across several linked servers can be logically accessed as a single large database. This scale-out solution requires servers to be configured as linked servers and for queries to be changed slightly by including a four-part name that includes the server name. For example, a query against an HR database located on a linked server would look as follows:

```
SELECT * FROM HRServer.HRDB.dbo.Employees
```

A linked server scale-out approach provides the ability to segregate databases by subject area, but still provide the ability to report across all subject areas if required. For example, a dedicated database for an Inventory data warehouse and a dedicated database for a Sales data warehouse might exist on separate SQL servers. By linking these servers, a query can bring data from both databases together into a consolidated Inventory and Sales report. Figure 1-40 shows a logical representation of linked servers.

Local
SQL Server

Linked
SQL Server

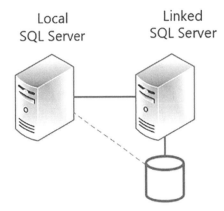

FIGURE 1-40 Illustration of linked servers

A fourth approach is to implement distributed partitioned views. Just like partitioned views covered previously, data is partitioned among tables, but in this case, the tables are distributed across several databases. The check constraints in each table tell SQL Server which table, and therefore which database, to get the data from. Distributed partitioned views rely on queries using the partitioning key as part of the filter criteria. Queries that don't use the partitioning key result in each table from all databases being read.

A distributed partition view scale-out approach works well in data warehouses where historical data is archived in one or more historical databases. For example, some organizations might choose to archive data in yearly databases. Queries can take advantage of partition elimination by using this approach if they commonly filter data for particular years as part of the WHERE clause predicate.

A fifth scale-out solution involves the use of a middleware service to route queries to the correct database. In this approach, a software application acts as the middleman between the user or the reporting application and the database. This type of scale-out solution is referred to as data-dependent routing. Queries are then routed by the middleware to the appropriate database containing the data. This scale-out approach requires a more complex management of the data.

For example, a data warehouse database can be broken down into separate databases that contain all information about customer sales by region. When a query is executed for sales data about a customer that belongs to a country, the middleware service routes the query to the corresponding database. Figure 1-41 shows a data dependent routing scale-out solution.

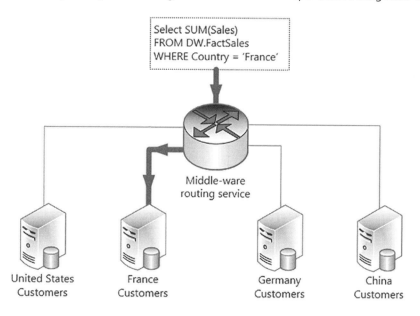

FIGURE 1-41 Illustration of data-dependent routing scale-out solution

Notice in Figure 1-41 that the query that sums the sales for customers in France is executed by routing it to the France Customers database.

The sixth scale-out solution commonly implemented is through

. SQL Server stretch databases allow you to dynamically place transactional data into an Azure database. In this approach, you end up with a hybrid. This scale-out solution allows you to store cold or warm data in the Azure cloud while maintaining data that is accessed more frequently in on-premise servers. Stretch databases allow you to move data out of large tables based on a simple filter function specified on one or more tables. After a table is defined as a stretch table and a filter function is defined, you can gradually start to migrate data to the Azure database.

A stretch database is seamless and transparent to the user. Queries are executed normally against the local table. SQL Server can eliminate reading the rows stored in Azure if they are not required in the query results. The filter function specified in the table acts, in this case, as a partition key. Figure 1-42 shows an illustration of a stretch database.

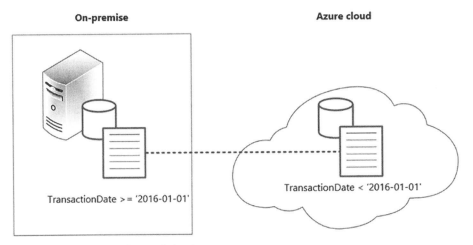

FIGURE 1-42 Illustration of a stretch database

Notice that in Figure 1-42 a table has been defined as a stretch table in the Azure cloud. The rows that are physically stored on-premise include data with a transaction date greater than or equal to '2016-01-01'. Data with a transaction date older than this is moved to the Azure cloud.

Thought experiment

In this thought exercise, demonstrate your skills and knowledge of the topics covered in this chapter. You can find the answer to this thought experiment in the next section.

You are tasked to create a logical star schema diagram that models the Wide World Importers purchasing business process. The business is interested in creating an analysis to compare the quantity of stock items ordered vs. the quantity of stock items received for all their purchase orders and corresponding suppliers over time.

The Wide World Importers sample database contains a dedicated schema for the Purchasing related tables. An entity relationship diagram of the source tables needed for your requirements is shown in Figure 1-43.

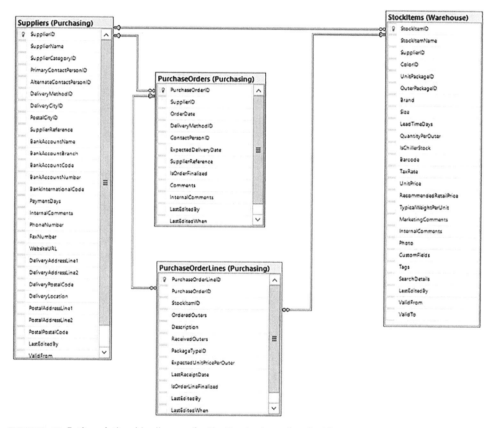

FIGURE 1-43 Entity relationship diagram for the Purchasing related tables

Notice that there is a PurchaseOrders parent table and a PurchaseOrderLines child table. The PurchaseOrderLines child table tracks the individual stock items that were ordered in the purchase order. The [OrderedOuters] column tracks the stock item quantity that was ordered.

The [ReceivedOrders] columns track the stock quantity that was received. The PurchaseOrders parent table tracks order level information, such as the supplier, delivery method, and order date.

With the information provided, complete the following tasks:

1. Identify the dimensions and attributes required to satisfy the analysis requested by the business.

2. Identify the measures required to satisfy the analysis requested by the business.

3. Identify the source columns for dimension attributes and measures.

4. Design dimension tables and a fact table required to satisfy the analysis requested by the business.

5. Create an entity relationship diagram showing a star schema model between the fact table and dimensions.

Thought experiment answer

This section provides the solution for each of the five tasks included in the thought experiment.

1. Identify the dimensions and attributes required to satisfy the analysis requested by the business.

   You were tasked to provide the ability to compare two measures across the following entities: purchase order, stock items, suppliers, and time. For the purposes of this exercise, you can assume that you only need bare minimum attributes, such as th name and ID of the entity members. The date dimension is a standard dimension and at a minimum, needs to include a date, month, quarter, and year. So far, the dimensions and attributes identified are listed in Table 1-16.

   TABLE 1-16 Dimension and attributes

Dimension	Attributes
Stock Item	Stock Item ID, Stock Item Name
Supplier	Supplier ID, Supplier Name
Purchase Order	Purchase Order ID
Date	Date, Month, Quarter, Year

   Identify the measures required to satisfy the analysis requested by the business.

2. The two measures requested for this analysis are ordered quantity and received quantity.

3. Identify the source columns for dimension attributes and measures.

You can create a data mapping document that shows the source table and column for each attribute and measure.

Table 1-17 maps dimension and attrributes to corresponding source tables and columns.

TABLE 1-17 Dimension attribute source mapping

Dimension Table	Attribute	Source Table	Source Column
StockItem	[StockItemID]	[Warehouse].[StockItems]	[StockItemID]
StockItem	[StockItemName]	[Warehouse].[StockItems]	[StockItemName]
Supplier	[SupplierID]	[Purchasing].[Suppliers]	[SupplierID]
Supplier	[SupplierName]	[Purchasing].[Suppliers]	[SupplierName]
PurchaseOrder	[PurchaseOrderID]	[Purchasing].[PurchaseOrders]	[PurchaseOrderID]
Date	Date	Autogenerated	Autogenerated
Date	Month	Autogenerated	Autogenerated
Date	Quarter	Autogenerated	Autogenerated
Date	Year	Autogenerated	Autogenerated

Table 1-18 maps measures to corresponding source tables and columns.

TABLE 1-18 Measure source mapping

Fact Table	Measure	Source Table	Source Column
Purchase	[OrderedQuantity]	[Purchasing].[PurchaseOrderLines]	[OrderedOuters]
Purchase	[ReceivedQuantity]	[Purchasing].[PurchaseOrderLines]	[ReceivedOrders]

Design dimension tables and a fact table required to satisfy the analysis requested by the business.

Table 1-19 lists the `[Dimension].[StockItem]` table definition.

TABLE 1-19 [StockItem] dimension table

Column	Data Type	ColumnType
[StockItemKey]	Int	Surrogate Key
[StockItemID]	Int	Alternate Key
[StockItemName]	nvarchar(100)	Attribute

Table 1-20 lists the `[Dimension].[Supplier]` table definition.

TABLE 1-20 [Supplier] dimension table

Column	Data Type	ColumnType
[SupplierKey]	Int	Surrogate Key
[SupplierID]	Int	Alternate Key
[SupplierName]	nvarchar(100)	Attribute

Table 1-21 lists the [Dimension].[Date] table definition.

TABLE 1-21 [Date] dimension table

Column	Data Type	ColumnType
[DateKey]	Int	Surrogate Key
[Date]	Date	Alternate Key
[Month]	nvarchar(10)	Attribute
[Quarter]	nvarchar(10)	Attribute
[Year]	int	Attribute

Table 1-22 lists the [Fact].[Puchase] table definition.

TABLE 1-22 [Fact.[Purchase] table

Column	Data Type	Column Type
[PurchaseKey]	Int	Surrogate Key
[Pu		
[DateKey]	int	Foreign Key
[SupplierKey]	int	Foreign Key
[StockItemKey]	int	Foreign Key
[OrderedQuantity]	int	Measure
[ReceivedQuantity]	int	Measure

Create an entity relationship diagram showing a star schema model between the fact table and dimensions as shown in Figure 1-44.

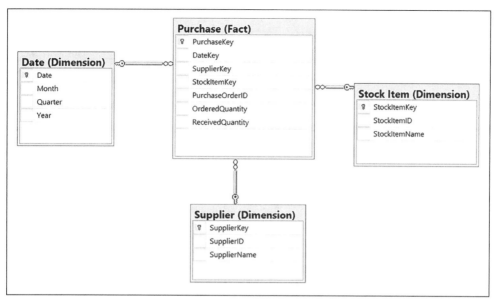

FIGURE 1-44 Star schema for the purchasing business process

Chapter summary

- Designing and implementing a data warehouse requires an understanding of the business processes and of the structures that make up a data warehouse.
- Dimension tables group related attributes that provide context to business processes.
- Dimension tables contain four types of columns: surrogate key, alternate key, attribute, and metadata columns.
- Hierarchies allow business users to perform drill-down analysis by using a predefined object that contains levels arranged in a logical order.
- Slowly Changing Dimensions allow users to report historical data.
- Table relationships can be classified as one-to-one (1:1), one-to-many (1:M), many-to-many (M:M), and self-referencing.
- Data lineage provides an audit trail of the data from its origin to its destination.
- The two common data warehouse schemas include star and snowflake schemas.
- Fact tables store measures that keep track of the business processes at a certain granularity.
- Fact tables contain four types of columns: primary key, foreign keys, measure, and metadata columns.
- The three types of measures include: additive, semi-additive, and non-additive

CHAPTER 2

Extract, transform, and load data

Y ou may know SSIS stands for SQL Server Integration Services, but what does integration mean? Integration means to combine or bring together, and in this instance, it means bringing all of the data together from various sources. In a nutshell, SSIS provides the orchestration to move data from source to destination (OLTP > DW), as well as transform and cleanse the data (replacing null values or correcting misspelled city names in a table).

What makes SISS powerful is its ability to move and transform data from various sources to various destinations. For example, SSIS can be used to extract financial data from an Oracle database and import it into a SQL Server database. You can also extract sales data from a SQL Server database and export it to an Excel, CSV, or flat file.

An important feature of SSIS is the built-in connectors for the most common database systems, platforms, and services used to store and analyze data. Some of these built-in connectors include ADO, ADO.NET, ODATA, ODBC, and OLEDB. A Hadoop connector is also available right out of the box to query Hadoop clusters.

Typically, SSIS is used in data warehousing projects for ETL (or ELT) development. These three interchangeable letters stand for:

- **E**   Extract (get data from the source)
- **T**   Transform (change/manipulate data)
- **L**   Load (copy the data to the destination)

We explain the difference between an ETL and an ELT development pattern in more detail in this chapter. For now, you should understand that in both of these development patterns the same work is being done, it is just the order in which the work is done that changes.

Skills in this chapter:

- Skill 2.1: Design and implement an extract, transform, and load (ETL) control flow by using a SQL Server Integration Services (SSIS) package
- Skill 2.2: Design and implement an ETL data flow by using an SSIS package
- Skill 2.3: Implement an ETL solution that supports incremental data extraction
- Skill 2.4: Implement an ETL solution that supports incremental data loading
- Skill 2.5: Debug SSIS packages
- Skill 2.6: Deploy and configure SSIS packages and projects

Skill 2.1: Design and implement an extract, transform, and load (ETL) control flow by using a SQL Server Integration Services (SSIS) package

Here we begin our adventure into building a new SSIS package and the basic tools involved. At the highest level, we have the Control Flow, which drives the whole package by showing the tasks that need to be executed, and the exact sequence they are executed. We review how tasks can be grouped into various types of containers so that their execution can be managed as a single unit. We review the different methods of utilizing the precedence constraints to control the flow of the tasks to be executed, but also how we can leverage variables to make the logic more sophisticated. We differentiate variables from parameters and review how they are created and used.

We look at how to use checkpoints in SSIS to mark how far a package has reached before failing so that it can be restarted and continue where it left off. Additionally, we can use the transactions feature within SSIS to bind database activity to the atomic units, which guarantee a successful completion to commit the change, or rollback. And we investigate the other types of containers that can loop a set number of times, or loop through a list of files in a filesystem folder to perform actions like move, or rename.

SSIS also has a component that makes it easy to analyze data in a table to see general information such as size of records, datatype, amount of blank, or null records, so that you can easily see the data composition of the table.

We then implement parallelism for scaling data loading by improving performance and concurrency in packages, followed by how we can use SSIS logging options to audit the loading process.

> **This skill covers how to:**
> - Design and implement ETL control flow elements, including containers, tasks, precedence constraints, and connection manager
> - Create variables and parameters
> - Create checkpoints, sequence and loop containers, and variables in SSIS
> - Implement data profiling, parallelism, transactions, logging, and security

Understanding new terminologies

Before we dive in, let's make sure you have a basic understanding of the main terminologies being used in this chapter to avoid any confusion or misunderstanding. Here we review the specific meanings of these terms as they relate to SSIS.

- **SSIS Package**   The SSIS file that contains the control flow, data flows, transforms, etc.

- **Connection Manager** This is basically a connection string that holds the credentials (username and password) to connect to a data source or data destination. You have one connection manager for every connection:
  - **Data Source** This is the source location where the data is extracted from, which could be a file, database table, spreadsheet, etc.
  - **Data Destination (Target)** This is the location to which the data is loaded—the destination or target database, file, etc.
- **Control Flow (Tab)** This contains the control flow tasks that manages the order in which the tasks within it execute; it is analogous to a workflow or process flow diagram. It contains the following to manage and direct all activities:
  - **Precedence Constraint** These are simply the arrows that indicate the direction and sequence of how one tasks calls the next task, but you can add additional checks and logic (constraints) to manage the flow.
  - **Containers** This allows the break up of large packages of logical groups of related tasks to run together. They can also be used to loop in order to process multiple items, e.g. moving all files from one folder to another.
- **Data Flow (Tab)** This contains data flow tasks that manage the work of copying, moving, loading, and transforming data.
- **Tasks** This refers to the various types of actions and work that can be performed by a component within SSIS.
  - **Control Flow Tasks** This refers to the various types of actions and work that can be performed only within the Control Flow tab.
  - **Data Flow Tasks** This refers to the various types of actions and work that can be performed only within the Data Flow tab and is related to moving and transforming data.
- **Variables** This is used to store values, strings, table objects, and can be updated and changed within a package.
- **Parameters** These are also variables, but are passed from a parent SSIS package to a child SSIS package. Parameter values cannot be changed or altered by the child package.
- **SSIS Expression (Language)** This is SSIS-specific expression language containing many prebuilt functions to manipulate strings, load variable and for dynamically changing connection strings that connect to servers, databases, and files.

SSIS is useful because of its ability to organize all of your tasks (loading, transforming, etc.) to run in a predefined sequence, either serially or in parallel. The term package essentially refers to an SSIS file and all of the components contained inside of the SSIS design file. It is similar to how we use the term document to refer to a word-processor file, or spreadsheet to refer to a file containing rows and columns of data.

When you first create your DW, you need to load all of the data from the source to the destination server. But once all of the data has been brought over, only new or changed data has to be brought over from the source database.

Therefore, we have two main types of loading:

- **Full load**
  - This is the initial data loading that requires bringing over all of the data from the source, which is normally done only once when creating the DW.
  - A full load can also be done if you want to refresh the destination by truncating all of the destination tables and loading it again. For example, you need to retest the loading process from the beginning or in case of data corruption requiring a reload.
  - Used in some cases where there have been significant changes made to the database schema, or the ETL loading process that requires reloading the data from scratch to include more information from the source database, or if additional data transformations (changes) have been added that would require all of the data to be reloaded to bring in the new changes.

- **Incremental loads**
  - Used once the full load has brought over all of the data from the source to the destination, only data that has been subsequently added or changed on the source system after the full load has to be added incrementally to the DW.
  - How often you run incremental loads depends on the nature of your business. In a DW environment, the incremental loads are normally done nightly to bring over all of the new and changed data from that day.
  - For time-sensitive data, this load can occur every five minutes, depending on the infrastructure capacity.

Slowly Changing Dimension (SCD) is a term used to identify which dimension tables you track historical changes, for example, DimCustomer, DimProduct, or DimEmployee tables.

In a data warehouse, you sometimes want to keep track of historical changes that happen to your data. For example, if a customer has a change of address or phone number; or if a product name or product code changes; or if an employee changes departments, title, salary, etc. You may need to keep track of this so that if you were to run a report today and you want the report to be consistent to when you ran it one year ago before a customer's address changed, the report would show you the same results. Otherwise, if you did not have the customer's old address and the date of change, and you ran the same report today, you would get different counts and sales numbers for that city (assuming the customer moved to a different city).

In data warehousing and dimensional modeling there are three types of SCDs:

- **SCD Type 0**   Fixed, absolutely no updates or changes allowed
- **SCD Type 1**   Replaces/updates changes to record
- **SCD Type 2**   Keeps historical record by inserting a new record and expiring the old record

- **SCD Type Inferred**   An inferred infemember exists when a fact table references a dimension member that is not yet loaded. A minimal inferred-member record is created in anticipation of relevant dimension data, which is provided in a subsequent loading of the dimension data. Here are some examples of data transformation tasks:

- **Data Conversion Task**   This is used to convert source column datatype, e.g. from string to integer.

- **Aggregate Task**   Applies aggregate functions to source columns, e.g. SUM, COUNT, AVERAGE, MIN, MAX.

- **Sort Task**   Sorts source.

- **Pivot Task**   Pivots source table columns.

- **Lookup Task**   Used to populate fact tables by looking up the business key to get the surrogate key.

Now that you have an overview and foundational understanding of SSIS and its core aspects, here is what you review in this chapter.

In skill 2.1, we begin by showing you how to start your SSIS design by building a control flow, which is the blueprint that controls how data is moved and transformed along its path from source to destination. In skill 2.2, we delve into the nuts and bolts of connecting to and moving data using a data flow, which is contained within the control flow design. It is within the data flow that we implement the data transformations that changes, updates, removes the records and columns from the incoming sources, before it is inserted into the destination tables. It is also inside the data flow that we add Slowly Changing Dimension Tasks and Lookup Tasks as part of the full load into the DW. In skill 2.3 we look at a different aspect of data flow to perform an incremental load so that we can continue to load our DW with the latest data from our source systems. This includes how we can track changes using Change Data Capture (CDC). Skill 2.4 ventures into debugging and error handling for the SSIS packages, including logging, and purveying data in realtime as it goes through the packages via Data Viewers. You also see how to easily perform the complex task of profiling data to see what types of data is contained in tables and columns to make sure your DW has the correct column datatypes and sizes. Skill 2.5 explains the various ways to deploy and run your SSIS packages.

Design and implement ETL control flow elements, including containers, tasks, and precedence constraints

There are several major components of SSIS that should be understood to get a good understanding of how SSIS works. We start by looking at the top-level structure of the SSIS package framework—the Control Flow. It is called "control flow" because this is where you design the sequence of steps in your package and direct how they flow from one to the next. If you have ever seen a "process flowchart" or a "workflow" diagram (Figure 2-1), this gives you a general idea and understanding of how Control Flow works. You decide how the tasks will progress from one to the next. Sometimes they flow sequentially, from one task to the next, or in parallel to run multiple tasks concurrently.

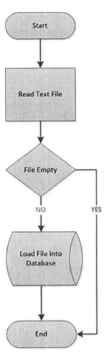

FIGURE 2-1 Flowchart to load text file into a database

There are four main types of items and objects in the Control Flow tab.

- Control Flow Tasks
- Precedence Constraints
- Containers
- Connection Managers

SSIS comes with many built-in Control Flow tasks that allow you to orchestrate flows of data and other activities. The most commonly used Control Flow tasks are grouped under the *Common* section in the SSIS Toolbox window. These tasks are all of the actions that can be taken in the Control Flow canvas for moving or manipulating your data. This task can be done against the Filesystem level, Database level, Analysis Services level, Package level, Hadoop level, etc. to consume, transform, and load data (Figure 2-2).

FIGURE 2-2 Control Flow tasks grouped under the Common section of the SSIS Toolbox

The following is a brief description of each Control Flow Task:

- **Analysis Services Processing Task** Processing SSAS cubes.
- **Bulk Insert Task** Inserts data from file into table with minimal logging.
- **Data Flow Task** Moves and transforms data from source to destination.
- **Data Profiling Task** Analyzes the data contained in the tables and saves results to an XML file, which can then be viewed using the Data Profile Viewer program.
- **Execute Package Task** Used by the parent package to call a child package.
- **Execute Process Task** Used to run external programs by calling them from SSIS package.
- **Execute SQL Task** Executes SQL scripts, including calling SPs.
- **Expression Task** Executes SSIS expression-language tasks.
- **File System Task** Performs operations on files and directories (create/delete a directory).
- **FTP Task** Executes FTP tasks to download and upload data files.
- **Hadoop File System Task** To copy files from, to, or within a Hadoop cluster.
- **Hadoop Hive Task** To run Hive scripts on a Hadoop cluster.
- **Hadoop Pig Task** To run Pig scripts on a Hadoop cluster.

- **Script Task**   Create and execute custom functionality by writing custom code. This uses a built-in script editor to write your custom code in either Visual Basic or C#.

- **Send Mail Task**   To send emails from within the SSIS package.

- **Web Service Task**   To execute web service methods.

- **XML Task**   To work with XML data, retrieve, merge, compare, and save XML documents.

In addition to the tasks listed under the Common section, additional management tasks are grouped under Other Tasks. These are administrator related tasks, which include tasks such as the Rebuild Index task, and the Backup Database task. Figure 2-3 show the tasks grouped under the Other Tasks section in the SSIS Toolbox.

FIGURE 2-3 Control Flow Tasks grouped under the Other Tasks section

A brief description of each of these Control Flow Tasks listed under the Other Tasks section includes:

- **Analysis Services Execute DDL Task**   To execute SSAS DDL tasks, e.g. create, alter, drop cubes, dimension tables, and data mining models.

- **Back Up Database Task**   Perform database backups.

- **CDC Control Task**   Handles all aspects of the Change Data Capture (CDC) process to do an initial full load and subsequent incremental loads.

- **Check Database Integrity Task**   Checks allocation and structural integrity of all database objects.

- **Data Mining Query Task**   Runs prediction queries based on data mining models in SSAS.
- **Execute SQL Server Agent Job Task**   To run SQL Agent jobs.
- **Execute T-SQL Statements Task**   Runs any SQL Statement including stored procedures.
- **History Cleanup Task**   Clears old historical information from tables within the msdb database.
- **Maintenance Cleanup Task**   Removes historical maintenance plan files, e.g. database backups and maintenance plan report files.
- **Message Queue Task**   Uses Message Queuing (MSMQ) to send and receive messages between SSIS packages.
- **Notify Operator Task**   Sends notification messages to SQL Server Agent operators.
- **Rebuild Index Task**   Rebuilds indexes ina SQL Server database.
- **Reorganize Index Task**   Reorganizes indexes in a SQL Server database.
- **Shrink Database Task**   Reduces the size of a SQL Server database data and log files.
- **Transfer Database Task**   Transfers a SQL Server database between two instances of SQL Server.
- **Transfer Error Message Task**   Transfers SQL Server user-defined error messages between instances of SQL Server.
- **Transfer Jobs Task**   Transfers SQL Server Agent jobs between instances of SQL Server.
- **Transfer Logins Task**   Transfers logins between instances of SQL Server.
- **Transfer Master Stored Procedures Task**   Transfers user-defined master databases stored procedures between instances of SQL Server.
- **Transfer SQL Server Objects Task**   Transfers various types of objects between instances of SQL Server.
- **Update Statistics Task**   Updates distribution of key values for statistics groups (collections) in table or indexed view.
- **WMI Data Reader Task**   Runs queries using Windows Management Instrumentation (WMI) Query Language to return information from WMI about a computer system.
- **WMI Event Watcher Task**   Watches for a Windows Management Instrumentation (WMI) events of interest.

An important object in Control Flows include Precedence Constraints. These objects serve as pointers to execute the next step to be taken when the current step completes as show in Figure 2-4. You can control the sequence of tasks that get executed based on completion, success, or failure of a task. Usually you want to move ahead only when the current step completes successfully. In other cases, you may only want to send out an email when the current step fails. Or you may want to move to the next step regardless if the current step succeeds or fails.

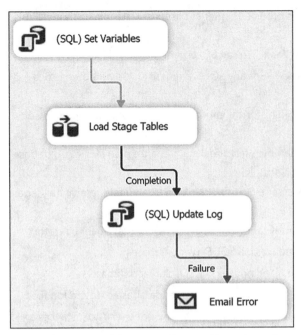

FIGURE 2-4 Example of three several types of Precedence Constraints

- **On Success (Green arrow)**   Proceeds to the next step only if the current step completes with Success. As seen in the earlier example, we move forward to "Load Stage Tables" only if the "(SQL) Set Variables" step completes successfully, otherwise it fails and stops.

- **On Completion (Black arrow)**   Proceeds to the next step regardless if current step completes with a Success or Failure. In the earlier example, regardless if "Load Stage Tables" succeeds or fails, it moves to the next step "(SQL) Update Log."

- **On Failure (Red arrow)**   Proceeds to the next step only if the current step Fails. As shown earlier, if the "(SQL) Update Log" step fails, only then will the next step run to send "Email Error" message, otherwise, no email is sent if it is successful.

There is an additional layer of condition that can be applied to the precedence constraints by using Expressions, and expressions can be combined with Success/Failure/Completion requirements. For example, if you wanted to check for both:

- "(SQL) Set Variables" = Successful completion
- "ServerName" variable = NOT NULL

You can do this using the following Precedence Constraint Editor settings, as shown in Figure 2-5.

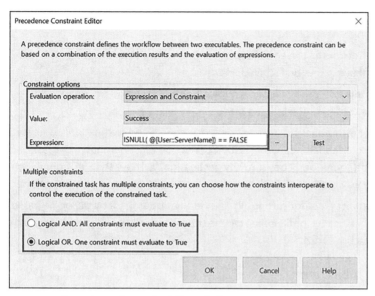

FIGURE 2-5 Precedence Constraint Editor window

Under the Evaluation Operation drop-down, you can select which variation of Expressions and Constrains you want to use for each precedence constraint (Figure 2-6).

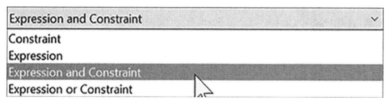

FIGURE 2-6 Evaluation Operations available for Constraints

The following are the four evaluation operations:

- **Constraint** The precedence constraint is evaluated using only the option selected in the Value property.

- **Expression** The precedence constraint is evaluated using only the expression in the Expression text box, which must evaluate to either TRUE or FALSE.

- **Expression AND Constraint** The precedence constraint is evaluated based on BOTH the Value property AND the given expression. To proceed, both must evaluate to true.

- **Expression OR Constraint** The precedence constraint is evaluated based on EITHER the Value property OR the expression. To proceed, only one of these properties must evaluate to true.

Containers are used for organizing and grouping units of work that run together. There are three types of containers:

- **For Loop Container**   Used to loop through and run everything inside the container a fixed number of times (e.g. 1 to 100).
- **ForEach Loop Container**   Used to loop through and run for each item (e.g. all the files in a folder that need to be archived).
- **Sequence Container**   Used only for grouping items that should be run together only one time (e.g. load all the Staging files).

A Connection Manager establishes the connection to the source and destination (database or file) with the necessary credentials needed. It is the Connection Manager that makes SSIS able to connect to any data source and copy it to any destination. Without the SSIS Connection Manager, there is no easy way to move data between disparate data sources and destinations.

SSIS can use both constant values for settings like server name, database name, or file name. Or the server name, database name, or file name can be set dynamically using parameters and variables when the SSIS package runs.

Built-in connection managers

Table 2-1 lists the connection manager types that SQL Server Integration Services provides.

Table 2-1 SSIS connection manager types

Type	Description
ADO	Connects to ActiveX Data Objects (ADO) objects.
ADO.NET	Connects to a data source by using a .NET provider.
CACHE	Reads data from the data flow or from a cache file (.caw), and can save data to the cache file.
DQS	Connects to a Data Quality Services server and a Data Quality Services database on the server.
EXCEL	Connects to an Excel workbook file.
FILE	Connects to a file or a folder.
FLAT FILE	Connect to data in a single flat file.
FTP	Connect to an FTP server.
HTTP	Connects to a webserver.
MSMQ	Connects to a message queue.
MSOLAP100	Connects to an instance of SQL Server Analysis Services or an Analysis Services project.
MULTIFILE	Connects to multiple files and folders.
MULTI FLAT FILE	Connects to multiple data files and folders.
OLEDB	Connects to a data source by using an OLE DB provider.
ODBC	Connects to a data source by using ODBC.
SMOServer	Connects to a SQL Server Management Objects (SMO) server.
SMTP	Connects to an SMTP mail server.
SQLMOBILE	Connects to a SQL Server Compact database.
WMI	Connects to a server and specifies the scope of Windows Management Instrumentation (WMI) management on the server.

To access any database source object, a connection manager needs to be initially configured to authenticate with the source database server . Once the connection manager is configured, any SSIS task using this Connection Manager can access database objects such as tables, views, functions and stored procedurest within the source database. Figure 2-7 shows an OLEDB connection manager window.

FIGURE 2-7 Connection Manager settings for OLE DB

In addition to database connection managers, SSIS provides the ability to use files as a source or destination. These files can be flat text files, comma-separated value (CSV) files, Excel files or XML files. The File Connection Manager specifies the path, filename, text qualifier, text delimiter and other properties that SSIS requires to parse the file properly. Figure 2-8 shows a Flat File Connection Manager.

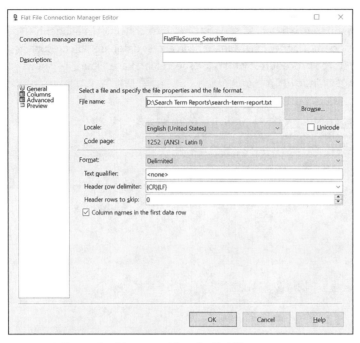

FIGURE 2-8 Connection Manager settings for Flat File

Now to demonstrate how this all comes together, let's build a Control Flow using Tasks, Precedence Constraints, Connection Manager, and a Sequence Container.

We do this by using the WideWorldImportersDW database. You can follow along with this demo by downloading and installing the following:

- *https://github.com/Microsoft/sql-server-samples/releases/tag/wide-world-importers-v1.0*
    - **WideWorldImporters DB** (WideWorldImporters-Full.bak)
    - **WideWorldImportersDW DB** (WideWorldImportersDW-Full.bak)
    - **Daily ETL SSIS Package** (Daily.ETL.ispac)
- *https://docs.microsoft.com/en-us/sql/ssdt/download-sql-server-data-tools-ssdt*
    - **SSDT for VS 2015 (Get latest build for SQL Server Data Tools 17.x for Visual Studio 2015)**
- *https://docs.microsoft.com/en-us/sql/ssms/download-sql-server-management-studio-ssms*
    - **Management Studio (Get latest build for SQL Server Management Studio 17.x)**

In this exercise, we look at how to set up two connection managers:

- Source
- Destination

When you move data from one place to another, you have the source location where you get the data from, and the destination location where the data is copied to, which could be the same or different servers.

Setting up a Connection for Connection Manager:

1. Right-click in the Connection Manager pane at the bottom center of the Visual Studio.

2. Select New OLE DB Connection from the menu (Figure 2-9).

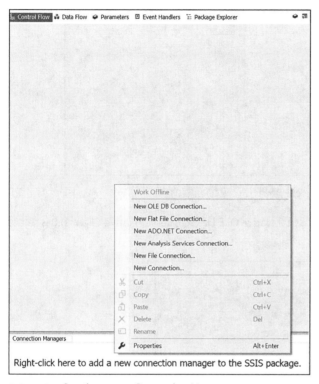

FIGURE 2-9 Creating a new Connection Manager

3. Press the New button to create a new Connection (Figure 2-10).

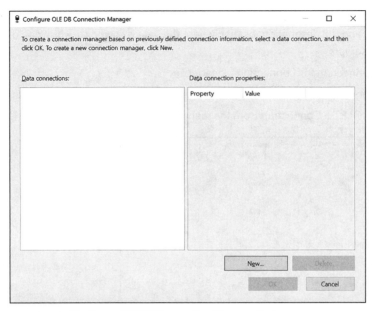

FIGURE 2-10 Configure OLE DB Connection Manger window

4. Under Provider, confirm that Native OLE DB\SQL Server Native Client 11.0 is selected (Figure 2-11).

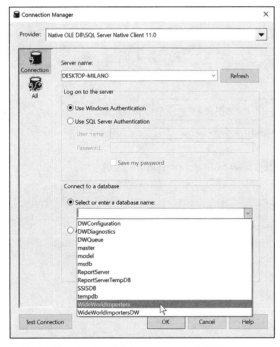

FIGURE 2-11 Selecting database name in OLE DB Connection Manager

5. Under Server Name enter your Server Name.

6. Under the drop-down Select Or Enter A Database Name: select WideWorldImporters.

7. Click the Test Connection button to verify that the connection is successful.

8. Click the OK button to see the new OLE DB Connection.

9. Click the OK button to complete the creation of the new WideWorldImporters Connection.

10. Under Data connections, you now see the newly created connection (Figure 2-12).

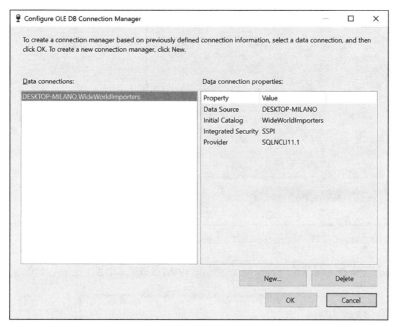

FIGURE 2-12 Creation of New WideWorldImporters OLE DB connection

11. The new LE DB Connection shows up in the Connection Manager pane (Figure 2-13).

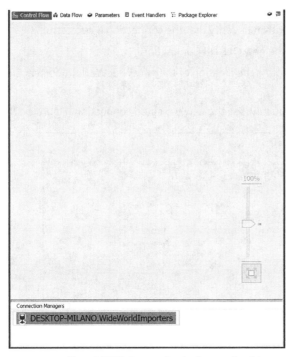

FIGURE 2-13 New OLE DB Connection in Connection Manager

12. To rename the Connection, press F2 and type **WWI_Source_DB** (Figure 2-14).

FIGURE 2-14 Renamed OLE DB Connection in Connection Manager

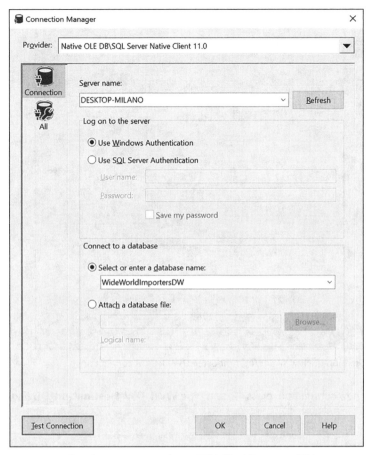

FIGURE 2-15 Creating new connection to WideWorldImportersDW

13. Click the Test Connection button to verify that the connection is successful.

14. Click the OK button to see the new OLE DB Connection.

15. Click the OK button to complete the creation of the new WideWorldImportersDW Connection.

16. Under Data connections, you now see the newly created connection (Figure 2-16).

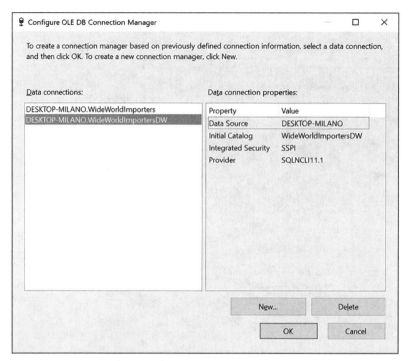

FIGURE 2-16 Creation of New WideWorldImportersDW OLE DB connection

17. Rename the new connection, press F2, and type **WWI_DW_Destination_DB** (Figure 2-17).

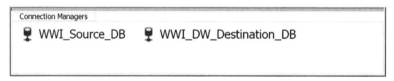

FIGURE 2-17 Renamed OLE DB Connection in Connection Manager

In this next exercise, you create a Control Flow using two Execute SQL Tasks to show how work can be organized and controlled using SSIS. In this simple example, we first truncate the destination table, and then load it with the FullNames from the source table.

Create an Execute SQL Task in the Control Flow Task:

1. To create a new SSIS package, in the Solution Explorer, right-click SSIS Packages > New SSIS Package (Figure 2-18).

FIGURE 2-18 Create new SSIS Package

2. In the Control Flow tab, click and drag the Execute SQL Task.

3. Double-click, or right-click and select Edit on the Execute SQL Task.

4. This opens the Execute SQL Task Editor (Figure 2-19).

5. In the Execute SQL Task Editor make the following changes:

    A. Change the name to Create Table for FullName.

    B. Confirm the ConnectionType = OLE DB.

    C. In the Connection drop-down, select WWI_Source_DB.

    D. Confirm SQLSourceType = Direct Input.

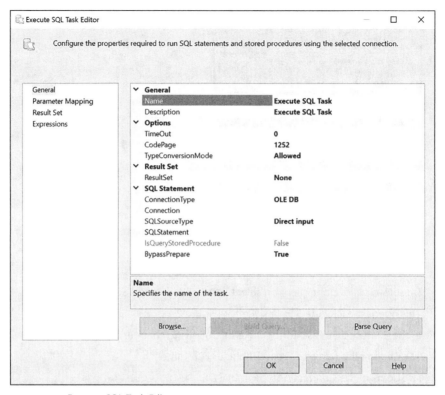

FIGURE 2-19 Execute SQL Task Editor

6. Click the ellipses for SQLStatement and enter the SQL Script from Listing 2-1 into the Enter SQL Query window (Figure 2-20).

LISTING 2-1 SQL Query for Execute SQL Task

```
SELECT DISTINCT FullName

INTO [Application].[People_FullName]

FROM [WideWorldImporters].[Application].[People]
```

FIGURE 2-20 Add SQL Script to Execute SQL Task

7. The completed Execute SQL Task Editor should look like Figure 2-21.

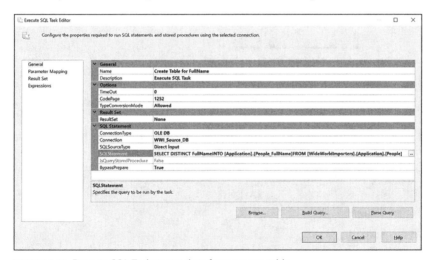

FIGURE 2-21 Execute SQL Task to get data from source table

8. Now drag a second Execute SQL Task onto the Control Flow tab (Figure 2-22).

9. Then connect the green precedence constraint arrow from the first Execute SQL Task to the newly added Execute SQL Task.

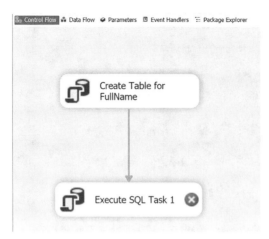

FIGURE 2-22 Creating a Control Flow with Execute SQL Tasks

10. You can right-click a task to select the Autosize option to automatically adjust the size of the tasks to give your layout a nice clean look (Figure 2-23).

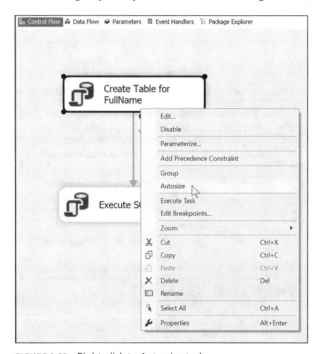

FIGURE 2-23 Right-click to Auto-size task

11. The task size is extended to fit the complete name on a single line (Figure 2-24).

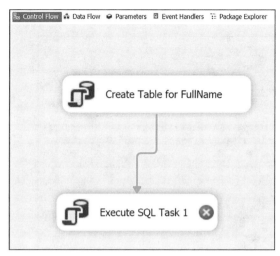

FIGURE 2-24 Auto-sized task

12. To set up the second Execute SQL Task, follow steps 3-5.

13. Click the ellipses for SQLStatement, and enter the SQL Script from Listing 2-2 into the Enter SQL Query window (Figure 2-25).

LISTING 2-2 SQL Query for Execute SQL Task

```
SELECT DISTINCT [SearchName]
INTO [Application].[People_SearchName]
FROM [WideWorldImporters].[Application].[People]
```

FIGURE 2-25 List Num-Caption

14. The completed Execute SQL Task Editor should look like Figure 2-26.

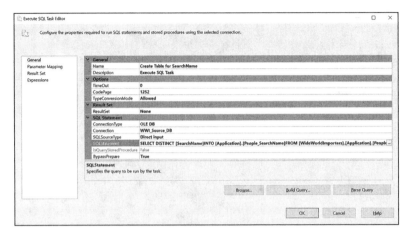

FIGURE 2-26 Execute SQL Task to insert data into the [Application].[People_SearchName] table

15. Your completed package in the control flow will look like Figure 2-27.

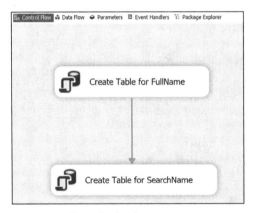

FIGURE 2-27 Auto-sized task

Create variables and parameters

Both variables and parameters are similar in their usage, but with one major difference—parameter values cannot be changed when the package is running (at runtime). Parameter values are fixed for the duration of the package execution. Alternatively, variables' values can be changed at any time. Variables are also used to assign values dynamically at runtime, e.g. the server name can be gotten at runtime and put into a variable that can be used to change the connection string in the Connection Manager. This can be very useful when you are running the same package on different servers (Development, QA, Production) so the package won't have to be manually updated every time it is executed on a different server—or break if you forget to change the server name.

System variables and user variables

SSIS contains many system variables that contain values, which contain system-type information that can be used at runtime (Figure 2-28).

FIGURE 2-28 System variables

Some commonly used System Variables are:

- **MachineName**   Name of the server where this package is currently running
- **PackageName**   Name of the current package
- **TaskName**   Name of the Task currently running within the PackageName
- **UserName**   User that started the package
- **StartTime**   DateTime the package was started
- **VersionBuild**   Version number of package (automatically versioned)

These variables are extremely useful because they can be put anywhere and will dynamically generate their values at runtime.

Aside from System Variables, there are User Variables that are created as needed to store values to be used and possibly shared across the different components of the SSIS package (Figure 2-29).

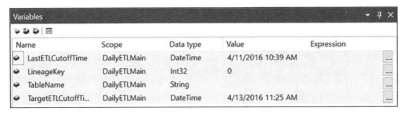

FIGURE 2-29 User variables

When creating variables, you can specify the following:

■ Name of the variable.

■ Scope indicates which components in the package the variable is visible to. By default, the scope contains the name of the package, which means that any object within the whole package can view and access this variable. But if the variable is created to be visible to a sequence container, only it is local to the sequence container and only the sequence container and all of the objects within the sequence container can see and access this variable (this is similar to private and local variables in most programming languages). But any object outside of the sequence container would not be able to see or access this local variable.

■ Data type is the SSIS datatype.

■ Value can be a default value or left empty and populated during runtime, e.g. the current datetime or servername.

■ Expression allows the value of the variable to be set by an expression using the SSIS expression language.

The SSIS expression language allows you to concatenate strings and convert datatypes, as well as assign values to variables. The following is an example of using the SSIS expression editor.

Here are some general expression language syntax and usage guides:

■ The strings must be enclosed with double-quotes.

■ You can drag-drop any of the System Variables or User Variables into the expression builder window (Figure 2-30).

■ You can concatenate strings using the plus (+) symbol between each string value in double quotes (Listing 2-3).

■ Use the Evaluate Expression button to check that your expression syntax is valid and preview the results of the expression to make sure it's what you expected the value to be.

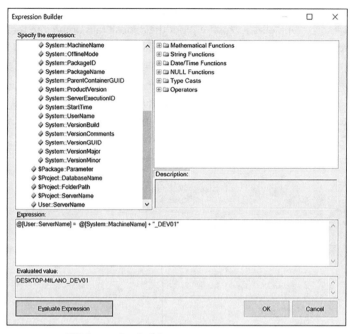

FIGURE 2-30 SSIS Expression Builder syntax

LISTING 2-3 SSIS Expression Language syntax

```
@[User::ServerName] =  @[System::MachineName] + "_DEV01"
```

Package vs. project parameters

SSIS has two different deployment models:

- Project deployment
- Package deployment

The package deployment model means nothing is shared and that everything is maintained separately within each individual SSIS package—variables, connection manager, etc.

The project deployment model enables you to deploy your SSIS project as a single unit with shared resources, including parameters, and packages. It is deployed to either file, or to the SSISDB database catalog within SQL Server.

Create checkpoints, sequence and loop containers, and variables in SSIS

In a database environment, you have a *transaction*, which is a logical unit of work that has to be completed in full (all the steps) to be deemed successful. In case there is a failure in any one of those steps, the whole transaction is deemed unsuccessful and any of the completed steps have to be undone (rolled back). This is done to maintain the integrity of the data. Using the simple example of money being transferred from one bank account to another bank account: if the money withdrawal step completes successfully, but the deposit fails going into the other account, the withdrawal step must be undone, otherwise the withdrawal amount would be "lost." In the same manner, SSIS has a built-in feature to manage these transactions.

Within SSIS, you can set the scope of the transactions at the entire package level, or for any individual control flow container, or task level. SSIS transactions require Windows Distributed Transaction Coordinator (DTC) service to be running on the machine for this feature to work.

To enable transactions within a package, set the TransactionOption property to Required for the container or task (Figure 2-31). This property can be set at any scope of the package:

- Package Level
- Container Level
- Control Task Level

FIGURE 2-31 **Setting the TransactionOption property to Required for Containers or Tasks**

Any tasks inside of the container will also be a part of the transaction as long as each individual task has the TransactionOption property set to Supported, which is the default.

If there are some tasks that you do not want to rollback within a container, in case of failure, set the TransactionOption to NotSupported. This can be useful where you have tasks that handle audits or record error statuses to review after the failure.

One thing to keep in mind is that the transactions only work at the Control Flow level tasks, not within the task inside of the Data Flow, which means that all of the steps inside of a Data Flow either complete in their entirety, or all of the steps are rolled back.

If you only want a subset of the Control Flow tasks to be run transactionally, place them inside of a container that is configured for transactions.

In cases when there is a package failure, it may only be necessary to rerun a portion of the package that failed instead of rerunning the whole package. This can save a lot of time if a large data loading step completed successfully, but a subsequent update step failed. You would then only need to restart the package at the update step. This is what SSIS checkpoints allow you to do—restart a package for the point of the failure forward. Checkpoints work in conjunction with transactions discussed above.

A word of caution to database administrators, the SSIS term checkpoint does not mean the same thing as it does in a database environment. In SSIS it is simply marking the point at which SSIS tasks completed successfully so it can keep track of where to continue running from.

You specify the scope of the restartability of transactions. If a package fails at a certain point, it can be configured to restart from the point of failure, or from an earlier step at the next attempt to run the package. This configuration process is called checkpoints. Checkpoints and transactions work together to enable package restartability.

The following are the setting for Checkpoints at the Control Flow tab (Figure 2-32):

- **CheckpointFileName**   Enter the path and filename where SSIS saves the checkpoint run status information.

- **CheckpointUsage**   By setting to IfExists, the checkpoint file is created if one does not already exist, otherwise it updates the existing file.

- **SaveCheckpoints**   Set this to True to enable checkpoints.

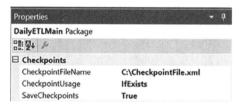

FIGURE 2-32 Checkpoint settings

Once the checkpoint has been enabled for the package, the last step is to update each container or task that you want to checkpoint by setting its FailParentOnFailure property to True. This activates checkpointing for each individual object you want to track (Figure 2-33).

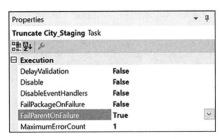

FIGURE 2-33 Activating checkpoints for a task or container

When you have multiple tasks that need to be run as a group, either sequentially or in parallel, SSIS provides three types of containers and each of these have their own unique benefit.

- **Sequence Container**   Grouping and organizing tasks.
- **For Loop Container**   Iterating tasks multiple times.
- **Foreach Loop Container**   Iterating through each object or file.
- **Sequence Container**   Provides a way to group several tasks together that need to be run as a single unit of work or simply for grouping related tasks together for easier understanding of the design flow (Figure 2-34).

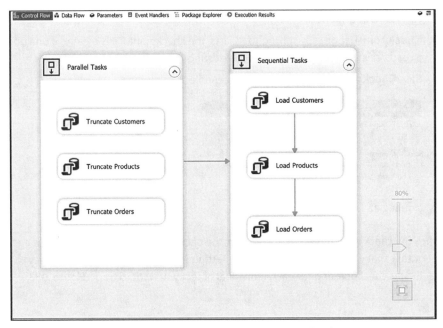

FIGURE 2-34 Sequence containers grouping parallel and sequential tasks

For Loop Containers allow you to loop and execute a set of tasks within the container a given number times. This value can be set as a variable at run time, for example the number of days in a month. Let's say we wanted to insert a new record into a table for each day of the month. This is done based on the evaluation of the For Loop properties.

- As an example, the following is what we would do if we wanted to insert records into a table for a specific number of days based on a variable:

1. Create a table (Listing 2-4).

LISTING 2-4 SQL Script for Days table

```
CREATE TABLE Days (
    DayNumber INT,
    NextDate DATE)
```

2. Create a variable. See Figure 2-35.

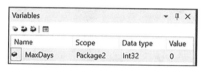

FIGURE 2-35 Create a new variable

3. Add Execute SQL Task to Control Flow and under SQLStatement insert the corresponding SSIS Expression (Listing 2-5) and Figure 2-36. Note the difference from the SQL Script:

- **SQL Script** INSERT INTO Days (DayNumber, NextDate) VALUES (@ MaxDays,DATEADD(DAY,@MaxDays,GETDATE()))

- **SSIS Expression** INSERT INTO Days (DayNumber, NextDate) VALUES (?,DATEADD(DAY,?,GETDATE()))

LISTING 2-5 SQL Script for Days table

```
INSERT INTO Days (DayNumber, NextDate) VALUES (?,DATEADD(DAY,?,GETDATE()))
```

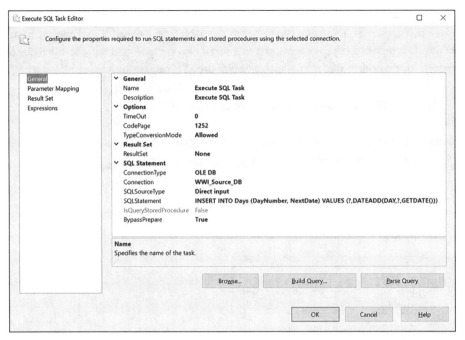

FIGURE 2-36 Creating Execute SQL Task with OLE DB connection and SQLStatement with parameters using "?".

When using the ConnectionType = OLE DB, the parameters are replaced by question marks in Figure 2-36. This can be confusing at first, but each question mark (?) represents a different variable from the Parameter Mapping page. (See Figure 2-37). Here the same variable is listed twice, once for each "?" in the SQLStatement line. Each of the ConnectionTypes have their idiosyncrasies. When using the ADO.NET ConnectionType, you can simply use a variable name like @MaxDays.

- Add the input parameter.

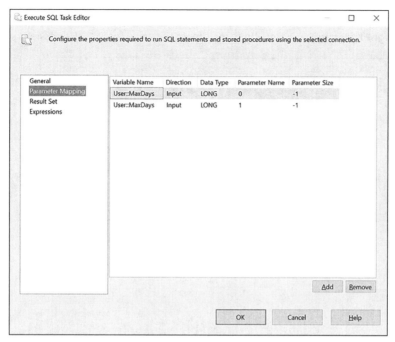

FIGURE 2-37 Create new input parameter

■ Add the For Loop Container and move the Execute SQL Task into it (Figure 2-38).

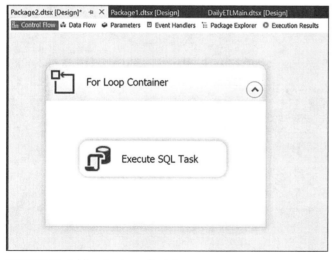

FIGURE 2-38 Adding For Loop Container

■ For Loop properties is where we set the values to iterate through as shown in Figure 2-39. The properties include:

■ **InitialExpression** Sets the initial value

- **EvalExpression**   Runs until this condition evaluates to TRUE

  - **AssignExpression**   Expression to increment the value for InitialExpression

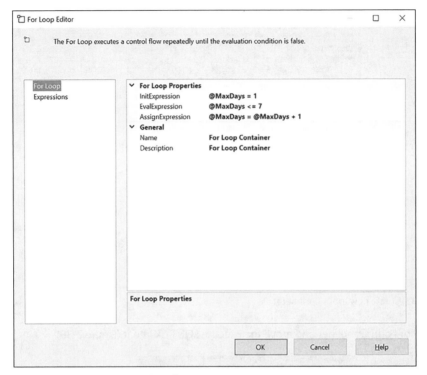

FIGURE 2-39 For Loop properties values

And when we run the For Loop Container we see the following results (Figure 2-40):

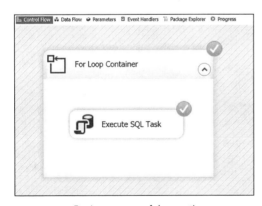

FIGURE 2-40 For Loop successful execution

As you can see (Figure 2-41), the For Loop Container ran until the value of the variable exceeded 7 and then stopped.

FIGURE 2-41 For Loop execution results

Implement data profiling, parallelism, transactions, logging, and security

Data profiling allows you to evaluate the content, structure, and quality of the source dataset. It cannot identify inaccurate or bad data, just metrics about the existing data to see how useful or difficult it will be to use the data. This includes the frequency of the values, the datatypes, NULLs, and length of data in the columns.

SSIS has a Data Profiler Task that can assist with profiling your data. This task saves the results of the data analysis in an XML file that can be accessed by another program, Data Profile Viewer (Figure 2-42), which is included with your installation of SQL Server.

Here are the types of information you can glean from it:

- Column Length Distribution Profile
- Column Null Ratio Profile
- Column Pattern Profile
- Column Statistics Profile
- Column Value Distribution Profile
- Candidate Key Profile
- Functional Dependency Profile
- Value Inclusion Profile

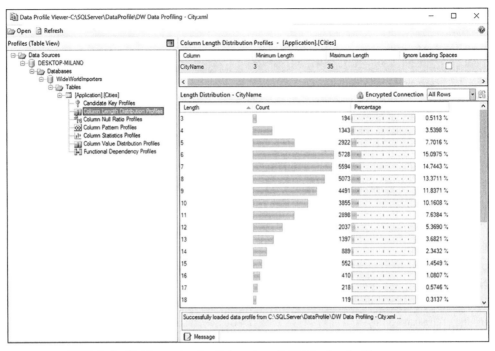

FIGURE 2-42 SSIS Data Profile Viewer showing Column Length Distribution Profile

To set up the Data Profiler Task, drag it into your Control Flow tab and right-click or double-click to edit it to see the Data Profiling Task Editor (Figure 2-43). In the General page, specify:

- **DestinationType**   FileConnection (or variable if this will be set dynamically at runtime).

- **Destination**   Choose a file connection manager where the XML file will be saved. If you don't have an existing connection manager, you can create a new one and specify the path and filename.

- **OverwriteDestination**   If you want to reuse the same XML file multiple times, you can choose to overwrite it the next time it is written to.

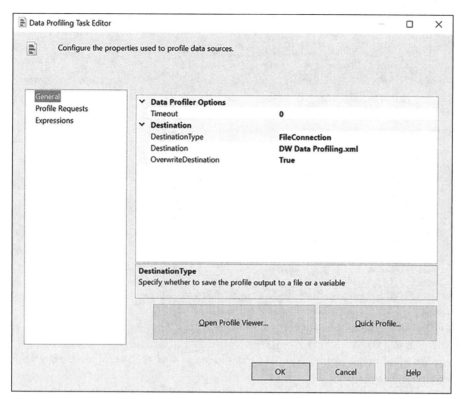

FIGURE 2-43 SSIS Data Profiling Task Editor settings

Next click the Quick Profile button to open the Single Table Quick Profile Form (Figure 2-44). Here you select the source table to use for data profiling and what types of profiling to do with the table data. Select the desired check boxes, and press OK.

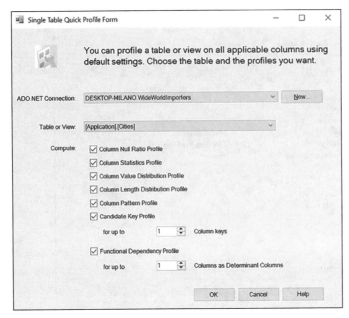

FIGURE 2-44 Single Table Quick Profile Form

Now you are taken to the Profile Requests page and see a list of all the profiles you checked in the previous window (Figure 2-45).

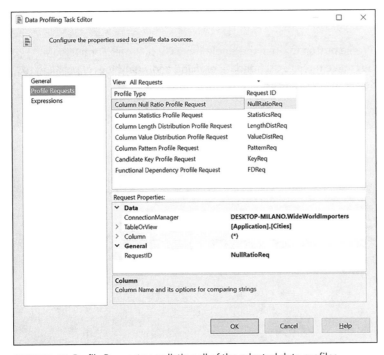

FIGURE 2-45 Profile Request page listing all of the selected data profiles

Notice that at the bottom of this window in the Request Properties pane, it shows the specific table and column names to be analyzed, and the asterisk (*) means get all of the columns. In this example, we chose the Quick Profile so the Profile Requests page in this window was automatically populated for us. But you can also do this manually for any specific table or column. Additionally, you can also limit the type of profiling for each of the selected tables and columns in the View All Requests pane in this window.

You can use Quick Profile to quickly set up a data profiling task, and then go to the Profile Requests page to add or change the Profile Type, tables, and columns. You can remove a Profile Type by selecting it and pressing the delete button on your keyboard.

Let's click OK to complete this step. Right-click this Data Profiling Task, and select Execute Task to run it. Upon successful completion, the profiling XML file is created in the location specified in the Destination parameter. To open this file you need to go to your Windows programs under Microsoft SQL Server 2016, and open SQL Server 2016 Data Profile Viewer. From here you can open the XML file to view the results of the data profiling analysis.

What is parallelism in SSIS?

Parallelism is simply running multiple SSIS tasks concurrently (together in parallel). So when you have multiple tables to be loaded that don't depend on each other for their data (Customers, Products, Cities), they can be loaded at the same time, instead of loading Products, then loading Cities, and finally Customers. Running SSIS packages in parallel can be a big time saver, but can also be resource intensive depending on the number of tasks running in parallel, the table sizes, complexity of the transforms, network bandwidth, CPU, and disk IO speeds. As with all development, when you create packages to run in parallel, you need to monitor your server resources to see if the parallelization is maxing out any of the resources, which could cause everything to run slower thereby defeating the purpose of parallelizing tasks in the first place.

In the package below (Figure 2-46), first we are truncating all of the tables in parallel, after that completes successfully we then load all of the tables in parallel and monitor the server resources.

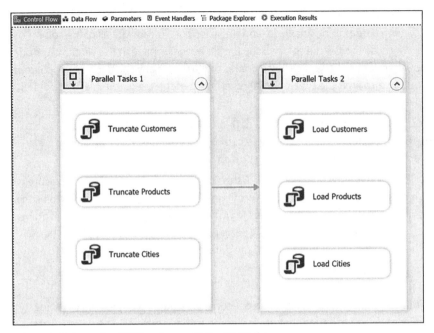

FIGURE 2-46 Example of SSIS package with Parallel Tasks

Control flow properties for parallelism

The performance of the Control Flow of an SSIS package can be optimized by setting a very important property known as MaxConcurrentExectutables. MaxConcurrentExecutables is a package-level property in the Control Flow tab and is used to throttle the amount of parallelism. Figure 2-47 shows the -1 default setting of the MaxConcurrentExectutables property.

MaxConcurrentExecutables sets the number of tasks that can run concurrently in the Control Flow. When you use the default value MaxConcurrentExecutables (-1) that tells SSIS to set the number of parallel tasks to equal the number of Logical Processors in your CPU + 2 (it over-commits a bit in default mode). If your server has 16 logical processors, the maximum number of parallel tasks is 18 (16 + 2). But if you set MaxConcurrentExecutables = 10, it only allows a maximum of 10 tasks to run at the same time. This allows you to leave some CPU resources for other services. Keep in mind the MaxConcurrentExecutables setting has no affect if all of your tasks run in serial, one after the other.

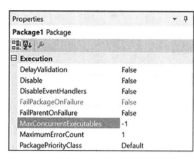

FIGURE 2-47 MaxConsurrentExecutables in Control Flow tab

Data flow properties for parallelism

EngineThreads is a property of each data flow that tells how many threads the data flow engine can create and run in parallel (Figure 2-48). The default value for EngineThreads = 10, which sets the amount of threads for the source (10) and for the worker threads (10), so the default setting can spawn 20 threads. A good rule of thumb is not to run more threads in parallel than the number of available processors. Having excessive threads running in parallel can cause context-switching between threads. The maximum number of EngineThreads is twice the number of logical processors. So if your server has 16 logical processors, the maximum EngineThreads is 32 (16 * 2).

FIGURE 2-48 EngineThreads in Data Flow tab

The control flow tasks run in parallel until it reaches the MaxCuncurrentExecutable number of control flow items (18 for your sever, 16+2). But if the DataFlow EngineThreads limit is reached by the Control Flow tasks (EngineThread = 10 & DataFlow1 uses 6 EngineThreads & DataFlow2 uses 4 EngineThreads), none of the other DataFlows can run until some of the EngineThreads get released. So the parallelization depends on the number of available DataFlow EngineThreads and the ControlFlow MaxCuncurrentExecutable value.

In order to see the number of logical processers on your machine, open Task Manager, go to the Performance tab, and look under the CPU graphs to see how many logical processor are on your server (Figure 2-49).

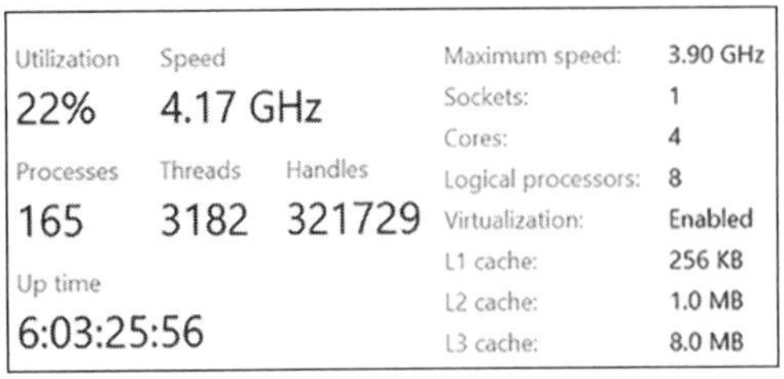

Utilization	Speed		Maximum speed:	3.90 GHz
22%	4.17 GHz		Sockets:	1
			Cores:	4
Processes	Threads	Handles	Logical processors:	8
165	3182	321729	Virtualization:	Enabled
			L1 cache:	256 KB
Up time			L2 cache:	1.0 MB
6:03:25:56			L3 cache:	8.0 MB

FIGURE 2-49 Checking the number of Logical Processors on the server

SSIS packages can be secured with a password. In doing so, there are a few options in securing your packages (Figure 2-50):

- **DontSaveSensitive**   Removes sensitive information upon saving
- **EncryptSensitiveWithUserKey**   Encrypts sensitive information with user profile key
- **EncryptSensitiveWithPassword**   Encrypts sensitive information with a password
- **EncryptAllWithPassword**   Encrypts the whole package with a password
- **EncryptAllWithUserKey**   Encrypts the whole package with user profile key

Security	
PackagePassword	
ProtectionLevel	**EncryptSensitiveWithUserKey** ⌄
Transactions	DontSaveSensitive
IsolationLevel	EncryptSensitiveWithUserKey
TransactionOption	EncryptSensitiveWithPassword
Version	EncryptAllWithPassword
VersionBuild	EncryptAllWithUserKey

FIGURE 2-50 Setting SSIS package Security ProtectionLevel

When the package is password-protected, you have to enter the password when opening the package to view and edit it. By default, there is a password used to secure the package, which is fine for development. But packages being put into production can use password protection. This can be difficult when working with individual packages, but as we'll see later in the package deployment section, you can use Project level deployment, which can include all of the project items to secure and deploy the whole project.

Skill 2.2: Design and implement an ETL data flow by using an SSIS package

Now that you understand the SSIS Control Flow, which is what orchestrates all of the control tasks, and their flow sequence and logic, we can now delve in to see the power of how SSIS transfers and transforms data from a source location to the target location using the Data Flow tasks. Just like there is a Control Flow tab, there is also a separate Data Flow tab. When you click the Data Flow tab, all of the items in the context-based SSIS Toolbox change to show tasks related to data movement and transformation. You can get data from various sources, including flat files, spreadsheets, databases, and XML files. In turn, these can be modified and then copied to the same or different destinations. What really makes SSIS powerful is its ability to connect to disparate data sources located on different servers, or different locations. As long as your account has permission to connect to the sources and destinations, you can get the data, transform it, and load it into the target.

This skill covers how to:

- Implement slowly changing dimension, fuzzy grouping, fuzzy lookup, audit, blocking, non-blocking, and term lookup transformations
- Determine the appropriate transform object for a given task
- Remove extra rows or bad rows by using deduplication
- Data flow source and destination column mappings
- Determine appropriate scenarios for Transact-SQL joins versus SSIS lookup

---

Implement slowly changing dimension, fuzzy grouping, fuzzy lookup, audit, blocking, non-blocking, and term lookup transformations

SSIS is very powerful in transforming incoming source data before loading it into the destination data stores. For example, here are some types of transformations that can be performed within data flow tasks, including:

- Removing duplicates
- Replacing values
- Looking up tables
- Cleaning the data
- Counting rows affected for audit purposes

Here is a complete list of all the data flow transforms available (Figure 2-51).

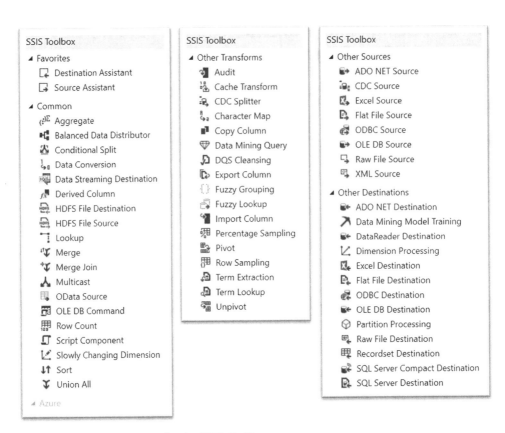

FIGURE 2-51 Data Flow Tasks in SSIS Toolbox

The SSIS Toolbox groups the data flows into various groups. The Common and Other Transforms groups contain all of the tasks used to perform lookups and data transformations. But the groups for Other Sources and Other Destinations are where you pick the type of data store that you get data from and send data to.

If the business requirement is to keep track of historical changes happening to your data so that a report you ran last year shows the same results as the same report run today before the customers' addresses changed, without Slowly Changing Dimensions (SCD) transform, you would have to create the complete process of tracking these changes manually.

Just to review, here are the three types of Slowly Changing Dimensions (SCD):

- **Fixed Attribute Output (SCD Type 0)**   Fixed, absolutely no updates or changes allowed.

- **Changing Attributes Updates Output (SCD Type 1)**   Replaces/updates changes to record.

- **Historical Attribute Inserts Output and New Output (SCD Type 2)**   Keeps historical record by inserting a new record and expiring the old record.

- **Inferred Member Updates**   An inferred member exists when a fact table references a dimension member that is not yet loaded. A temporary inferred-member record is created, which is provided in a subsequent loading of the dimension data. This record is a placeholder until the actual record arrives.

The built-in Slowly Changing Dimension transform component allows you to implement all three of these types.

To create a new SCD transform, you need to make sure that in the dimension tables, your DW has two additional metadata columns for tracking changes:

- ValidFrom column
- ValidTo column

You can name these anything you like, but functionally they would be used to capture when the records were created and retired. To implement Slowly Chaning Dimensions using the SSIS SCD components, followe these steps.

1. In your Control Tab, add a Data Flow task.
2. Edit the Data Flow task and add an OLE DB Source
3. Double-click the OLE DB Source and connect to your source table, either in the OLTP environment, or a staging table within the DW.
4. Add a Slowly Changing Transform and connect it to the precedence constraint from the OLDE DB Source as shown in (Figure 2-52).

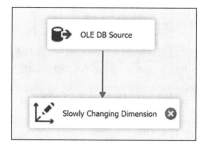

FIGURE 2-52 Connecting OLE DB to Slowly Changing Transform

5. Next, Double-click the Slowly Changing Dimension transform to start the Slowly Changing Dimension Wizard, and click Next.
6. On the Select A Dimension Table And Keys window, select Connection Manager to connect to the destination DW.
7. Select Table Or View for the destination table.
8. Map the Input Columns to the Dimension Columns.
9. Make sure that only one column is marked as "Business Key", which is the key from the source table.
10. Ensure all of the other Key Type columns are marked as "Not A Key Column" as shown in (Figure 2-53). Click Next.

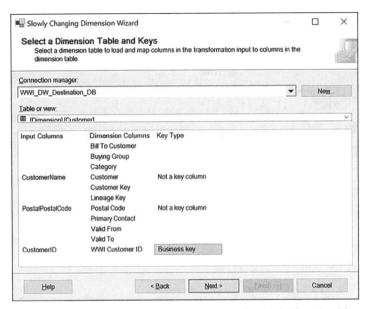

FIGURE 2-53 Selecting a Dimension Table and Keys for Slowly Changing Dimension transform

11. Next, select the change type option for each of the Slowly Changing Dimension Columns as shown in Figure 2-54 and then click Next. The options available include:

- **Dimension Columns**   Pick the columns to be used for SCD.

- **Change Type**   Select what SCD Type you want each column to be:

- **Historical attribute (Type 2)**   Keeps all old values—no overwriting.

- **Changing attribute (Type 1)**   Keeps only current value--overwrites old value.

- **Fixed Attribute (Type 0)**   Value cannot be changed.

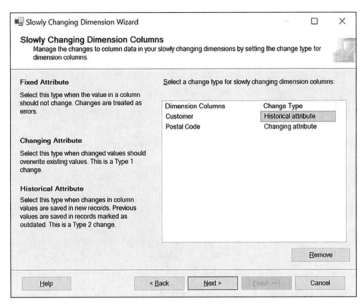

FIGURE 2-54 Slowly Changing Dimension Columns – Type 0, 1, or 2

- Select the Fixed and Changing Attribute option as shown in Figure 2-55. The options include:

    - **Fixed Attributes**   If you have fixed attributes in your SCD transform, you can check this option (fail the transformation if changes are detected in a fixed attribute) so that any change to a fixed attribute fails the transform with an error. But if this is unchecked, it simply ignores the change and does not bring it into the DW and doesn't give an error.

    - **Changing Attributes**   If you check this option (change of all the matching records, including outdated records, when changes are detected in a changing attribute), the new value being updated for a column also updates earlier historical values. This basically overwrites the current value into all of the earlier historical values for that column.

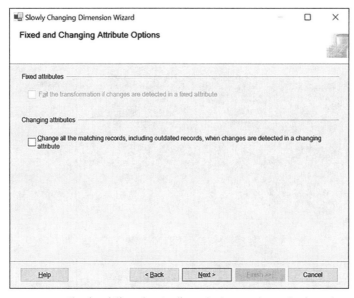

FIGURE 2-55 Fixed and Changing Attribute Options to determine how changes are handled

In our example, make sure both are unchecked.

12. Next, select the Historical Attribute Options as shown in Figure 2-56. As mentioned earlier, both options require having either one or two additional columns available for historical tracking of changes for each record.

- **Use A Single Column To Show Current And Expired Records**   This option only uses a single string column and marking it as either:
  - Current / Expired
  - True / False
- **Use Start And End Dates To Identify Current And Expired Records**   This option uses two columns to mark the beginning and ending dates of the record's life:
  - Start date column
  - End date column
- **Variable To Set Date Values**   Here you can select where the date values for above Start and End dates are gotten from. These can be gotten from the user variable defined by you or these system variables:
  - **CreationDate**   DateTime the package was created
  - **ContainerStartTime**   Start DateTime of the container
  - **StartTime**   The DateTime the package started to run

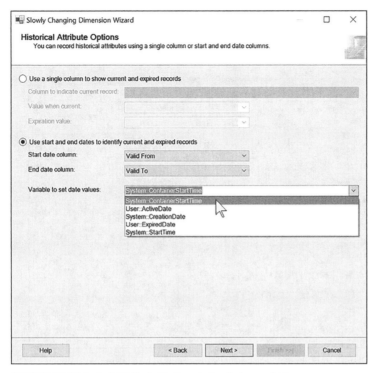

FIGURE 2-56 Historical Attribute Options to track change history

13. Next, select the Inferred Dimension Members option. This allows for handling of an inferred member when you have late arriving dimension table records (or early arriving fact tables).

- For this example, uncheck this option, then click Next and then click Finish.

The output of the Slowly Changing Wizard is the fully designed SCD tasks as shown in Figure 2-57 and described below.

- **Historical Attribute Inserts (Output)** Manages inserting new rows and expiring old rows.
- **New (Output)** Manages inserting new rows.
- **Changing Attributes Updates (Output)** Manages updating rows without any history.

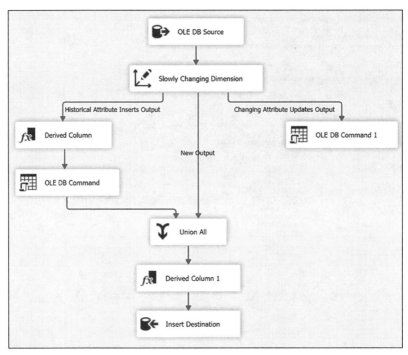

FIGURE 2-57 Slowly Changing Dimension Data Flow created by the wizard

A frequent problem that you may experience when you bring data from multiple sources that need to be unified and consolidated and/or needs to be deduplicated. In the case of an enterprise maintaining multiple customer or product sales information in for various business entities, e.g. retail and web sales, or possibly different CRM programs that are a result of a company merger, all of this information has to be brought under one roof within the data warehouse.

SQL Server provides two fuzzy transformations to help with such scenarios:

- Fuzzy grouping
- Fuzzy lookup

These transformations can be used independently or in concert to assist with unification and deduplication of your data. Both the fuzzy transformation algorithms create and utilize temporary tables created within SQL Server.

Fuzzy grouping is used primarily for deduplicating and standardizing values in column data. Fuzzy grouping has input parameters and this transformation algorithm adds output columns, which are included to its results (Fig 2-58).

- Input parameters
    - **Token delimiter**   Identifies which characters are used to break up the string into smaller units to be compared (e.g. spaces, tabs, new line, comma, etc.).

- **Similarity thresholds** Value range is from 0 to 1 (1 being an exact match).
- Output columns
  - **_key_in** Contains a unique identifier key for each row.
  - **_key_out** Contains a group identifier key for duplicate rows; all duplicate rows have the same value for this column.
  - **_score** This indicates the similarity to the row, which Fuzzy Grouping has identified as the canonical (correct) row. The score ranges from 0 to 1. Only the canonical row has a score value of 1.

The term *canonical row* here refers to the row that has been determined by the Fuzzy Grouping algorithm to be the most correct row data among all the similar (duplicate) rows. And so the *_key_in* & *_key_out* values are the same for a canonical row.

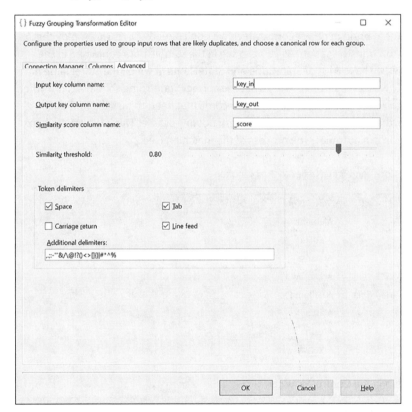

FIGURE 2-58 Fuzzy Grouping Transformation Editor

Fuzzy Lookup is used for identity mapping to look up values in a reference table using a fuzzy match where the data may have different spellings for customer names, street names, or city.

Fuzzy lookup has input parameters and this transformation algorithm also adds output columns which are included to its results.

- Input parameters
  - **Maximum Number Of Matches To Output Per Lookup**   Set this value to any value >= 1.
  - **Token Delimiter**   Identifies which characters are used to break up the string into smaller units to be compared (e.g. spaces, tabs, new line, comma, etc.).
  - **Similarity Thresholds**   Value range is from 0 to 1 (1 being an exact match).
- Output columns
  - **_Similarity**   This value indicates the similarity between input value and reference column value. The range is between 0 to 1 (1 being an exact match).
  - **_Confidence**   This indicates the level of confidence or quality of the match between the input value and the reference column value.

Now let's look at an example of comparing data from a new file containing a list of states. Because we only want to bring in new records, which we don't already have, we employ the use of the fuzzy lookup transformation. As you can see in the sample data contained in the source text file below, we have a list of StateCode and StateName in which the StateName have misspellings. Visually we can see from this list what the correct StateName should be, but when you have source data with thousands or millions of records that need to be validated against your reference data, the task becomes very daunting, if not impossible. This is where the fuzzy lookup transformation can automate the process of the matching (see 2).

TABLE 2-2 List of StateCodes and StateNames for fuzzy lookup

StateCode	StateName
AL	Alabema
AK	Alaskka
AZ	Arizonia
AR	Arkansaw
AL	Aalabama
AK	Alasca
AZ	Arisona
AR	Arkensas

Open up Visual Studio in the Control Flow canvas.

- Add a Data Flow and open it.
- Now add a Flat File Source.
- Create a Connection Manager to the source text file.
- Next drag into the Data Flow canvas the Fuzzy Lookup transformation (to configure it to use the text file and compare it with the reference data, which is a StateProvinces table in the WideWorldImporters database).

- Double-click the Fuzzy Lookup transformation and select the Reference Table tab.
- Under the OLE DB Connection Manager, select the connection to the WideWorldImporters database.
- Click the first radio button for Generate New Index.
- Check the box to Store New Index.
- Under the Reference Table Name drop-down, select Application.StateProvinces.
- Now select the Columns Tab.
- Here you link the column names between the source and reference tables.
- You can also select additional columns to include by checking them in the table Available Lookup Columns (Figure 2-59).
- On the bottom of the window you see the list of the select Lookup Columns and their Output Alias names, which can be changed, in case you want these names to be different.

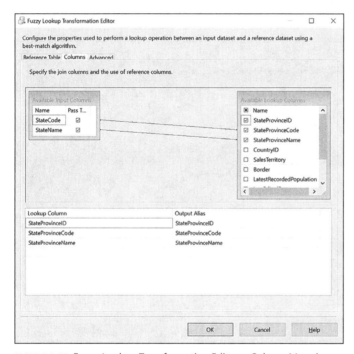

FIGURE 2-59 Fuzzy Lookup Transformation Editor—Column Mapping

- Now select the Advanced tab, which is where all the Fuzzy Lookup settings are made to determine the quality of the match.
- Set Maximum Number Of Matches To Output Per Lookup to 1.
- Set the Similarity Threshold to 0.80 (80 percent). The higher the Similarity Threshold value, the more strict the algorithm is in its matching. And vice versa, the lower the

Similarity Threshold value, the more relaxed the algorithm is in matching between source and referenced data. To avoid allowing too many inaccurate matches to occur by setting the Similarity Threshold value too low, it is better to start with a higher Similarity Threshold value to get the best matches first, and then lessen the Similarity Threshold value to go after the stragglers.

- Finally, under the Token Delimiters, you can choose all the various characters contained in your data by which the Fuzzy Lookup algorithm can parse and breakup the column values to compare the source data with the reference data. As an example, if your data contains spaces and commas, each column value is broken up into smaller values separated by spaces and commas. And each one of these smaller separated values is a "token" used by the algorithm to better analyze and compare source and reference data. So "123 Main St, Chicago, IL 61234" is broken up into the following tokens: 123 / Main / St / Chicago / IL / 61234 (tokenized by spaces and commas). You can see under Additional Delimiters, several more delimiters are added to further improve the matching be breaking the column values into smaller and smaller tokens (see Figure 2-60).

- Click OK to complete the Fuzzy Lookup transformation.

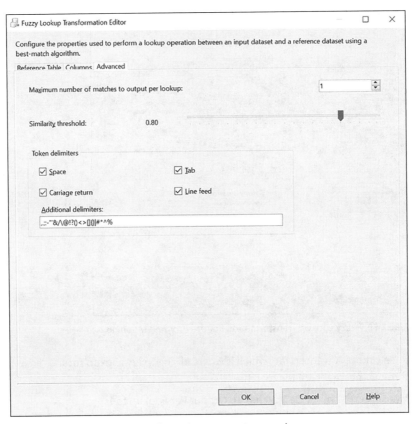

FIGURE 2-60 Fuzzy Lookup Transformation, parameter mapping

- In the Data Flow transform, add the Union All transform, and connect the Fuzzy Lookup to it.

- Right-click the Data Flow Path between the Fuzzy Lookup and Union All, and Enable Data Viewer (Figure 2-61) so that we can see the resulting output data within Visual Studio.

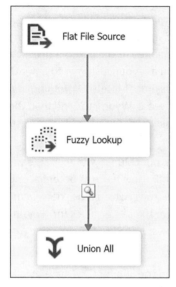

FIGURE 2-61 Fuzzy Lookup Transformation

- Run the package by clicking the Start (Play) button in Visual Studio.
- You should see the following results in the Data Viewer pop-up window (Figure 2-62).

Fuzzy Lookup Output Data Viewer at Fuzzy Lookup

StateCode	StateName	StateProvinceID	StateProvinceCode	StateProvinceName	_Similarity	_Confidence	_Similarity_StateCode	_Similarity_StateName
AL	Aalabama	1	AL	Alabama	0.9322138	0.5	1	0.8746017
AL	Alabema	1	AL	Alabama	0.9223574	0.5	1	0.8563682
AK	Alasca	2	AK	Alaska	0.9237109	0.8653358	1	0.8314797
AK	Alaskka	2	AK	Alaska	0.934948	0.8609884	1	0.8562314
AZ	Arisona	3	AZ	Arizona	0.9291965	0.5	1	0.8562314
AZ	Arizonia	3	AZ	Arizona	0.9382113	0.5	1	0.8745314
AR	Arkansaw	4	AR	Arkansas	0.9384457	0.5	1	0.875
AR	Arkensas	4	AR	Arkansas	0.9382113	0.5	1	0.8745314

Attached Total rows: 0, buffers: 0   Rows displayed = 8

FIGURE 2-62 Fuzzy Lookup Transformation—matching results

Here you see how the first two columns from our source text file is matched to the three columns of our reference table. The remaining columns are the output of the Fuzzy Lookup algorithm comparisons.

The _Similarity and _Confidence values, as described earlier, are a combined score for all the columns being compared (StateCode and StateName). But you also get a more granular similarity comparison for each of the columns in the comparison: _Similarity_StateCode and _Similarity_StateName. This allows you to apply special logic if needed to handle the column match results individually, like possibly running all the columns with _Similarity_StateName < 0.80 through another Fuzzy Lookup with a lower Similarity Threshold equal to 0.65 (65 percent) to try and match the remaining stragglers that did not match the first time.

On the other hand, Fuzzy Grouping does not use a reference data set like Fuzzy Lookup does. It only compares the source data with itself to determine which of the column values are the most valid based on how many times it occurs in the data set. Therefore, if a column value is spelled incorrectly for the majority of the records, it is deemed as the authoritative spelling for that term—even if it is wrong. As an example, if you ask your customer to enter the city and state of their dream vacation, and most customers enter Metetse, Wyoming as their dream destination (instead of the correct spelling of Meeteetse, Wyoming), and then the Fuzzy Grouping algorithm will deem that the all similar city names be changed to the wrong spelling, of Metetse, Wyoming (Figure 2-63).

In the Data Viewer results for Fuzzy Grouping, the _key_out column with the same values will indicate duplicates. So the _key_out values of 3, 7, and 10 show these as potential duplicate records. The _score indicates how closely it matches to the rows, which it has determined to be the authoritative rows. These authoritative rows have the same values for _key_in and _key_out columns. These rows are called the canonical rows: 1, 2, 3, 5, 6, 7, and 10.

Additional columns included are:

- **CityName_clean**   The corrected and deduplicated spelling for CityName
- **StateProvinceName_clean**   The corrected and deduplicated spelling for StateProvinceName
- **_Similarity_CityName**   How similar it is to the canonical CityName
- **_Similiarity_StateProvinceName**   How similar it is to the canonical StateProvinceName

As you can see, the correct spelling for Meeteetse, Wyoming has been changed to Metetse as seen under column CityName_clean, which is the suggested spelling for this city.

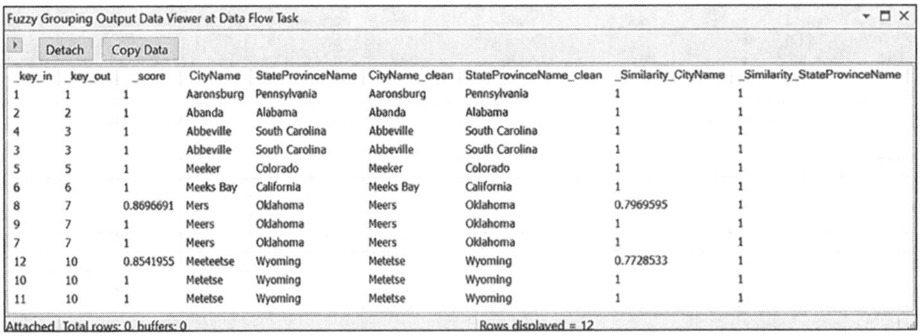

_key_in	_key_out	_score	CityName	StateProvinceName	CityName_clean	StateProvinceName_clean	_Similarity_CityName	_Similarity_StateProvinceName
1	1	1	Aaronsburg	Pennsylvania	Aaronsburg	Pennsylvania	1	1
2	2	1	Abanda	Alabama	Abanda	Alabama	1	1
4	3	1	Abbeville	South Carolina	Abbeville	South Carolina	1	1
3	3	1	Abbeville	South Carolina	Abbeville	South Carolina	1	1
5	5	1	Meeker	Colorado	Meeker	Colorado	1	1
6	6	1	Meeks Bay	California	Meeks Bay	California	1	1
8	7	0.8696691	Mers	Oklahoma	Meers	Oklahoma	0.7969595	1
9	7	1	Meers	Oklahoma	Meers	Oklahoma	1	1
7	7	1	Meers	Oklahoma	Meers	Oklahoma	1	1
12	10	0.8541955	Meeteetse	Wyoming	Metetse	Wyoming	0.7728533	1
10	10	1	Metetse	Wyoming	Metetse	Wyoming	1	1
11	10	1	Metetse	Wyoming	Metetse	Wyoming	1	1

FIGURE 2-63 Fuzzy Grouping—matching results

In today's day of social media and online reviews, you may want to scan a large piece of text for certain words and the frequency it is referred to in the text. *Term Lookup* can be used to look up terms in a reference table and count terms extracted from text.

To use the Term Lookup transform, your input source in the Data Flow will be the table or file containing rows of data that you want to search through, like reviews or Tweets. The next step is to add a Term Lookup to your Data Flow and point to a reference table, which contains the terms that you will be looking for in the source records. You can set the destination for the output results to another table where you see how many times each of the terms are found in the source data.

When using Term Lookup, keep in mind:

- **When using Singular Form of the term**   Term Lookup transformation considers both singular and plural forms of a word as the same (Shoe = Shoes) and counts them together.

- **When using Plural Form of the term**   Term Lookup transformation looks at both the singular and plural forms as different terms (Shoe <> Shoes) and counts them separately.

- **Case Sensitivity**   If you have chosen to use Case-Sensitive matching, the only exception is allowance for the first letter of a sentence to be capitalized. If the case-sensitive term is "shoe" and the source contains, "If the shoe fits. Shoe shine kit gift box", both occurrences of shoe are counted.

When moving any amount of data, we sometimes require an audit trail to show where the data is coming from and via whose account. This realm of data lineage, the identification of the source of data, including the machine name, package name, task name, execution time, etc., is handled by the Audit transform, Figure 2-64. And when used in conjunction with the Row-Count transform, you can also keep track of the number of records processed.

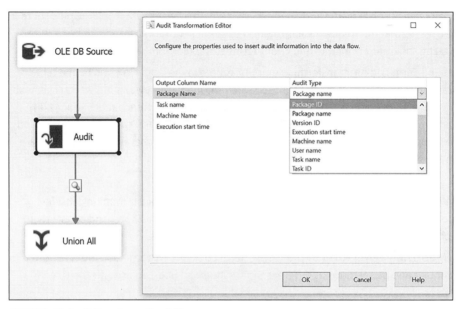

FIGURE 2-64 Audit Transformation Editor

Here is a sample output using a Data Viewer to show how the Audit Transform can append new columns with the additional audit information (Figure 2-65).

PersonID	FullName	PreferredName	Package Name	Task name	Machine Name	Execution start time
1	Data Conversion Only	Data Conversion Only	Audit Transform	Data Flow Task	DESKTOP-MILANO	2017-07-30 19:53:53.0000000
2	Kayla Woodcock	Kayla	Audit Transform	Data Flow Task	DESKTOP-MILANO	2017-07-30 19:53:53.0000000
3	Hudson Onslow	Hudson	Audit Transform	Data Flow Task	DESKTOP-MILANO	2017-07-30 19:53:53.0000000
4	Isabella Rupp	Isabella	Audit Transform	Data Flow Task	DESKTOP-MILANO	2017-07-30 19:53:53.0000000
5	Eva Muirden	Eva	Audit Transform	Data Flow Task	DESKTOP-MILANO	2017-07-30 19:53:53.0000000
6	Sophia Hinton	Sophia	Audit Transform	Data Flow Task	DESKTOP-MILANO	2017-07-30 19:53:53.0000000
7	Amy Trefl	Amy	Audit Transform	Data Flow Task	DESKTOP-MILANO	2017-07-30 19:53:53.0000000
8	Anthony Grosse	Anthony	Audit Transform	Data Flow Task	DESKTOP-MILANO	2017-07-30 19:53:53.0000000
9	Alica Fatnowna	Alica	Audit Transform	Data Flow Task	DESKTOP-MILANO	2017-07-30 19:53:53.0000000
10	Stella Rosenhain	Stella	Audit Transform	Data Flow Task	DESKTOP-MILANO	2017-07-30 19:53:53.0000000
11	Ethan Onslow	Ethan	Audit Transform	Data Flow Task	DESKTOP-MILANO	2017-07-30 19:53:53.0000000
12	Henry Forlonge	Henry	Audit Transform	Data Flow Task	DESKTOP-MILANO	2017-07-30 19:53:53.0000000
13	Hudson Hollinworth	Hudson	Audit Transform	Data Flow Task	DESKTOP-MILANO	2017-07-30 19:53:53.0000000
14	Lily Code	Lily	Audit Transform	Data Flow Task	DESKTOP-MILANO	2017-07-30 19:53:53.0000000

Attached | Total rows: 0, buffers: 0   Rows displayed = 1111

FIGURE 2-65 Audit Transformation—sample output

You can also use the Derived Column transformation to add any customized columns to the output to be included downstream. The new Derived Column Names can either be added or used to replace existing columns. In Figure 2-66, we have added new columns using system variables to create an alternative method for generating audit-related columns.

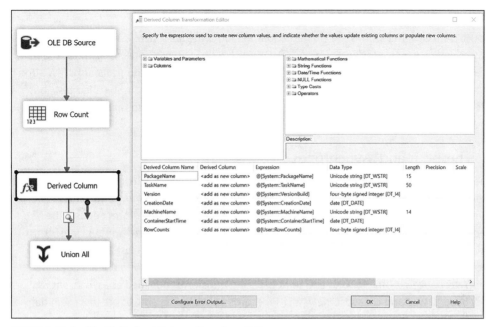

FIGURE 2-66 Audit with Derived Column Transform Editor

In Figure 2-67, you can see the Data Viewer output with addition columns generated by the Derived Column transform.

PersonID	FullName	PreferredName	PackageName	TaskName	Version	CreationDate	MachineName	ContainerStartTime
1	Data Conversion Only	Data Conversion Only	Audit Transform	Data Flow - Audit Transform	13	2017-07-30 19:48:50.0000000	DESKTOP-MILANO	2017-07-30 20:23:34.0000
2	Kayla Woodcock	Kayla	Audit Transform	Data Flow - Audit Transform	13	2017-07-30 19:48:50.0000000	DESKTOP-MILANO	2017-07-30 20:23:34.0000
3	Hudson Onslow	Hudson	Audit Transform	Data Flow - Audit Transform	13	2017-07-30 19:48:50.0000000	DESKTOP-MILANO	2017-07-30 20:23:34.0000
4	Isabella Rupp	Isabella	Audit Transform	Data Flow - Audit Transform	13	2017-07-30 19:48:50.0000000	DESKTOP-MILANO	2017-07-30 20:23:34.0000
5	Eva Muirden	Eva	Audit Transform	Data Flow - Audit Transform	13	2017-07-30 19:48:50.0000000	DESKTOP-MILANO	2017-07-30 20:23:34.0000
6	Sophia Hinton	Sophia	Audit Transform	Data Flow - Audit Transform	13	2017-07-30 19:48:50.0000000	DESKTOP-MILANO	2017-07-30 20:23:34.0000
7	Amy Trefl	Amy	Audit Transform	Data Flow - Audit Transform	13	2017-07-30 19:48:50.0000000	DESKTOP-MILANO	2017-07-30 20:23:34.0000
8	Anthony Grosse	Anthony	Audit Transform	Data Flow - Audit Transform	13	2017-07-30 19:48:50.0000000	DESKTOP-MILANO	2017-07-30 20:23:34.0000
9	Alica Fatnowna	Alica	Audit Transform	Data Flow - Audit Transform	13	2017-07-30 19:48:50.0000000	DESKTOP-MILANO	2017-07-30 20:23:34.0000
10	Stella Rosenhain	Stella	Audit Transform	Data Flow - Audit Transform	13	2017-07-30 19:48:50.0000000	DESKTOP-MILANO	2017-07-30 20:23:34.0000
11	Ethan Onslow	Ethan	Audit Transform	Data Flow - Audit Transform	13	2017-07-30 19:48:50.0000000	DESKTOP-MILANO	2017-07-30 20:23:34.0000
12	Henry Forlonge	Henry	Audit Transform	Data Flow - Audit Transform	13	2017-07-30 19:48:50.0000000	DESKTOP-MILANO	2017-07-30 20:23:34.0000
13	Hudson Hollinworth	Hudson	Audit Transform	Data Flow - Audit Transform	13	2017-07-30 19:48:50.0000000	DESKTOP-MILANO	2017-07-30 20:23:34.0000
14	Lily Code	Lily	Audit Transform	Data Flow - Audit Transform	13	2017-07-30 19:48:50.0000000	DESKTOP-MILANO	2017-07-30 20:23:34.0000
15	Taj Shand	Taj	Audit Transform	Data Flow - Audit Transform	13	2017-07-30 19:48:50.0000000	DESKTOP-MILANO	2017-07-30 20:23:34.0000
16	Archer Lamble	Archer	Audit Transform	Data Flow - Audit Transform	13	2017-07-30 19:48:50.0000000	DESKTOP-MILANO	2017-07-30 20:23:34.0000
17	Piper Koch	Piper	Audit Transform	Data Flow - Audit Transform	13	2017-07-30 19:48:50.0000000	DESKTOP-MILANO	2017-07-30 20:23:34.0000
18	Katie Darwin	Katie	Audit Transform	Data Flow - Audit Transform	13	2017-07-30 19:48:50.0000000	DESKTOP-MILANO	2017-07-30 20:23:34.0000
19	Jai Shand	Jai	Audit Transform	Data Flow - Audit Transform	13	2017-07-30 19:48:50.0000000	DESKTOP-MILANO	2017-07-30 20:23:34.0000
20	Jack Potter	Jack	Audit Transform	Data Flow - Audit Transform	13	2017-07-30 19:48:50.0000000	DESKTOP-MILANO	2017-07-30 20:23:34.0000
21	Reio Kabin	Reio	Audit Transform	Data Flow - Audit Transform	13	2017-07-30 19:48:50.0000000	DESKTOP-MILANO	2017-07-30 20:23:34.0000
22	Oliver Kivi	Olly	Audit Transform	Data Flow - Audit Transform	13	2017-07-30 19:48:50.0000000	DESKTOP-MILANO	2017-07-30 20:23:34.0000
23	Hanna Mihhailov	Hanna	Audit Transform	Data Flow - Audit Transform	13	2017-07-30 19:48:50.0000000	DESKTOP-MILANO	2017-07-30 20:23:34.0000
24	Paulus Liopmaa	Paulus	Audit Transform	Data Flow - Audit Transform	13	2017-07-30 19:48:50.0000000	DESKTOP-MILANO	2017-07-30 20:23:34.0000

Attached Total rows: 0, buffers: 0   Rows displayed = 1111

FIGURE 2-67 Audit with Derived Column Transform—sample output

Non-blocking, semi-blocking, and blocking transforms

Not all Data Flow transforms are created equal. In fact, some are much faster and require a lot less memory (non-blocking transforms). Others are slower while consuming much more memory (blocking transforms), and some are in between (semi-blocking transforms). We don't always have a choice if we need to use a certain transform to do a certain specified task, but it is good to know the differences between these types of transforms so that we can better understand performance and resource utilization issues.

Synchronous and asynchronous

There is another related aspect about Data Flow transforms, which is their ability to quickly process a row as they are coming into the transform, independently of any other rows that came before or after (synchronous transforms). The other type of transform needs to be dependent on some or all of the rows that come before and after (asynchronous transforms). On the whole, non-blocking transforms are also synchronous, thus are fast and require less memory; they process a row as soon as it arrives and sends it on its way to the next destination. Alternatively, both blocking and semi-blocking transforms qualified as asynchronous; they need to wait and collect some or all the records before being able to process them before sending them to the next destination.

The output of a synchronous component utilizes the same buffer as the input component because the output of a synchronous component always contains exactly an equal number of records as the input component. This reuse of buffers makes it faster. Alternatively, the output of an asynchronous component uses new buffers. New buffers are required because an asynchronous component can have more or less output records than input records.

It's important to note that all source adapters are asynchronous; they create two buffers: one for the success output and the other for the error output. Destination adapters are synchronous.

An example of a non-blocking, synchronous Data Flow transform would be the Derived Column or Data Conversion, both of which can add or convert columns for the active record and pass it along and move on to the next record. And an example of a fully-blocking, asynchronous Data Flow transform would be Sort, which requires all of the data to be collected before outputting the final sorted set of records.

Here is a list of all the various types of transforms and performance.

- Non-Blocking Synchronous Transformations (Very Fast)   Rapid streaming
    - Audit
    - Cache Transform
    - Character Map
    - Conditional Split
    - Copy Column
    - Data Conversion

- Derived Column
- Lookup (Full Cache enabled)
- Multicast
- Percent Sampling
- Row Count
- Non-Blocking Synchronous Transformations (Fast)   Row-based processing
  - DQS Cleansing
  - Export Column
  - Import Column
  - Lookup (Partial Cache or No Cache enabled)
  - OLE DB Command
  - Script Component, if configured to use an outside resource
  - Slowly Changing Dimension (SCD)
- Semi-Blocking Asynchronous Transformations (Intermediate)   Some data collection
  - Data Mining Query
  - Merge
  - Merge Join
  - Pivot
  - Term Lookup
  - Union All
  - Unpivot
- Fully Blocking Asynchronous Transformations (Slow)   Full data collection
  - Aggregate
  - Fuzzy Grouping
  - Fuzzy Lookup
  - Row Sampling
  - Script Component (if aggregating records)
  - Sort
  - Term Extraction

Although it would be great if we could always use the fastest, rapid-streaming transforms for all of our DW data processing that would not be plausible because each transform has an inherent functionality needed when transforming data. Below is a guideline with an overview of all of the transforms and their basic usages. This helps to direct you to the transforms best suited for your task at hand in the moving and processing from the source systems into the DW.

- DW and BI transformations
  - Data Mining Query
  - DQS Cleansing
  - Fuzzy Grouping
  - Fuzzy Lookup
  - Slowly Changing Dimension
  - Term Extraction
  - Term Lookup
- Row and column data transformations
  - Character Map
  - Copy Column
  - Data Conversion
  - Derived Column
  - Export Column
  - Import Column
  - OLE DB Command
  - Script Component
- Aggregations, sorting, sampling, and pivot transformations
  - Aggregate
  - Percentage Sampling
  - Pivot
  - Row Sampling
  - Sort
  - Unpivot
- Combining, splitting, broadcasting, looking-up, caching transforms
  - Balanced Data Distributor
  - Cache Transform
  - Conditional Split
  - Lookup
  - Merge
  - Merge Join
  - Multicast
  - Union All

- Logging and row count transformations
  - Audit
  - Row Count

Data flow source and destination column mapping

Data being brought into the DW can come from various sources, flat file, excel, xml file, or database. These source columns need to be mapped to the correct, corresponding columns in the destination table. Within the Data Flow task, nearly every transform requires a mapping of the source columns to the target columns. Most often, the transform itself automatically maps these columns based on matching column names. The auto matching is usually correct in general, as long as both the source and target column names are the same. If some of the column names are not the same, they will not be matched, thereby excluding those columns from being including in the transformation. That is why it is important to always check that all the required columns have been mapped correctly. Alternatively, the auto matching may include columns that should be excluded from the transformation, so check the column mapping is an important step to avoid loading errors due to additional and/or missing columns.

In Figure 2-68, you can see the OLE DB Destination Editor auto mapping between the Input and Destination columns. You right-click the gray area around the table columns and choose from one of the following options:

- **Select All Mappings**   This selects all the mapping lines so they can be deleted.
- **Delete Selected Mappings**   This deletes any of the select mapping lines.
- **Map Items By Matching Names**   This is the auto-matching option in case you delete any of the mappings.

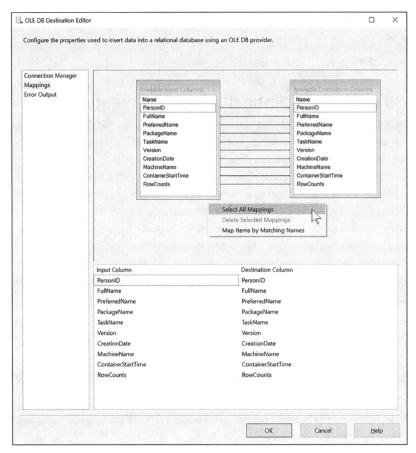

FIGURE 2-68 Column Mapping—OLE DB Destination Editor

Determine appropriate scenarios for Transact-SQL joins versus SSIS lookup

Some common design patterns for data warehouse loads invlove extracting data from one or more sources and performing business and dimension key column lookups and joins. In most instances, SSIS packages can be optimized to perform these lookups and joins efficiently by tuning package control and data flow properties. In addition, it might be necessary to ensure that database object maintenance activities are done in a regular basis including, index de-fragmentation and statistics update.

The SSIS Lookup transform comes very handy when doing lookup of dimension keys. For example, when loading a fact table with customer transactions, we lookup the customer's business key against the business keys stored in the customer dimension. If we find a match, we retrieve the customer's surrogate key and insert it in the fact table along with the corresponding transactions.

In this case, the SSIS Lookup transform would be appropriate to use if we can cache all customer dimension records in the SSIS memory buffer. By default, the SSIS Lookup transform uses the Full Cache mode. If there is not enough memory available to cache all customer records, the SSIS package execution will fail. Some alternatives to overcome a cache limitation, include changing the default cache mode to Partial Cache or No Cache or using a Cache Connection Manager. For more information on Lookup cache modes visit: *https://blogs.msdn.microsoft.com/mattm/2008/10/18/lookup-cache-modes/*. Although, originally written for SSIS 2008 this article still applies to SSIS 2016.

In some cases, the best alternative to overcome SSIS Lookup limitations is to use T-SQL joins. Joins peformed using T-SQL can perform much better in those instances in which the SSIS server cannot fit an entire table in its buffer. The SQL Query Optitmizer can make use of indexes and statistics to produce a more efficient query plan to process large datasets in less time than it would take SSIS to cache all the data. Partition elimination can further improve large query performance.

In addition to lookups and joins, merge operations can scale better using T-SQL than the SSIS Merge, Merge Join or SCD transformations. This is true when staging large volumes of data that need to be merged to identify what needs to be inserted, updated or deleted. Using the SSIS Merge, Merge Join or SCD transformations means that the data needs to be brought into the SSIS server's memory buffer to apply merge and join operations. This can be very costly when processing large volumes of data or when more complex business rules need to be applied.

In some scenarios in which you are joining and merging data from sources other than SQL Server, SSIS may be the only viable solution if the data is not being staged in a SQL Server database or not being staged at all.

Other scenarios that may influence the decision when to use SSIS over T-SQL may include:

- Complexity of business rules and data transformations
- Number of lookups
- Developer skillsets
- Organization standards and regulations

Skill 2.3: Implement an ETL solution that supports incremental data extraction

Once all the data has been fully loaded into the DW, this completes your full load, also known as the initial load that populates the target database. The next step is setting up an incremental loading SSIS package so that you do not have to reload all the data over and over again, only the new or changed data. This is especially necessary source data sizes are in hundreds of gigabytes, terabytes, or even petabytes. We look at different techniques to load incremental data depending how your source data keeps track of changes. If there is no reliable method of determining which records have change or have been inserted into the source environment, you can use the native Change Data Capture (CDC) feature to let SQL Server keep track of those changes for you, thereby assisting the incremental loading process.

This skill covers how to:
- Design fact table patterns
- Enable Change Data Capture
- Create a SQL MERGE statement

Desgin fact table patterns

Fact tables used in data warehouses can become the very large, very fast by order of magnitude. It's important to implement best practices for fact table design at the onset, even if your fact table does not contain billions of rows. Here are some things to be aware and include in your fact table design:

- Consider partitioning your fact tables when they are larger than 100 GB. The partitions can be by any column, which provides a fairly equal distribution of your data. Usually the Date columns (not DateTime columns) are good candidates.
  - This provides more granularity when creating indexes, loading, updating, and deleting data (by partitions).
  - Faster data access for queries by limiting the IO to specific partitions.
  - Utilize partition switching to move data in and out almost instantaneously.
  - Implement sliding window using partition splitting and partition merging.
- Build clustered indexes on the Date Key of the fact tables (not DataTime).
  - This allows for more efficient queries when accessing historical data and loading SSAS cubes.
  - When working within a maintenance window the following settings for the fact table clustered index will speed up the scan operations during query times by minimizing granular-level locking on the table:
  - ALLOW_ROW_LOCKS = OFF
  - ALLOW_PAGE_LOCKS = OFF
- Build nonclustered indexes on each of the fact table foreign keys to allow for faster selection of records when joining again the corresponding dimension tables.

You have two main stages when loading the fact tables in your DW. The initial load, or full load, is relatively straightforward because all of the relevant data from your source systems are extracted, transformed, and loaded into the DW. Once the full load is complete, it's the ongoing Incremental load that keeps the DW up-to-date.

One of the most vital design processes for a data warehouse ETL (extract, transform, and load) solution is the incremental load. Incremental loading is the ongoing process that is done after completing the initial (full) load of the data warehouse fact tables from the source systems. Once your dataset gets beyond a few hundred gigabytes, it is no longer feasible, nor prudent to reload all the data, especially if less than two percent of the data has actually been added or changed. If the full load took 15 hours to populate all the DW fact tables, then loading only the incremental changes may take 15-60 minutes depending on the amount of changes and the complexity of the transformations required to prepare the staging data to populate the fact tables. But it certainly won't take anywhere as long as the initial load. On one project where we had a DW that was nearly 50 terabytes, even the incremental loads were taking a few hours nightly.

Once all of the data has been initially populated into the DW, probably over the weekend, the incremental loads are set up as a repeating job that will run nightly, or throughout the day, depending on the business requirement for refreshing the data warehouse.

The incremental loading can be done using SSIS with two different methods:

- **CDC Control Task** This is the *Change Data Capture* component within SSIS.
- **Execute SQL Task** This can be implemented via the T-SQL MERGE statement.

Enable Change Data Capture

Change Data Capture (CDC) is a SQL Server built-in audit-tracking system that can automatically track and record any change activity to a table: INSERT, UPDATE, DELETE, which can be used for the purpose of incremental loading. In order to use CDC, someone with sysadmin level permissions must enable CDC for the database, which contains the tables that need to be tracked. Once it is enabled on the database level, someone with at least dbo_owner level permissions can enable CDC on the specific table that will be tracked for changes.

To enable CDC at the database level, sysadmin has to run this command:

```
-- ===============================
-- Enable Database for CDC
-- ===============================
USE WideWorldImporters
GO
EXEC sys.sp_cdc_enable_db
GO
```

The next step is to enable CDC for the specific table:

```
-- =====================================================
-- Enable a Table for Net Changes Queries
-- =====================================================
USE [WideWorldImporters]
GO
EXEC sys.sp_cdc_enable_table
     @source_schema = N'Application',      -- Schema name
     @source_name   = N'People',      -- Table name
     @role_name     = N'cdc_db_role',      -- Role name will be created if it does not
exist
     @supports_net_changes = 1      -- Only the Net/Final Changes are brought over
GO
```

If the @role_name does not already exist, SQL Server attempts to create it if the user has the appropriate permissions, otherwise this SP fails unless the @role_name is preexisting.

CDC does all the housekeeping for tracking table-level changes so you don't have to setup any custom tracking tables or processes. This is especially useful if you don't have an easy way of tracking changes on the source system, like an InsertedDate, or a TimeStamp that you can reference to know where you last left off in your loading process. For CDC to work, SQL Agent must be running because when CDC is enabled, it creates SQL Agent jobs to do its work. We delve further into the actual setup of CDC later in the chapter.

Create a SQL MERGE statement

Alternatively, if you do have a way to keep track of which records have changed at the source system, you can implement the simple, yet powerful T-SQL MERGE command. The MERGE command allows your table to be scanned once and checked for all changes: inserts, updates, and deletes. And you can choose if you want to affect changes for any one or all of these change types into your target table.

In Figure 2-69 you can see the structure of a MERGE statement. In this example the StudentSource and StudentTarget tables are matched on ID, which is their key column. The first clause, WHEN MATCHED performs and update when the IDs match. The next clause, WHEN NOT MATCHED BY TARGET THEN, checks the TARGET table to see if any IDs don't exist in the StudentTarget and inserts the new records, but in this case, there are no new ID values to insert. The last clause, WHEN NOT MATCHED BY SOURCE THEN, checks the SOURCE table to see if any IDs have been removed, and deletes those records form StudentTarget. The MERGE statement can check either the Source or Target for MATCHED or NOT MATCHED, but the changes are only made to the target table.

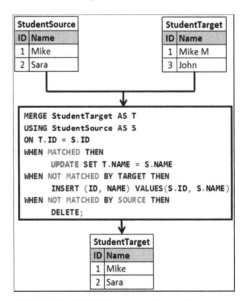

FIGURE 2-69 MERGE Statement Example

Skill 2.4 Implement an ETL solution that supports incremental data loading

For incremental loading to be successful you must identify which source system attribute or column will identify what was the last set of data that has already been loaded into the DW, possibly a Date column. Let's say you have a source system with an LastModifiedDateTime column, or something similar, then it can be used to filter out the last load cutoff time. So the next incremental load would begin after the latest ModifiedDate stored in the DW. Because ModifiedDate changes every time the incremental load runs, you can get the latest record date from the corresponding DW fact table and put that into a variable in SSIS, @LastModifiedDate = MAX(ModifiedDate) to get all the records after that date.

> **This skill covers how to:**
> - Design a control flow to load change data
> - Load data by using Transact-SQL Change Data Capture functions
> - Load data by using Change Data Capture in SSIS

Design a control flow to load change data

In creating an incremental load Data Flow, you can create a dynamic query within the OLE DB Source Editor under Connection Manager page, go to the Data Access Mode drop-down and select SQL Command. This opens up a free text pane below labeled SQL Command Text. Here we can enter the query against the source table with a variable parameter in the WHERE clause. The parameter is identified by the "?" in the SQL text. "?" is the syntax used by the SSIS expression language for a parameter (Figure 2-70). Even though you have a Preview button, you get an error since the parameter values only get evaluated at runtime, not here at design time.

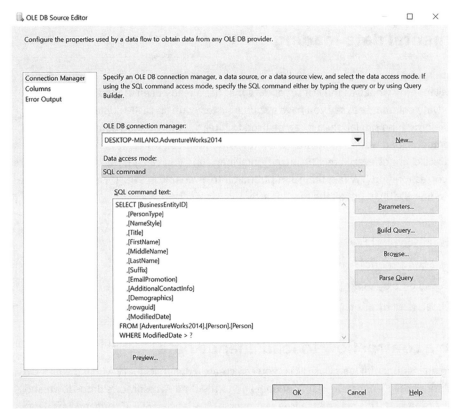

FIGURE 2-70 Incremental Loading—SQL Command Text with parameter

With the SQL query in place, click the Parameters button to map the SQL query parameter to the SSIS variable @LastModifiedDate, which will pass in the value of MAX(ModifiedDate) from the fact table (Figure 2-71). Make sure the Param Direction is set to Input because the SSIS variable value is being passed in to be used by the query.

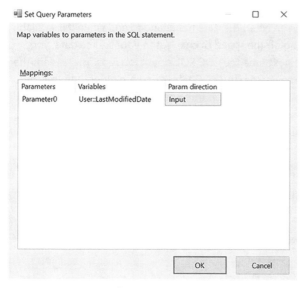

FIGURE 2-71 Incremental Loading—Mapping Query Parameter to SSIS User variable

Load data by using Transact-SQL Change Data Capture functions

In order to use Change Data Capture for automatic incremental load processing you need to make sure certain items are in place and specific tasks have been done. As mentioned earlier, CDC requires SQL Agent to function, if SQL Agent has been turned off or fails for any reason, the CDC process will be halted.

CDC needs to be enabled on the database level before it can be used. CDC also needs to be enabled on each table to be tracked. You can configure individual columns to be tracked, but by default all columns are select for tracking. CDC tracks the following changes:

- Rows inserted
- Rows updated (records column values before and after update)
- Rows deleted (records column values before delete)
- When the operation occurred

CDC works by creating a new CDC schema and new physical tables for each tracked table within the System Tables folder. These are the tables that contain the changes; there is a single row created for each INSERT and DELETE operation—and two rows created for each UPDATE operation: one row shows how the data looked before the update, and the second row shows the data after the UPDATE.

CDC is asynchronous, which means when a table data is changing, there is no contention with CDC, nor does it slow any transactions down. That is because CDC detects changes by reading the transaction log file, not the source tables. This is managed by the SQL Server Agent jobs. One of the jobs read the logs and records the changes, which means that when you query for changes, there may be a delay between when the data has changed and when it is available in CDC. Due to this delay, and depending on the speed of changes to your source data, you may not see all of the changes until the next time the CDC SQL Agent job runs. There is another SQL Server Agent job that removes the rows from the CDC tables that are older than the configured retention period. The default retention period is three days, which can be customized based on business retention requirements.

The basic structure of CDC Control Flow package is the same for both an Initial, full load and for an Incremental load (Figures 2-72 and 2-73):

- Truncate/clean out Staging Table.
- Use CDC Control Task to mark the Start of the CDC process.
- Use a Data Flow task to load the Staging Table with data from the Source table.
- Use CDC Control Task to mark the End of the CDC process.

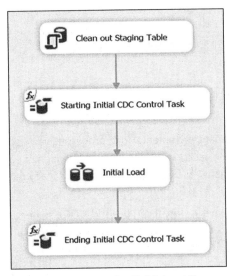

FIGURE 2-72 Initial Load—CDC Control Flow

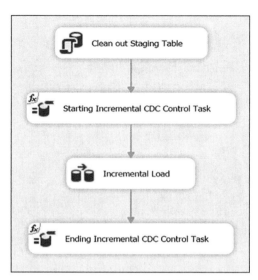

FIGURE 2-73 Incremental Load—CDC Control Flow

In the CDC Control Task Editor you specify the following items (Figure 2-74):

- The source database where the CDC tables are located.
- Specify the CDC Control Operation.
- The SSIS variable containing the CDC state.
- The database where the state is stored for the current CDC value.
- The Table to use for storing the state of the current CDC value.
- The State name to use to identify the table for which the state is being stored.

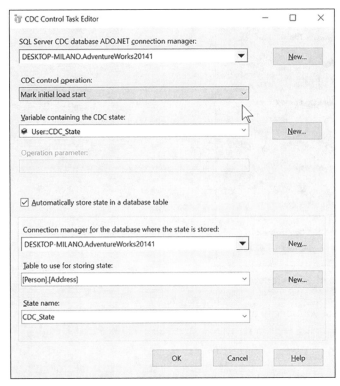

FIGURE 2-74 Initial Load—CDC Control Task Editor

Here are all of the options available for the CDC Control Operations drop-down, which is part of the CDC Control Task Editor (Figure 2-75).

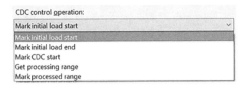

FIGURE 2-75 CDC Control Task Editor—CDC Control Operations Options

- **Mark Initial Load Start**   This option is used at the beginning of the initial load to record the current LSN from the source (non-snapshot) database before the package starts reading from the source tables. To use this option, the user account in the connection manager must have db_owner or sysadmin permissions.

- **Mark Initial Load End**   This option is used at the end of an initial-load package to record the current LSN in the source (non-snapshot) database after the package finished reading the source tables. This LSN is based on the time this operation occurred and querying cdc.lsn_time_mapping table in the CDC source database for any change occurring after that time. To use this option, the user account in the connection manager must have db_owner or sysadmin permissions.

- **Mark CDC Start** This option is used when the initial load is made from a snapshot database or a quiescence (not used) database. This option can take a parameter which is a snapshot LSN, or a snapshot database name; if left empty, it uses the current database LSN used as the starting LSN in order to process the changes. This is used in lieu of the Mark Initial Load Start/End operations. To use this option, the user account in the connection manager must have db_owner or sysadmin permissions.

- **Get Processing Range** This option is used in incremental loading prior to using the CDC Source data flow. This provides the range of LSNs used by the CDC Source data flow. The range value is stored in SSIS package variable used by CDC Source during data-flow processing.

- **Mark Processed Range** This option is used at the end of incremental loading, after the CDC data flow has completed successfully, to record the last LSN that was fully processed in the CDC run. The next time GetProcessingRange is executed, this position determines the start of the next processing range.

Load data by using Change Data Capture in SSIS

If you plan to load multiple tables simultaneously, in parallel, to maximize performance and fully utilize your sever resources, consider setting the State Name to the name of the table being loaded. In this way, you can track the individual loading of tables running in parallel (Figure 2-76). In the event that some of the tables fail to load, you can restart the package to load only the failed packages because each of their CDC states is stored individually. This allows each table to maintain its own Log Sequence Number (LSN).

name	state
CDC_State_Customer	ILEND/IR/0x0002DFC6000153A80002/0x0002DFC6000153B00002/TS/2017-07-24T00:04:58.4533122/
CDC_State_Product	ILEND/IR/0x0002DFC6000154B60002/0x0002DFC6000154B80002/TS/2017-07-24T00:24:29.9106828/
CDC_State_Order	ILEND/IR/0x0002DFC6000154C70002/0x0002DFC6000154CA0002/TS/2017-07-24T00:25:51.9476119/
CDC_State_Sales	ILEND/IR/0x0002DFC60001564D0002/0x0002DFC6000156500002/TS/2017-07-24T00:55:42.5322522/

FIGURE 2-76 CDC State Names for parallel running CDC table loading

CDC Control Task

The three major components of CDC and their primary functions are (see Figure 2-77).

- Manages the full cycle of the change data capture (CDC) packages.
- It handles CDC package synchronization for the initial load package, which includes managing of Log Sequence Number (LSN).
- Handles error scenarios and recovery.

- Maintains the CDC package state in an SSIS package variable and/or in a database table so states can be maintained across package activations and between multiple packages that perform a common CDC process together.
- Handles synchronization of the initial load and change processing.
- Manages change-processing range of LSNs for a run of a CDC package and keeps track of what was processed successfully.

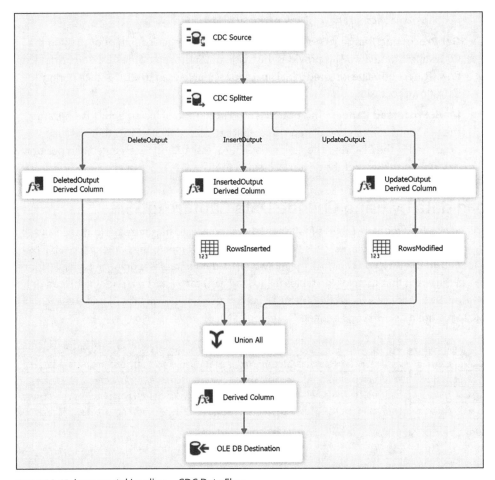

FIGURE 2-77 Incremental Loading—CDC Data Flow

CDC Source

- Reads change the data from the tables and deliver these changes to other SSIS components.
- Reads CDC Processing Range is derived from the value of a package variable, which maintains the CDC processing state for a group of tables.

- CDC source uses the following configurations (Figure 2-78):
  - SQL Server ADO.NET connection manager
  - CDC Enabled Table
  - Capture Instance for the selected table
  - CDC Processing Mode
  - The variable name holding CDC state

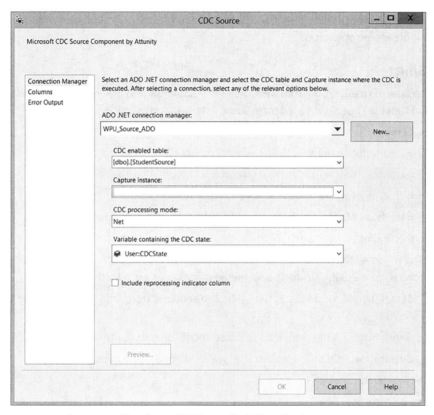

FIGURE 2-78 Incremental Loading—CDC Source Task (Data Flow)

CDC Processing Mode has five different processing options (Figure 2-79):

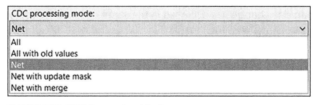

FIGURE 2-79 CDC Processing Modes

- **All**   Returns changes from current CDC range without *Before Update* values.
- **All with old values**   Returns changes from current CDC processing range along with the old values (*Before Update*). Each Update operation has two rows—before and after.
- **Net**   Returns only finally modified record from the current CDC processing range.
- **Net with update mask**   Like Net mode but adds Boolean columns with the name pattern __$<column-name>__Changed to indicate columns have changed in the current row.
- **Net with merge**   Like Net mode but Insert and Update operations processed into a single Merge operation.

CDC Splitter

Splits the flow of change rows from the CDC source data flow into different paths (Insert, Update, and Delete). The split is based the column __$operation as follows:

- 1 = Delete
- 2 = Insert (not available with Net with Merge mode)
- 3 = Update - Before-update row (available only with All with Old Values mode)
- 4 = Update - After-update row (follows the Before-update)
- 5 = Update - Merge row (only available with Net with Merge mode)
- Other = Error

   The Union All task combines the results sets from the Deleted, Inserted, and Updated rows (Figure 2-80). The additional metadata columns are added:

- **__$start_lsn**   Column stores the LSNs of the commit transactions that changed the records.
- **__$end_lsn**   Column reserved for future enhancements (currently always null).
- **__$operation**   Column specifies the type of change made to each record.
  - 1 = delete
  - 2 = insert
  - 4 = update
- **__$update_mask**   Columns are bit masks to indicate which columns have been changed (for insert or delete records, bit mask are all ones since all column changed).
- **__$seqval**   If more than one change has occurred in the same transaction, values in this column are used to order the changes.

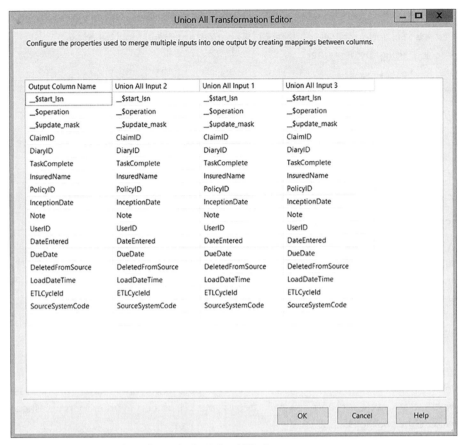

FIGURE 2-80 Incremental Loading—CDC - Union All Task

Skill 2.5: Debug SSIS packages

As with any development environment, we need tools to debug and resolve errors and discrepancies with data and logic. Not only will you experience problems with connection managers, package execution, but also performance-related issues loading large data sets. When dealing with incremental loading, but even more vital for full loads, it is important to architect a design with parallelization in mind so that you maximize concurrent loading into fact and dimension tables. SSIS allows for very extensive logging on a multitude of events to help isolate the errors. In addition, the usage of breakpoints provides the ability to step through each individual task and process and data viewers expose the records, which are mid-flight so you can see if the data being transformed by a task in the package is giving you the expected results. While all this is done at design time, you can also utilize the Data Tap feature to export in-flight data to a file from your production package.

Fix performance, connectivity, execution, and failed logic issues by using the debugger

When working with something as vast and powerful as SSIS, connecting to a multitude of data sources (databases, files, spreadsheets), designing complex ETL packages with Control Flows and Data Flows, Transformations and Tasks, you experience issues and errors while designing and testing your packages. Alternatively, you could have a package that has been deployed into production, which was running successfully for months and, all of a sudden, you get a call about the production ETL is failing to load data into the DW.

Any new software design experiences a period of development where you are testing and troubleshooting the logic and process to make sure you're getting the desired results from your SSIS packages. To assist with this, the Visual Studio design environment provides several ways to track, audit, log, and view each step of your ETL process in order to troubleshoot and validate the packages.

Some are basic validations like verifying that your Connection Manager is successfully connected to the data sources, while other methods allow you to do a full-scale deep dive and follow the breadcrumbs all the way back to the point of error. You use certain troubleshooting methods only during the design phase of the development lifecycle. Other methods facilitate you to constantly audit and log package execution activities in production to expedite forensic analysis when you get that 3 am call that the system is down and you're on call.

Features such as audit logging can provide some level of troubleshooting to your Level 1 Network Operations Center (NOC) support to attempt to investigate the failure and possibly find the cause and fix it—or advise you of the cause so you can hit the ground running when there is an issue. Our preference is to create a runbook for the NOC team with documentation on how to read the logs in case of an error and what types of errors or warnings to look for in those logs, and even the resolution if they have sufficient permissions. After some training, the NOC personnel can handle many common issues without having to call and wake up the developer, or more importantly, keep businesses running as usual with little delay.

Visual Studio provides a vast array of methods for tracking, monitoring, and troubleshooting SSIS packages, Control Flow tasks, and Data Flow tasks at design time, which is when you are creating or modifying the package. Some methods are displayed automatically by default, while others require some setup. Anything being run or executed in the Visual Studio environment is running in Debug Mode, which is the same as design-time.

When you run the package in Debug Mode, you can visually monitor the progress, success and failure of all package tasks by the icons displayed on the top right of each task (Figure 2-81 and Figure 2-82).

- Green Check = Completed Successfully
- Yellow Spinner = Processing / In-Progress
- Red Circle with X = Failed

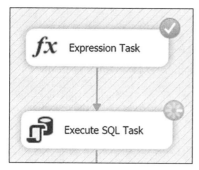

FIGURE 2-81 Execution Status in Debug Mode—Successful and In-Progress

By default, whenever the SSIS package encounters the first error, the package is stopped at that point with the red-circled X mark. This can be overridden by changing the MaximumErrorCount property at the package, container, or task level.

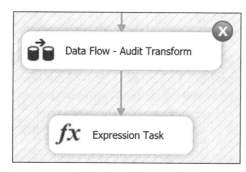

FIGURE 2-82 Execution Status in Debug Mode—Failure and Not Started

The icons during execution shouldn't be confused with the error and warnings that are displayed inside the task when there is a connection or data mapping issue that may not allow the package to be executed unless the issue is resolve. These show up before you ever try to run the package (Figure 2-83 and Figure 2-84).

- **Yellow triangle with exclamation point** Warning (e.g. data truncation possible)
- **Red circle with X** Error (e.g. datatype error)

FIGURE 2-83 Design Mode – Warning

FIGURE 2-84 Design Mode – Error

The errors must be fixed otherwise the package cannot be executed.

On the other hand, a package can still be executed when there is a warning on a Control Flow or Data Flow component (Figure 2-85).

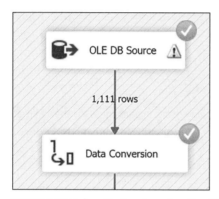

FIGURE 2-85 Debug Mode—Execute with a Warning

When the package is ready to run (no Warnings or Errors), you can press F5, or on the menu bar select Debug > Start Debugging, to begin execution. You can watch as each task starts running (yellow spinner) and completes successfully (green check mark). If there is an error while running on task, the package execution stops and the task is marked with a red X to show where the failure is located.

When you are using a For Loop or Foreach Loop container where the container iteratively processes the tasks within the container, you see a yellow spinner on the container for the full duration of its processing, but the individual tasks within the container will constantly be changing from yellow spinner to green check mark, and cycle back and forth for each success-ful iteration. Once the container completes successfully, the container and all its tasks will be marked with a green checkmark. In case any of the tasks in the container fail, then both the container and the failed task inside the container will have a red X mark on them. This shows where the error is in the container and the package execution stops.

In most cases, you want the execution to stop on the error so you can debug the cause and fix it. But on occasion, you may want to see if there are any more error and want the package to continue running to see if there are more downstream errors. If that is the case, you can change the value for the Control Flow property called MaximumErrorCount from its default value of 1 to the number of errors you want to allow before the package fails.

Checking your execution results progress tab

When you are testing your packages, and troubleshooting issues, the details of the execution results can be found in the last tab of the package design environment. A point of possible confusion can be how SSIS changes the name of this one tab depending on if the package is executing or the package execution has been stopped. The last tab is labeled as follows:

- **Execution Results tab**   When the package is not executing you can see the results of the last run.
- **Progress tab**   When a package execution is in-progress you can see the real-time execution results. Once the package execution has been stopped, you can still see these results under the Execution Results tab.

In either case, the information displayed here is the same. The execution details contained in this tab can be quite verbose, but useful and helpful in debugging package errors. It shows all warnings, validation statuses, informational details, and progress percentages. It also gives the start times, end times, run durations for each task, as well as for the complete package (Figure 2-86).

If your package fails during execution, you can hover the mouse over the red X error symbol on the failed task and a pop-up message displays the error message. This is a quick way to get a glimpse of the error, but usually the full error message doesn't display. The Progress / Execution Results tab is where you can see all of the package warnings, errors and execution statistics in one place. In case an error message is getting cut off, you can right-click and copy the message and paste it to any application to see the full message.

If the issue is with the data, such as data truncation error or datatype error, then you need to go to either the source or target adapter and open the Advanced Editor to compare the data sizes and datatypes for inconsistencies.

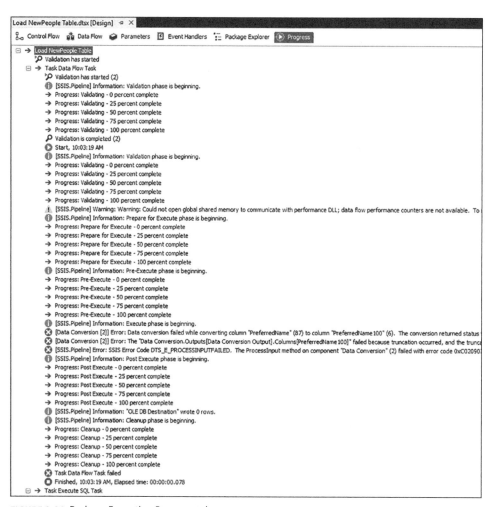

FIGURE 2-86 Package Execution Progress tab

Package execution reports in Management Studio

Once you have a package executing successfully, you want to monitor and track its progress. SQL Server Management Studio (SSMS) provides a very detailed, color-coded package execution report. This report can be accessed directly from within Management Studio (Figure 2-87):

1. Open the Integration Services Catalogs folder.
2. Open the SSISDB folder.
3. Open the Project Solution name folder that was created in Visual Studio.
4. Open the Projects folder.
5. Right-click the Package Name created in Visual Studio.
6. Select Reports from the pop-up shortcut menu.

7. Select Standard Reports from the submenu.

8. Finally select All Executions from the second submenu.

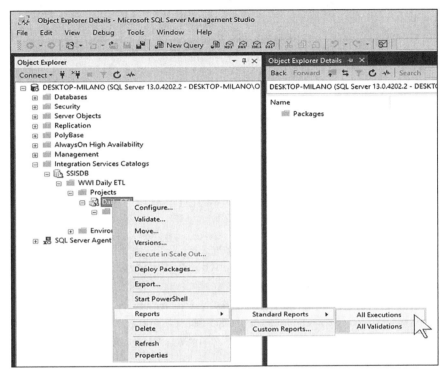

FIGURE 2-87 Management Studio Execution reports

This brings up the All Executions reports, which displays the package execution statistics number on top: Failed, Running, Succeeded (Figure 2-88). Below the overall statistics is a table with all of the details about each time a package was executed.

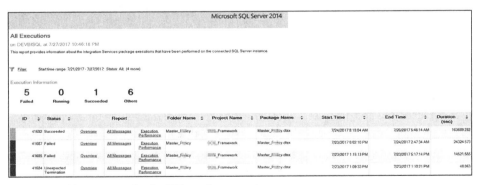

FIGURE 2-88 Management Studio All Executions report

The Status column shows if the package Succeeded, Failed, or was Terminated for some reason. The next three columns contain hyperlinks that take you to specific reports. The level of detail you see in this report strongly depends on your logging level. So if you don't see any information, or too much information, adjust your logging level. You can export the report results by right-clicking anywhere in the report.

Here is the information contained in each of the hyperlinks:

- Overview
    - Details about the execution: execution result, environment used, overall duration, who started the package, parameters, and values
    - The duration and result, master and child packages information
- All Messages
    - Displays warnings and error messages of the package executions
    - If Diagnostic logging is enabled, you may get pages and pages of details
- Execution Performance
    - The breakdown of package performance
    - It shows individual package executions duration, along with a three-month average and standard deviation

Most of these reports allow filtering by using the filter icon to limit or exclude information you don't want to see so you can focus on the actual issues and errors—or the information that matters to you most. This report can be accessed and viewed by anyone with access to the SQL server running SSISDB.

Performance

This execution metric is useful to gauge if the package runtime fits within your maintenance window. Knowing the run durations of each individual task makes it easy to address the low-hanging fruit by trying to improve the slowest running tasks first to get the best improvement. Keep in mind that these execution metrics are based on the server specs they run on.

If you are testing the runtimes on a development machine, it will not provide an accurate baseline when run in a production server that has more resources, such as faster storage in a SAN or SSD drive array or more memory and CPUs. But if it is running in 30 minutes on a development or QA machine, and your maintenance window is four hours, you should be safe. But it is still prudent to test it on the production server during the maintenance window to make sure there aren't other jobs and processes running on the server during the same time, which may cause resource contention and cause the SSIS package to take much longer.

SSIS can be very memory intensive and it could also be highly network and IO intensive if there is a lot of data being copied across the enterprise by the SSIS package. So, keep your network and database crew on call when deploying SSIS packages that will be handling a lot of data movement.

Parallelization

SSIS can increase performance by orders of magnitude by simply running tasks in parallel that operate on different or distributed datasets, as long as you are monitoring the server and testing to find the sweet spot between parallelization and resource utilization (CPU, Memory, IO). This can work for a data warehouse by loading dimension tables concurrently if they don't depend on each other for data. The same holds true for loading fact tables in parallel, but depending on their sizes, you may choose to load only a few of them concurrently.

Connectivity

The Connection Manager is responsible for providing the connectivity that allows for data to flow in and out of the SSIS packages. Before SSIS connecting to and getting and sending data between servers required setting up complex trusts between servers and creating linked servers—all of which made the data movement process very difficult. Add to that getting data from flat files, spreadsheets, XML files, files from FTP etc. all of which required additional third-party programs for each type of file. So aside from all of the wonderful transformations and data manipulations that can be done by SSIS, the Connection Manager significantly streamlines the inter-server data movement, which allows us to get on with the business of processing the data once it arrives at the SSIS server.

Setting up the Connection Manger is quite straightforward. Creating a new Connection Manger is done by right-clicking in the bottom pane of the Visual Studio design environment labeled Connection Managers and selecting New Connection and picking which type of connection you need to make in the pop-up window. These are some of the common connection types:

- **Database Connections**   ADO.NET, OLEDB
- **Flat File Connections**   FILE, FLATFILE
- **Excel Connection**   EXCEL
- **FTP Server Connection**   FTP
- **Webserver Connection**   HTTP
- **ODBC Connection**   ODBC
- **SSAS Connection**   MSOLAP100

If you are connecting to database, you provide the server name and authentication details, along with the database to connect to with this Connection Manager (Figure 2-89). You can use this same Connection Manager for both importing and exporting data. In the Data Flow page, you can create a Source and/or Destination task in which you select this Connection Manager for your database. If you need to connect to a flat file or an Excel spreadsheet, specify the location of the file to connect.

FIGURE 2-89 Connection Manager

In the OLE DB Connection Manager you can connect to your database by specifying the Server and database details:

- **Server name** The name of the database server.
- **Log on to the server** Choose the security mode to use (Windows or SQL Server account).
- **Select or enter database name** From the drop-down, select the database this Connection Manager will connect to. If you don't see a list of databases, verify that the server name is correct and that SQL Server service is running on that server. You may also need to make sure your Windows or SQL Server account has access to the server and database.
- **Test Connection** Pressing this button verifies that you can successfully connect to the specified database.

Add data viewers

One of the simplest and easiest methods of troubleshooting is using Data Viewers. These are literally windows into your data that can show you the actual data flowing through your package in real-time so you can easily validate and troubleshoot any dataset flowing between Data Flow tasks.

Setting up Data Viewers just requires selecting which Data Flow path you want to "wiretap." Right-click the Data Flow path and select Add Data Viewer (Figure 2-90).

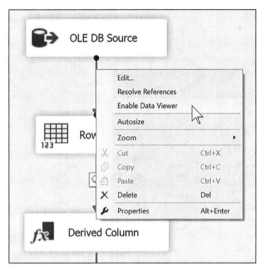

FIGURE 2-90 Enable Data Viewers

Once Data Viewers are enabled, you see a small box with a magnifying glass on top of the arrow of the Data Flow path. With that, you just run your package normally in Visual Studio to view your data flowing through that pipe.

After starting your package in Visual Studio, it runs normally until it runs up to a Data Flow path marked with a Data Viewers icon and then pauses to open a window. This window shows the rows and columns of data, which is the output from the previous Data Flow Task and will be going into the input of the next Data Flow task (Figure 2-91).

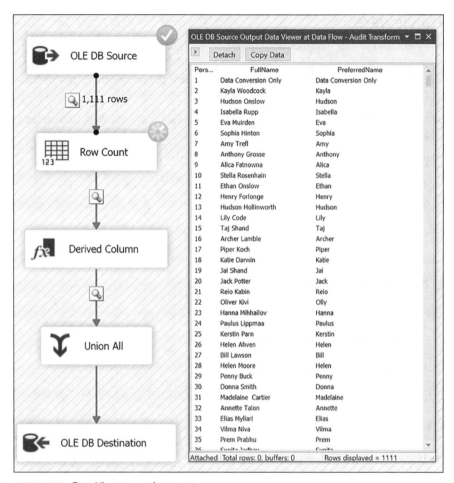

FIGURE 2-91 Data Viewer sample output

While this Data Viewer window is open, the package is paused. You are presented with these three options:

- **Copy**   Copies the data into the clipboard so that you can analyze and validate it to make sure all of the expected records are present and any required transformation or changes to the data have been performed correctly.

- **Detach**   This allows the package to continue running but the data in the viewer is no longer being updated to match the data in each buffer. In the event that your dataset is very large, this stops getting more data and allows the Data Flow to continue processing to the next task.

- **Play button**   Used to un-pause and continue running (playing) the tasks in the Data Flow. Because the package is automatically paused by the Data Viewer, this button allows it to continue moving forward.

Sometimes you want to use the Data Viewer, but the dataset has too many rows and you only want to focus on a handful of them. You can be selective about which columns get displayed in the Data Viewer. When you right-click the Data Flow path instead of selecting Enable Data Viewer, select Edit (Figure 2-92). Check the box to Enable Data Viewer. In the Data Flow Path Editor, select the Data Viewer page to see all of the available Columns to display. Using the arrows between the right and left panes, select which columns to be displayed in the Data Viewer window when it opens. In case you also wanted to see the metadata about the columns, select the Metadata pane to examine the column data types and sizes. There is a Copy To Clipboard button on the bottom right to copy the metadata grid into the clipboard for documentation or future review. Select OK to activate the Data Viewer.

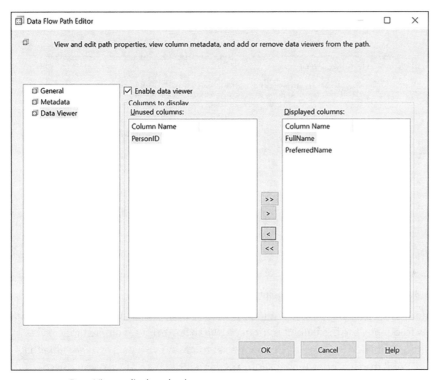

FIGURE 2-92 Data Viewer displayed columns

Implement breakpoints

Any good debugging environment needs the ability to set breakpoints. In SSIS, breakpoints can be set in the Control Flow on any individual Control Flow Task. In the Control Flow window, right-click a Control Flow task or container, and select Edit Breakpoints to open the Set Breakpoints window (Figure 2-93).

SSIS provides a list of various events to set breakpoint conditions on, some of the most common ones are:

- OnPreExecute event
- OnPostExecute event
- OnError event
- OnVariableValueChanged event

For Loop and Foreach Loop Containers have an added breakpoint condition:

- Break at the beginning of every iteration of the Loop

Enable the preferred breakpoint condition events from the list that would best help troubleshoot the package. Once the breakpoints have been added, a red dot is placed on the task or container.

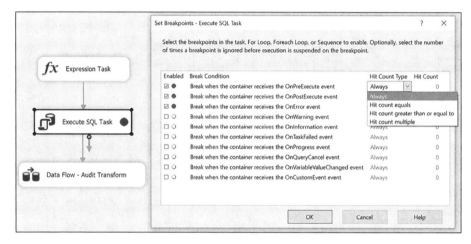

FIGURE 2-93 Breakpoints—Selecting Breakpoint Conditions

The Hit Count Type is another powerful addition to breakpoints. It allows more granular control on how frequently the breakpoint is triggered when it executes multiple times, as inside of a For Loop Container. By default, Hit Count is set to Always so it pauses every time that task tries to run. But if the Hit Count Type is set to anything other than Always, you can specify a Hit Count value to quantify the number of iterations to run through before invoking the Breakpoint. If the Hit Count Type is set to Hit Count Multiple and the Hit Count Value is set to 3, the Breakpoint condition would be invoked at every third execution. Alternatively, if the Hit Count Type is set to Hit Count Equals and the Hit Count Value is set to 5, the Breakpoint condition is invoked the fifth time the task or loop is executed. Note that you can specify different Hit Count settings for each breakpoint condition.

Here are descriptions of Hit Count Types:

- **Always** Suspends execution when the Breakpoint Condition occurs (default).
- **Hit count equals** Suspends execution only when the number of times the Breakpoint Condition occurs equals the Hit Count number.

- **Hit count greater than or equal to**   Similar to Hit Count Equals, but suspends execution only when the number of times the Breakpoint Condition occurs is equal to or greater than the Hit Count number.

- **Hit count multiple**   Suspends execution when multiples of the hit count occurs, every X times, where X is the Hit Count number.

Once you have set your breakpoints, start the package. The package runs normally until it reaches the Control Flow object with the breakpoint and suspends execution. The red dot on the object now has a yellow arrow inside of it indicating that it is waiting for you to continue (Figure 2-94). It only moves forward when you direct it to Continue by pressing the F5 shortcut key, the green play toolbar button, or going to the Visual Studio menu item Debug > Continue. When you elect to continue, the package proceeds to move forward until the end, unless you have additional breakpoints in the package.

In troubleshooting errors, the advantage of the breakpoint is to suspend packages at desired stages in the package execution to allow checking of the interim values of variables and locate where the flaw in design or logic is.

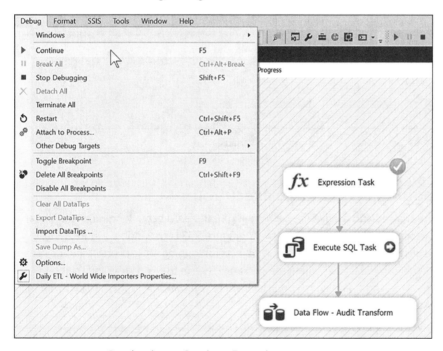

- **FIGURE 2-94** Breakpoints—Continue Execution

To troubleshoot, use breakpoints to see values of local and user variables during package execution and verify that they contain the correct values.

When the package is suspended because of the Breakpoints, or Data Viewer, go to the Visual Studio menu and select Debug > Windows. This shows a completely different menu with options only available during execution time (Figure 2-95):

- **Breakpoints** Opens the Breakpoints window, which shows package suspending events, including:
  - Breakpoint Events, along with task location
  - Data Viewer, along with task location
- **Watch** Where you can watch selected variables and see their values change during execution.
- **Locals** Displays the values and types of all variables that are within the scope of the currently executing procedure.

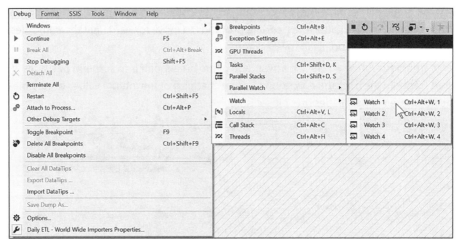

FIGURE 2-95 Debug Menu—Local and Watch Variables

Enable logging for package execution

Logging can be enabled and used at design time and runtime. To begin logging, in the Visual Studio menu select SSIS > Logging to open the Configure SSIS Logs window (Figure 2-96). In the Containers section, select the Control Flow objects for logging—the overall package itself and/or each of the individual tasks within the package. Then in the Providers and Logs tab, under the Add A New Log > Provider Type, select where you want the logging to be saved to, and click the Add button:

- SQL Server
- Windows Event Log
- Text Files
- SQL Server Profiler
- XML files

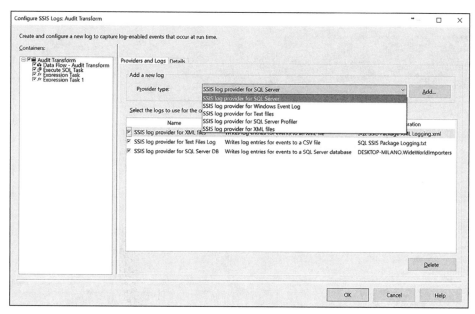

FIGURE 2-96 Configure SSIS Logs—Providers And Logs Tab

After adding each of the Provider Types selected you want to log to, go to the Select the Logs to Use for the Container section to set up the Connection in the Configuration column (Figure 2-97). In the case of a Text file, select a file to write to. For SQL Server DB as the target, simply select the target database. You are not limited to selecting only one target location for the logging, multiple destinations can be added and they will all be written to concurrently.

For every item checked in the Containers pane, you also need to individually select the check box under the section Select The Logs To Use For The Container, for each of the target SSIS Log Provider. If you don't check both sides, it won't create all the container logs you would expect to generate.

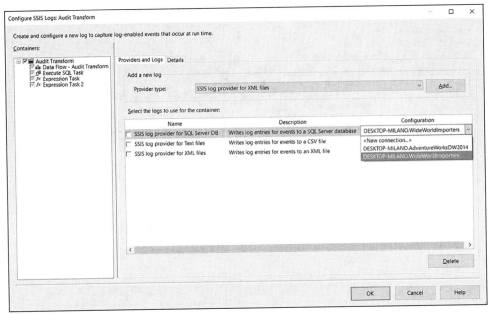

FIGURE 2-97 Configure SSIS Logs – selecting provider connection configuration

Next, go to the Details tab to choose all the events that will be logged for this container (Figure 2-98). All of these events are logged to all locations specified in the Providers And Logs tab.

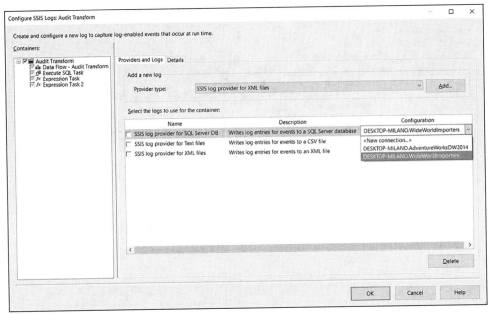

FIGURE 2-98 Configure SSIS Logs—Details Basic tab

In the Details tab, click the Advanced button to select which additional Event logging attributes to include or exclude from the logging (Figure 2-99).

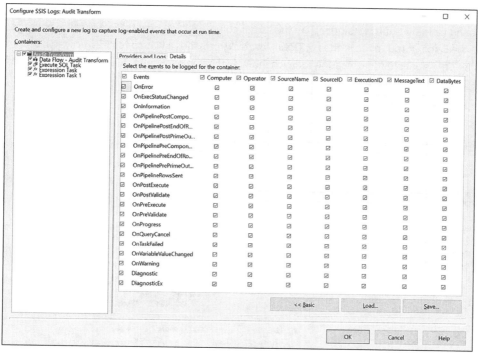

FIGURE 2-99 Configure SSIS Logs—Details Tab – Advanced

When logging to SQL Server, the log records are written to a system table, dbo.sysssislog (Figure 2-100). It automatically creates this default system table the first time it starts logging records to SQL Server. The table is located in the System Tables folder, not with user tables.

FIGURE 2-100 Configure SSIS Logs - SQL Server Provider Database

The dbo.sysssislog table can be easily queried and filtered by specific types of events, start and end times, as well as other details in the log table.

Any package logging sent to the file system (flat file, XML), can be viewed directly to see the package execution results. Searching his file is limited to string searches, you won't able to query and sort the data, but could be consumed by other applications for further analysis or zipped and archived for compliance requirements.

Implement error handling for data types

When data is being moved from a source to a destination, there you may experience different types of issues related to the datatype errors and column data truncation. When column data coming from the source is bigger than the target column it is going into, SSIS fails the package. But the Error Output page in the For Data Flow tasks provides a way to tell SSIS how to handle either errors or column truncation for each individual columns (Figure 2-101). The three options are:

- **Ignore Failure**   Continues processing on error or truncating and disregard any errors
- **Redirect Row**   Sends the offending row out to the output
- **Fail Component**   Fails the task when an error or truncation occurs

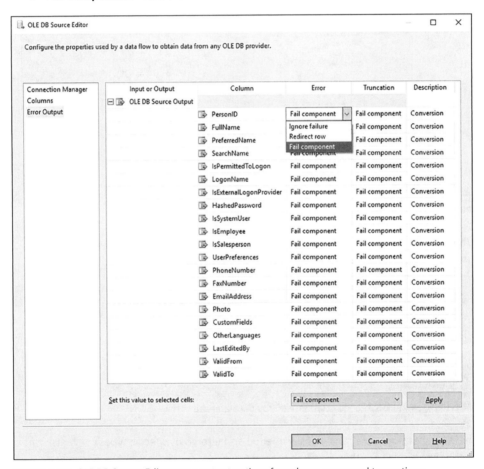

FIGURE 2-101 OLE DB Source Editor error output options for column errors and truncations

If you want to change the Error Output for multiple column names, you can do so by multi-selecting a range of rows under the Error or Truncation column, and then going to the drop-down list at the bottom of the window labeled Set This Value To Selected Cells and choose the error action to be taken and press the Apply button to update all the selected columns at one time (Figure 2-102).

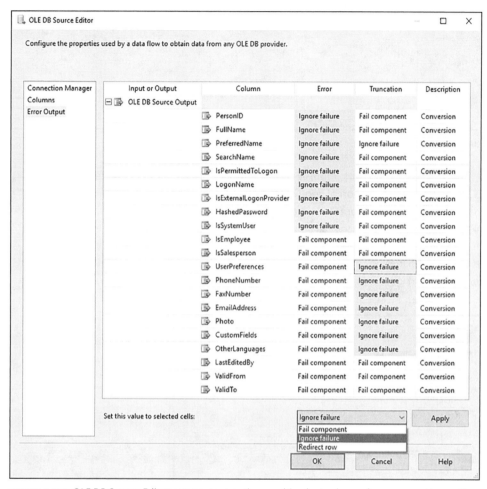

FIGURE 2-102 OLE DB Source Editor error output options multi-select columns for errors and truncations

If you want to just send the error or truncated records to an error file or table, you can change the setting to Redirect Row. In this way, you can set up an error output destination (Figure 2-103).

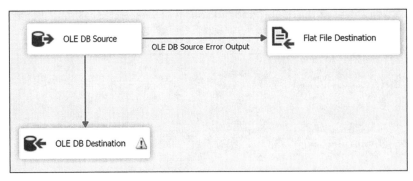

FIGURE 2-103 Error output destination

In the case of column truncation, you have another option to handle the truncation warning if you know the truncation of certain columns will not be an issue. For example, if your target table has a column for State which is CHAR(2) and the source has a State column as VARCHAR(5), but you know that all States should be abbreviated to CHAR(2). In this case, you can change the length of the string being output from the Source Data adapter. You can do this by right-clicking the OLE DB Source adapter and selecting Show Advanced Editor from the shortcut menu (Figure 2-104).

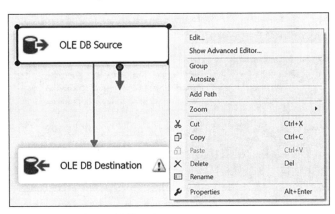

FIGURE 2-104 Advanced Editor shortcut menu

This opens the Advanced Editor for OLE DB Source (Figure 2-105). Here you go to the Input and Output properties tab. In the left pane under Inputs and Outputs, open the Output Columns folder. The Output Columns displays all the columns and their attributes, which are being sent out of the source adapter to the next Data Flow task (this is after the data has been pulled into the source adapter). If you want to see the attributes of the columns at the source, you can open the External Columns folder.

For our purposes of correcting the truncation error affecting the destination, we select the column name under Output Columns and on the right pane, scroll down to the Data Type

Properties section, down to Length. You can change the length to the appropriate size to match the target column size. You can press OK and the truncation warning should go away and you're ready to load your table.

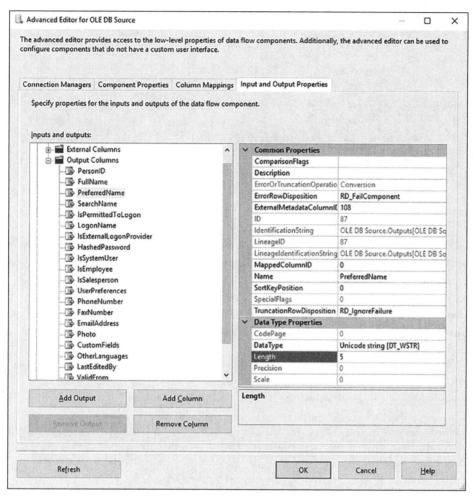

FIGURE 2-105 Advanced Editor for OLE DB to change Column Length value

Profile data with different tools

Another common issue occurs when we are making changes to the column mappings and some of the mappings go awry—or there is a datatype conflict. You notice the issue when you see a red X on the Data Flow path; this indicates that there is a problem with the column mapping. To correct this, right-click directly on the Data Flow path arrow to get a pop-up shortcut menu, select Resolve References from the menu (Figure 2-106).

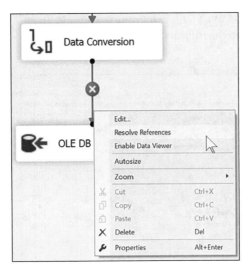

FIGURE 2-106 Resolve References shortcut menu

This opens up the Resolved References window (Figure 2-107). In the center of the window, you see all of the matched columns from the Source and Destination. On the left-most and right-most sides you are shown all of the unmatched columns that were automatically detected. There is a check box at the bottom left corner to automatically Delete Unmapped Input Columns after you press OK. In the case that you have a lot of column names to comb through, you can use the filter row underneath each of the four columns to make it easier to search for specific column names.

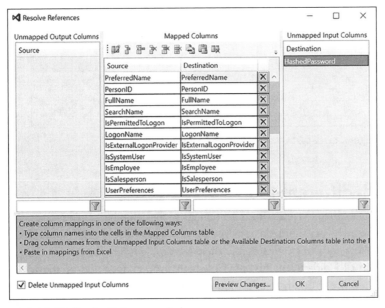

FIGURE 2-107 Resolve References window

At the top, in the center, there is a toolbar that makes it very easy to insert, delete, and match columns (Figure 2-108).

FIGURE 2-108 Resolve References Toolbar

Here are the actions that can be performed by the toolbar to expedite resolving column references:

- **Automap Columns** Maps input and output columns based on their matching names
- **Insert Cell** Opens a space to add either a Source or Destination column
- **Insert Row** Inserts a whole row to add both a Source and Destination column
- **Delete Cell** Removes the Source or Destination column
- **Delete Row** Removes the whole row of the Source and Destination column
- **Eliminate Blank Rows** Automatically removes all blank records
- **Copy Mappings to Clipboard (Excel Format)** Easily exports mapping
- **Paste from Clipboard (Excel Format)** Easily imports mapping
- **Clear All Mappings** Un-maps all Source and Destination columns so that you can manually map columns individually

After you have made all of the necessary changes to the column mappings, and maybe even selected the option to Delete Unmapped Input Columns, you can press the Preview Changes button to show all of the changes that will be made after you press OK. Once the column mappings have been updated, the red X should disappear from the Data Flow path and you're ready to run the package.

Error handling at package level

There are many causes of errors and failures when a package is running, either in Debug Mode or in Production. One of the best and simplest ways to manage error handling is with the Event Handler tab in the SSIS Visual Studio design environment. Under the Event Handler drop-down list, you can see all of the event types that can be triggered to fire off a notification, email, or insert the error details into a file, or a database table.

From this tab, you can choose from any (or all) of the components within your whole package to contain an event handler. Although each component can have its own custom event handler, generally the most common error handling method is to put the error handling at the highest level, the package, so that all of the errors float up and can be processed from one centralized location (Figure 2-109).

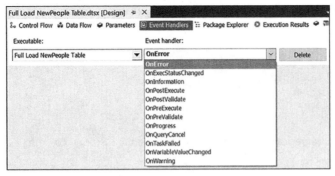

FIGURE 2-109 Event Handler—On Error

In every other respect, you create Event Handlers just like any package—with Control Flows and Data Flows. In Figure 2-110, we have added an Expression Task to populate a variable with Error Codes and Error Descriptions, which are then inserted into an ErrorLog table in a database table. Interestingly enough, the components within the Event Handler can have Event Handlers of their own to catch any problems with the error handling—for example maybe the database connection being used for the event handler is no longer available.

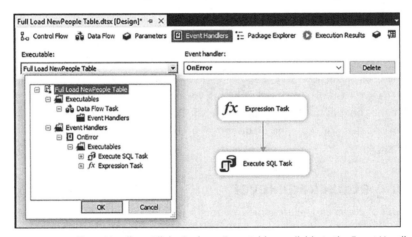

FIGURE 2-110 Event Handler – All the Package Executables available to the Event Handler

Skill 2.6: Deploy and configure SSIS packages and projects

Now that you have created all of your packages, how do you deploy it to your servers? What are the different ways you can deploy your packages, either one at a time, or all at once as a complete project? And deploying usually entails not just a single server but several servers—development, QA, production, and maybe even replicated servers.

After the packages have been deployed to all the respective servers, the next and most vital aspect of all the hard work to this point leads up to the package execution. Getting the packages to execute successfully to perform the complete ETL lifecycle is the finale.

In this chapter, you see the process of taking your completed packages and deploying them to a server; how to configure and change parameters so you can, for example, point to different sources and destination data sources without having to open the packages; and finally, the various ways to execute the package so it can move and process all the data as it was initially designed to do.

We also cover the difference between package-level verses project-level deployment.

> **This skill shows how to:**
> - Create an SSIS catalog
> - Deploy packages by using the deployment utility, SQL Server, and file systems
> - Run and customize packages by using DTUTIL

Create an SSIS catalog

SQL Server 2012 introduced a new paradigm in storing and deploying SSIS packages. Before that release, all packages were individually managed and deployed. So you would have to copy each package separately from your development environment to its final location where it would reside on the filesystem. At the very least this was cumbersome, but it also left room for human error in forgetting to copy some of the packages, or keeping all the packages in sync and up to date.

The SSIS DB catalog and SSISDB database serves as a centralized place where deployed SSIS packages can be stored along with everything related to it, including (Figure 2-111):

- Project and package parameters
- Configuring runtime values for packages
- Executing and troubleshooting packages
- Managing Integration Services server operations

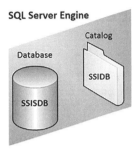

FIGURE 2-111 SSISDB database and catalog

You find the SSISDB catalog in the folder labeled Integration Services Catalogs. This is where you find the Projects folder containing each project with all its packages. And the Environments folder contains the package configuration and environment values, which can be set before executing the packages. Each SQL Server instance gets only one SSISDB (Figure 2-112).

FIGURE 2-112 SSISDB catalog

You also find another SSISDB in the Databases folder in SQL Server (Figure 2-113). This is essentially a system database containing all of the information about the projects and packages and their executions, parameters, logging, etc. Here you find tables and views that store a lot of information and details about environment and variable infomration; and stored procedures that can execute package-specific tasks. So you can see everything under the hood. By comparison, the SSISDB catalog shows us just the main working items needed to work on, such as the projects, packages, and environments.

FIGURE 2-113 SSISDB database

If you do not see the SSISDB catalog, you may have a newly installed SQL Server and SSISDB is not installed by default; it must be created. You can create it in Management Studio by right-clicking the Integration Services Catalogs folder and selecting Create Catalog (Figure 2-114).

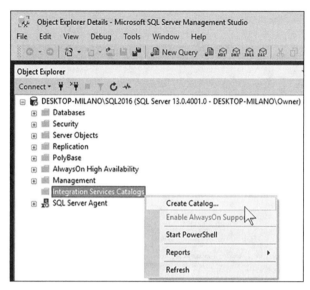

FIGURE 2-114 Create SSISDB catalog

In the Create Catalog window, you can perform the following (Figure 2-115):

- Enable CLR Integration. This is required for the creation of the catalog.

- Enable automatic execution of Integration Services stored procedures at SQL Server startup. This enables the catalog.startup stored procedure to run each time the SSIS server instance is restarted.

- Enter the Password to create an encryption key, which can be used to restore the catalog.

- Click Ok to create the SSISDB catalog.

- You should now see the SSISDB catalog and database.

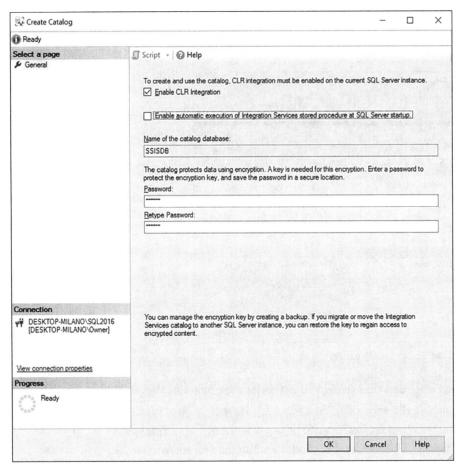

FIGURE 2-115 SSISDB catalog create options

You should be aware of some properties of the SSIS Catalog that can be configured if needed (Figure 2-116):

- **Clean Logs Periodically**   If logs should be cleared or retained (see Retention Period)
- **Retention Period (days)**   How long the longs should be kept before being cleared
- **Server-wide Default Logging Level**   The level of detail of the package execution log
  - **None**   No logging.
  - **Basic**   Event types are captured.
  - **Performance**   Captures events and each step of the execution.
  - **Verbose**   Includes events, each step, as well as statistics for component.
- **Maximum Number of Versions per Project**   Retains specified number of previous versions of the project within the SSISDB catalog
- **Periodically Remove Old Versions**   Specifies how many versions to retain

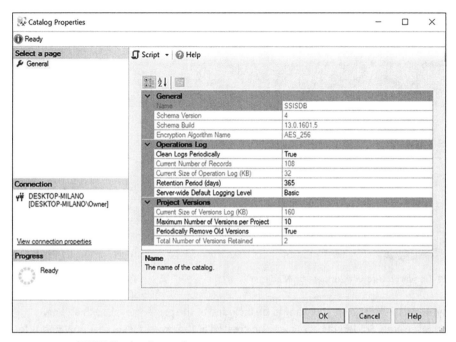

FIGURE 2-116 SSISDB Catalog Properties

Deploy packages by using the deployment utility, SQL Server, and file systems

When deploying packages, you have the option of deploying packages individually or deploying the complete project with all its included packages. For project deployment, you must ensure that all the related objects needed for the package execution are also part of the package. For example, when a Connection Manager is created, it is specific for the package within which it was created, unless it is promoted to a project-level Connection Manager by right-clicking it and selecting Convert To Project Connection (Figure 2-117). Now the name of the Connection Manager is prefixed with the word (project) to confirm it is now available at the project level. This includes the Connection Manager with all the projects in the solution when deployed. Another benefit of using a project-level Connection Manager is that you don't have to recreate the same connection for each and every package that also needs to use this Connection Manager; in effect it becomes shared among all the packages in the project and solution.

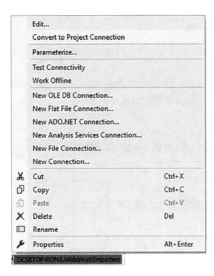

FIGURE 2-117 Convert to Project Connection Manager

Similarly, any parameter that you want to be included at the project level, such as, Server-Name, DatabaseName, FolderName, etc. can be created at the project level so it only needs to be changed in one place and will be available for all the packages in the project. And once the project has been deployed to a different server, for example to the Development, QA, or Production server, the parameter value only needs to be changed in one place. To add a project parameter, right-click Project.params and select Open, or just double-click it.

In Figure 2-118, you can see the Project.params tab opened with project parameters, and also under Connection Managers, you see the project level connections.

FIGURE 2-118 Project level parameters and Connection Managers

The project deployment options are:

- Deploy packages directly to server using a wizard.
- Create an ISPAC file using a wizard; deployment can be handed off to be done by an administrator.

The start the project deployment, right-click the project name and select Deploy to open the Integration Services Deployment Wizard. On the Select Destination page, enter the Server Name and Path from the SSISDB Catalog; you can create a new project folder in the SSISDB Catalog by selecting New Folder (Figure 2-119). Now press the Deploy button to have the packages deployed to the selected SSISDB project folder. You see the newly deployed packages under the Integration Services Catalog folder > SSISDB Catalog > Project Name.

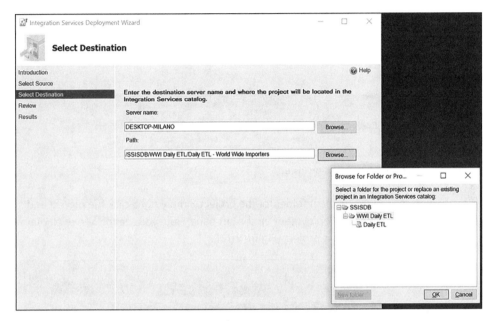

FIGURE 2-119 Deploying to SSISDB Catalog

As mentioned earlier, project versions are retained as part of the project versions history. If you deploy a project multiple times to the same SSISDB catalog, you are able to see all the versions, including the Current version when you right-click the project name under the Projects folder and select Versions. The Project Versions window displays (Figure 2-120). The current version has the check box selected. If you ever need to rollback, just highlight the row for the version you want to revert to and press the button Restore To Selected Version.

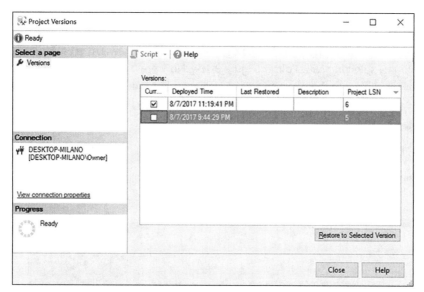

FIGURE 2-120 Project deployment version history

If you need to see the deployment folder for the project, simply right-click the project and select Properties and select the Deployment on the left pane. Here you see the Server Name and the Server Project Path for this project (Figure 2-121).

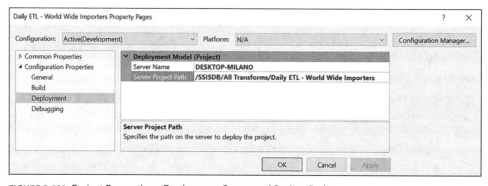

FIGURE 2-121 Project Properties—Deployment Server and Project Path

In the corporate enterprise, a developer cannot simply connect to a production server and deploy packages. Usually production is a highly restricted zone cordoned off to the production administrators who need to follow a well-defined production rollout procedure before putting anything into the production environment.

For this reason, SSDT can create an ISPAC project deployment file to allow deployment of packages into production without developer involvement. The project deployment file is a self-contained unit of deployment, which includes information about the packages and parameters in the project. It does not contain all of the information in the Integration Services project file (.dtproj extension). The steps to create the ISPAC project deployment file is by right-clicking the project name and selecting Build or Rebuild. The location of the file is contained in the properties of the project, which can be opened by right-clicking again on the project name and selecting Properties (Figure 2-122). If you're not sure of the folder path where your project is located, just open you project in SSDT and select Save As from the File menu, and you should see all the packages and the Output Path inside one of those folders.

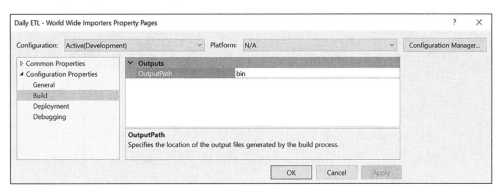

FIGURE 2-122 Project Properties—Build Output Path

You can also use Management Studio to deploy packages from your SSISDB catalog to different target servers, or another project folder, or even create an ISPAC file. By right-clicking the Project's folder, which is located under the name of your deployment project folder, select Deploy Project (Figure 2-123).

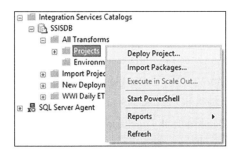

FIGURE 2-123 SSMS project deployment

From here you get options to create either a Project or Package deployment. These are the options you need to fill out, depending on your choice of deployment (Figure 2-124).

FIGURE 2-124 Integration Services Deployment Wizard

- Project deployment
    - **Project Deployment File**   Select the path to create the ISPAC file.
    - **Integration Servers Catalog**   Select the target Server and Folder where to deploy the packages into the SSISDB catalog.
- Package deployment
    - **Packages Folder Path**   Select the folder where package .dtsx files are located.
    - **Package Name**   Select the check boxes for each of the packages to deploy.
    - **Password**   Enter the password initially used to create the packages.

After completing Project Deployment steps, it deploys the packages to the target server, or creates the ISPAC file in the specific location. If you chose the Package Deployment, the package files are installed in the target folder path location.

If you want to create new environment variables, simply right-click the Environments folder under the project name in the SSISDB catalog. Here you can go to the Variables page of the Environments Properties window and create new variables (Figure 2-125). These can be used to replace values in the package for Project Parameters, Package Parameters, and Connection Managers.

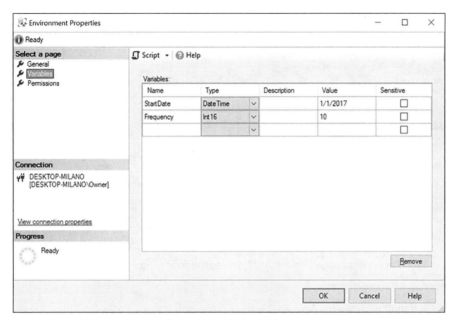

FIGURE 2-125 SSISDB catalog, adding environment variables

After creating the environment variables, you need to associate the variables to the packages. To do this, right-click the project name and select Configure. In the Configure window, go to the References page on the left, and press the Add button to add the newly created variables from the Browse Environments window, and click OK. If you selected variables for the Local Folder you will see a dot (.) under the Environment Folder heading, indicating it is a relative reference, but if you selected a variable from one of the SSISDB project folders, you will see the project name under the Environment Folder heading (Figure 2-126).

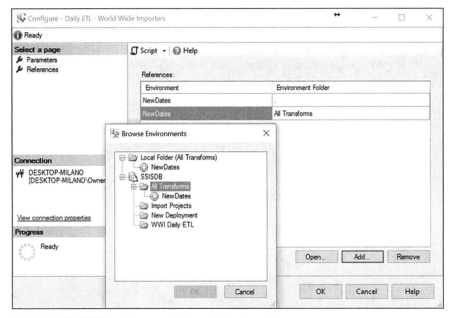

FIGURE 2-126 SSISDB catalog, associating variables to packages

Next, go to the Parameters page (Figure 2-127) to see the following:

- Container = Package names
- Name = Variable names
- Value = Default or Assigned values

Click the ellipsis in the Value column to set each of the parameter values to be used when the package runs. Click OK to accept and close the Configure window.

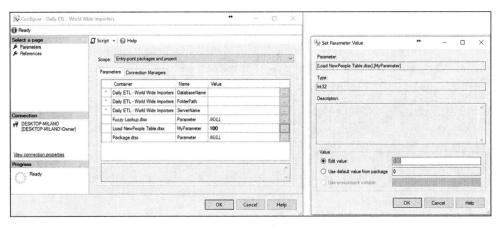

FIGURE 2-127 SSISDB catalog, associate parameters to packages

Package deployment model

The legacy deployment model was at the package level. Each package is required to be managed individually by copying them to the appropriate server and folder location form where they would be executed or copied to a SQL Server database. There is a Deployment Utility to assist in the deployment of these packages. Before using the Deployment Utility, make sure your project is set up for the package deployment model. If not, you need to convert the project by right-clicking the project and selecting Convert to Package Deployment Model (Figure 2-128).

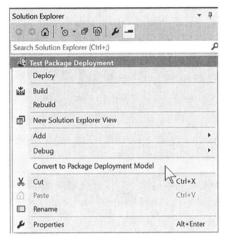

FIGURE 2-128 Convert to Package Deployment Model

Open the properties of the project and go to the Deployment page (Figure 2-129). Here you want to make sure that CreateDeploymentUtiltiy is set to True. Also, note the location of the DeploymentOutputPath so you can see where the deployed files are sent. It's important that you right-click the project and select Build to create all of the necessary deployment files. To verify, go to the Bin\Deployment folder and make sure there is a file with an .SSISDeployment-Manifest extension, because this is the file used to run the Deployment Utility. You can right-click the file with the .SSISDeploymentManifest extension and Open With and select Package Installation Wizard application, or you can double-click the file.

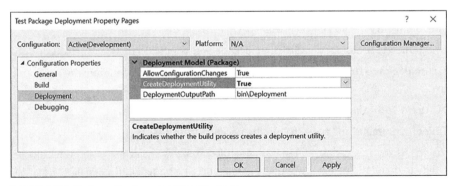

FIGURE 2-129 Package Deployment Property page

Now you can choose to deploy to the file system or to SQL Server by following the prompts (Figure 2-130).

FIGURE 2-130 Package Installation Wizard

Run and customize packages by using DTUTIL

If you have a need to deploy packages using a command line tool to copy, move, delete, and encrypt packages, you can use the DTUTIL.EXE utility.

Package execution

After a package has been deployed, it needs to be executed to perform all of the tasks contained in the packages. Depending on your design, you may have a master package, which is executed and in turn, calls all the child packages contained within it. Alternatively, the packages can be called individually as needed to perform the required tasks on-demand, or on a schedule.

There are four main ways you can execute a package as follows:

- **Management Studio** Right-click the package and select Execute.
- **Execute Package Utility** Enter all of the values in the utility to generate the execution.
- **SQL Agent Job** Create a job pointing to the SSIS package.
- **DTExec** Command line utility to run the package from a script.

When using DTExec, it is easiest to generate the full command line syntax using the Execute Package Utility to generate the full script in the Command Line page (Figure 2-131).

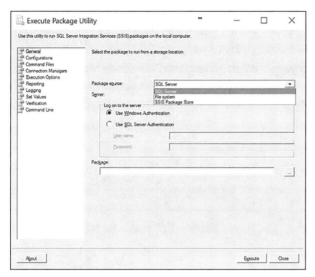

FIGURE 2-131 Execute Package Utility

The Execute Package Utility can be found in the Start Menu under the Microsoft SQL Server 2016 program folder. Using this user interface, it is much simpler to provide all of the values and information in a step-by-step fashion to prepare your package for execution. You can provide:

- Package source, location, and credentials
- Package configuration files
- Command files
- Connection Manager connection strings
- Execution Options (including MaxConcurrentExecutables and enabling checkpoints)
- Report messages as the packages execute
- Logging activation
- Property values
- Verification
- Command line syntax that can be used in the DTExec utility (Listing 2-6).

LISTING 2-6 Command line output from SSIS Execute Package Utility

```
/FILE "\"D:\SQL Server\Visual Studio 2015\Projects\WorldWideImporters\Daily
ETL\DailyETLMain.dtsx\"" /CHECKPOINTING OFF  /REPORTING EW  /LOGGER "\"{F9EC8DD0-
598D-4DC6-AC74-8D8675E77680}\"";"\"DW Data Profiling.xml\""
```

From the UI, you can click Execute to kick off the package or save the Command Line output for later use or to put into a script to be used for automation.

When creating a SQL Server Agent job to execute an SSIS package, the main thing is to specify when creating the job step is the Type = SQL Server Integration Services Package (Figure 2-132). In the Package tab you give the details about the package source, location, and the name. In the Configuration tab, you provide the Parameters, and Connection Managers. In the Advanced tab you can set up overrides, logging level, as well as 32-bit runtime. Make sure the SQL Agent service account has permissions to access the packages depending on their location: SQL Server or the file system.

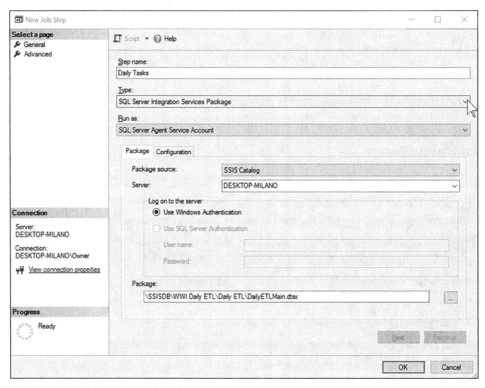

FIGURE 2-132 SSIS SQL Agent Job – Job Step

Thought exercise

In this thought exercise, let's assume that you oversee the incremental loading of a data warehouse. As part of your tasks, you need to ensure that all records from the source system make it to the data warehouse and that you implement a mechanism to facilitate troubleshooting of errors. Provide a solution to the following scenarios and requirements:

1. How could you keep track of the number of rows extracted from the source and rows inserted into the data warehouse for each data load?

2. What solution could you provide to detect records that have been inserted, updated or deleted from a SQL Server database source?

3. How would you troubleshoot a package that executes without failing, but produces no new or changed rows?

Thought exercise answer

1. The RowCount transform could be added in a Data Flow to count the number of rows extracted from the data source and number of rows inserted or updated in the destination. A variable can be added to store the row counts.

2. Change Data Capture (CDC) can be configured in the source SQL Server instance to track changes to the data. The SSIS CDC tasks can be added to the package to process records that have been deleted, updated or inserted.

3. You could debug the package by adding breakpoints and watch variable and parameter values. By analyzing run-time values, you could pinpoint errors such as incorrect source query parameter values, incorrect handling of lookups or incorrect join and filter criteria. You could also add Data Viewers between different transformation to analyze column values before and after a transformation is applied.

Chapter summary

- We described the the initial full-load stage and the incremental load stage of a data warehouse (DW). We then considered the nature of slowly changing dimensions and how they are handled differently than fact tables.

- The distinct categories and types of Control Flow and Data Flow tasks were explained and their functionality and usages, along with audit, blocking, non-blocking, fuzzy transforms, term lookup transformations, sequence, and loop containers so you can determine which transform is the best for the given task.

- We describe the proper usage of variables and parameters and provide an explanation when to use each. Checkpoints and transaction were implemented for restartability, so packages can resume where they left off in case of failure. We also explored how we can use logging to track package progress and execution results.

- An example of the SSIS data profiling task was provided to identify patterns of the data, null value ratios and distribution of data values in each column. We then described the concept of parallelism and the SSIS package properties available to improve concurrency and performance.

- We looked at when to use SSIS to perform tasks vs. T-SQL for performance, including using the MERGE statement. Change Data Capture was implemented to track changes at the source so only changed records are processed to avoid re-processing the entire data source.

- We looked at troubleshooting common performance, connectivity, and logic issues using the debugger. We saw how to handle datatype issues in the Data Flow Advanced editors. We overviewed how to implement breakpoints and data viewers to analyze records flowing through, watching variable values and datasets.

- We looked at how to deploy the packages to SSISDB catalog or the filesystem, and we went over the several ways packages can be executed using SQL Agent and the DTExec utility.

CHAPTER 3

Build data quality solutions

I n this Chapter, we cover the installation and configuration of Data Quality Services and MDS. Data Quality Services is knowledge-drive data quality application that allows you to perform a variety of critical data quality tasks including correction, enrichment, standardization and deduplication of data. Master Data Services is a master data management solution that allows you to maintain master data.

DQS and MDS are part of the Microsoft SQL Server platform and are key components of the Enterprise Information Management (EIM) framework. DQS and MDS are designed to support an organization's EIM framework with an integrated approach to data management and governance. DQS and MDS along with the rest of the SQL Server platform enable organizations to capture, integrate and distribute data that is credible, reliable, and accurate to support daily operations and to derive meaningful insights.

In Skill 3.1, we provide instructions to install and configure SQL Server 2016 Data Quality Services. We cover the process of creating and maintaining a knowledge base and provide appropriate use cases for a knowledge base in an organization's data lifecycle. We then provide the steps to perform a knowledge discovery and domain management.

Skill 3.2, covers in detail how to perform data quality activities such as matching and deduplication. We also walk-through data cleansing activities using the DQS client and the SSIS DQS Cleansing Task.

In Skill 3.3, we provide instructions to install and configure SQL Server 2016 Master Data Services. We cover how to create and configure an MDS web application and MDS database using the MDS Configuration Manager. We then provide step-by-step instructions to implement and deploy MDS objects including entities, attributes, and hierarchies and to import and export data using MDS Manager and the Excel MDS add-in.

In Skill 3.4 we show how to use MDS tools along with how to create a Master Data Manager database and web application, and illustrate how to use the application. We'll show you how to take advantage of the Master Data Services Add-in for Excel, and finally how to create a Master Data Management hub.

Skills in this chapter:

- Skill 3.1: Create a knowledge base
- Skill 3.2: Maintain data quality by using DQS
- Skill 3.3: Implement a Master Data Services (MDS) model
- Skill 3.4: Manage data by using MDS

Skill 3.1 Create a knowledge base

Follow along as we detail the process of creating and maintaining a knowledge base, providing relevant use cases based on an organization's data lifecycle. We'll then walk you through the steps needed to perform a knowledge discovery and domain management. Let's get started.

> **This section covers how to:**
> - Install DQS
> - Create a Data Quality Services (DQS) knowledge base
> - Determine appropriate use cases for a DQS knowledge base
> - Perform domain management
> - Perform knowledge discovery

Install DQS

The installation of DQS is a two-step process which consists of running the SQL Server 2016 Setup wizard and a command prompt based application called the Data Quality Server Installer. To start the installation process, locate the SQL Server 2016 installation media and run Setup.exe. This will open the SQL Server 2016 Installation Center. Click on Installation menu option and then click on New SQL Server Stand-Alone Installation Or Add Features To An Existing Installation to launch the SQL Server 2016 Setup wizard.

On the Microsoft Update window of the SQL Server 2016 Setup wizard, you may check the option box to enable Microsoft Updates if you want updates to be downloaded automatically through Automatic Updates. You can leave this option box unchecked if you don't want Windows Update to automatically check for SQL Server updates. Click Next. On the next window, select the installation type option Perform A New Installation of SQL Server 2016, if SQL Server 2016 Database Engine has not been previously installed. In this case, you will also need to install SQL Server 2016 Database Engine as it is required for Data Quality Services.

If there is already an installation of SQL Server 2016 Database Engine and you would like to add DQS to the existing instance, select Add Features To An Existing Instance Of SQL Server 2016. In this case, you will need to select the instance to which you will be adding Data Quality Services as seen in Figure 3-1.

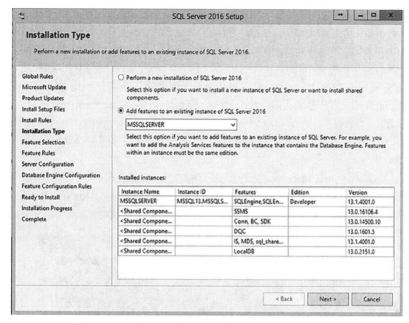

FIGURE 3-1 SQL Server 2016 Installation Type options

Once you have chosen the installation type, click Next. In the Feature Selection window, select Data Quality Services and Data Quality Client from the list as seen in Figure 3-2.

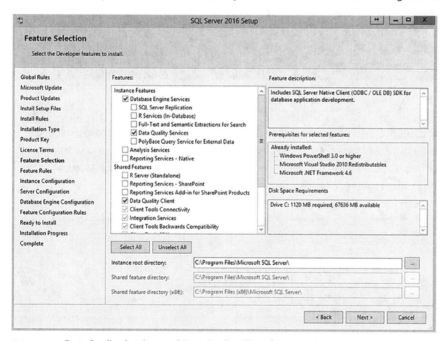

FIGURE 3-2 Data Quality Services and Data Quality Client feature selection

Click Next. If installing a new instance of SQL Server, complete the setup process to configure the new instance name, instance id, users and default data directories. On the Ready To Install window, verify the SQL Server features to be installed and click Install to start the installation process. Once installation completes, click Close to exit the SQL Server setup wizard.

The next step is to complete the Data Quality Services installation by running the Data Quality Server Installer. You can find a shortcut to this application in the Start menu under Microsoft SQL Server 2016>Data Quality Services folder. You can also find the application executable (DQSInstaller.exe) under "C:\Program Files\Microsoft SQL Server\MSSQL13.MSSQLSERVER\MSSQL\Binn\".

Execute the Data Quality Server Installer application. The DQS Installer runs on in command prompt window and displays the default values that will be used during the installation. Type **Yes** and press Enter to continue with the installation process, as shown in Figure 3-3.

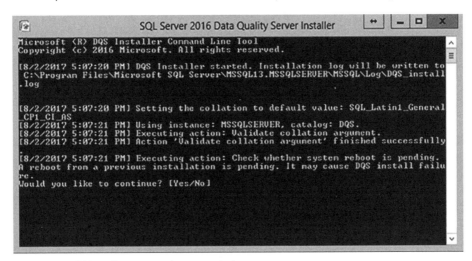

FIGURE 3-3 DQS Installer command prompt window

When prompted, type a password and confirm the password for the database master key and press Enter. A series of progress messages will be displayed in the command prompt window. You will see a confirmation the all assemblies have been successfully registered and that DQS installer finished successfully as shown in Figure 3-4.

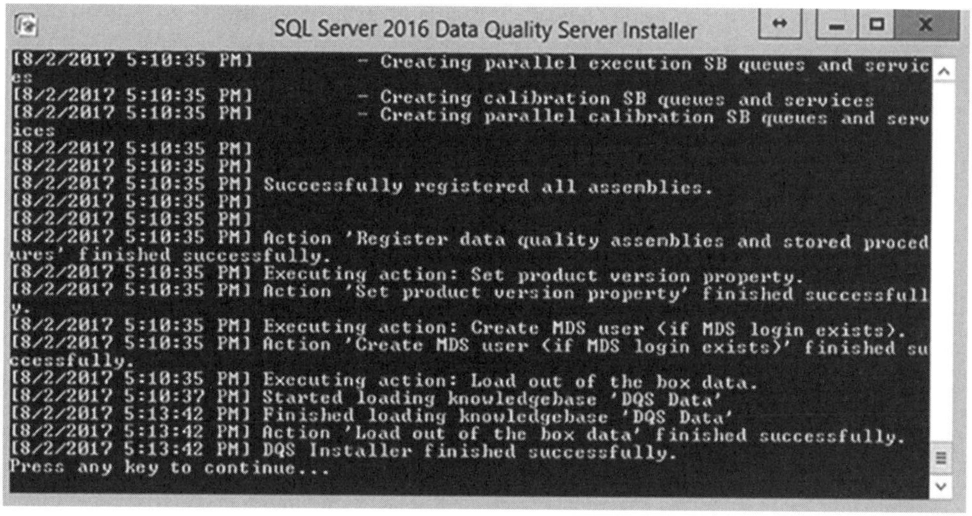

FIGURE 3-4 DQS Installer completion

As part of the installation process performed by DQS Installer, the following three databases get created on the SQL Server Database Engine instance:

1. DQS_MAIN
2. DQS_Projects
3. DQS_STAGING_DATA

Create a Data Quality Services (DQS) knowledge base

A Data Quality Knowledge Base (DQKB), is a repository of knowledge and metadata that describes and defines the data domains and rules to cleanse and match data. The DQKB is used in an organization to identify and correct invalid or incorrect data to ensure that data is consistent, and trustworthy. A DQKB stores domain values that have been validated along with terms, spelling errors, business rules, and reference data that can be used to perform data quality cleansing and matching actions on the data.

A Data Quality Services knowledge base can be created as a new and empty knowledge base or by importing an existing DQS knowledge base from a DQS (.dqs) file. In our example, we will be creating a Suppliers DQS Knowledge base. To create a new and empty DQS knowledge base, follow these steps:

1. Open the Data Quality Services client and connect to the DQS instance.
2. Click on New Knowledge Base button from the Knowledge Base Management section.
3. Type the following information in the New Knowledge Base window:
   - Name: Suppliers
   - Description: Suppliers knowledge base from the WWI database.

4. Select None from the Create Knowledge Base from drop-down list.

5. Click on Domain Management from the Select Activity section, then click Next.

6. Click Finish, then click Publish to exit.

Figure 3-5 shows the New Knowledge Base window of the Data Services client.

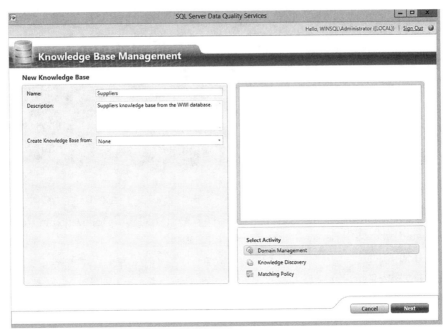

FIGURE 3-5 New Knowledge Base window of the Data Services client

At this point, the new and empty Suppliers Knowledge Base has been created. The next step is to create one or more domains by performing domain management.

Determine appropriate use cases for a DQS Knowledge Base

Data Quality Services can be used for a wide variety of use cases to ensure that the data is suited for business usage. Data can be cleansed manually or computer-assisted by establishing matching and cleansing rules or by leveraging cloud-based services of reference data providers.

Incorrect or bad data is often a symptom of weak or lack of data validation rules during data entry. Other forms of inconsistent data can arise from data integration processes and data corruption. Bad, incorrect and inconsistent data create inefficiencies in the business processes and can lead to loss of revenue and increased operational costs. Bad data is often amplified during data analysis, reporting, data mining and data warehousing.

The main use cases for a DQS Knowledge Base involves the need for business users, information workers or IT professionals to create, maintain and execute data quality operations resulting from data incompleteness, inconsistency, inaccuracy, invalidity, duplication and non-conformity.

Data that is incomplete or incorrect can be cleansed using a DQS Knowledge Base by processing and analyzing how data conforms to the knowledge. The data steward can review, approve, reject or modify the computer-assisted process results. For example, incomplete data such as addresses can be enriched by reference data. Addresses missing or with invalid zip code values can be corrected with address validation services.

Fixing incorrect and non-standardized data is a common use case for DQS Knowledge Base. This is particularly important when integrating data from multiple sources. For example, different applications may store and display values for gender in multiple ways. Some of the most common values for gender may include 'M' for Male and 'F' for Female, others may store the word 'Male' or 'Female' or the values '0' or '1'. These values can be automatically standardized by implementing term-based relationships or domain value synonyms in DQS. In addition, other rules can be put in place, such as null or blank values can be converted to 'Unknown' and values other than the ones expected above can be converted to 'Other'.

In some cases, it can be hard to know all the different values that are expected for a domain. An example of this includes incorrect or alternate spellings of words. In this case, a Matching Policy can be created to programmatically correct misspelled domain values. Once a Matching Policy is defined, you can run a Data Quality Matching Activity Project with a new dataset to match misspelled values based on the Matching Policy's weight and similarity thresholds.

Perform domain management

A knowledge base consists of domains. Each domain represents the data in a data field. Each value in a data field or domain is known as a domain value. DQS provides the ability to validate, cleanse, match and deduplicate values from any dataset against domain values in the DQS Knowledge Base.

Domains are created by performing a domain management activity. To create a DQS domain for valid supplier names in the Suppliers Knowledge Base, follow these steps:

1. Open the Data Quality Services client and connect to the DQS instance.
2. Click on Open Knowledge Base button from the Knowledge Base Management section.
3. Select Suppliers from the Knowledge Base list
4. Click on Domain Management from the Select Activity list, then click Next.
5. Click on the Create A Domain icon.
6. Type the following information on the Create Domain window:
   - Domain Name: SupplierName
   - Description: List of valid Supplier Names.
   - Select String from the Data Type drop-down list.
7. Check the Use Leading Values option.

8. Check the Normalize String option.

9. Select None from the Format Output To option.

10. Select English from the Language drop-down list.

11. Check the Enable Speller option.

12. Un-check the Disable Syntax Error Algorithms option, then Click OK.

Figure 3-6 shows the Create Domain window of the Data Services Client.

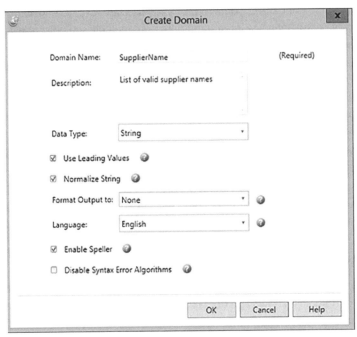

FIGURE 3-6 Create Domain window of the Data Services client

Once the domain is created, the Domain Management activity window opens. You can open the Domain Management activity directly by clicking on the Open Knowledge Base button in the main DQS Client menu, then selecting the Knowledge Base and Domain Management from the Select Activity section.

In the Domain Management activity, you can set field-wide properties, create rules, configure reference data services, or setup term-based or cross-field relationships. The domain properties shown in Figure 3-6 above can be modified under the Domain Properties tab.

In the Reference Data tab of the Doman Management activity window, you add service providers from a Microsoft DataMarket subscription to standardize, correct, cleanse and enrich data. Unfortunately, the Microsoft DataMarket was retired on March 31, 2017 and you can no longer configure this service. At the time of this writing, no alternative service is available.

In the Domain Rules tab of the Doman Management activity window, you add rules that the domain values must pass in order to be deemed correct. For example, you can set up a rule the validates that the length of the domain value should be greater than or equal to five characters. All new domain values will be checked against this rule. If a domain value is added with less than five characters, the value will be marked as Invalid.

For a complete list of all the domain rules available in DQS, please visit the Microsoft Documentation titled Create a Domain Rule at: *https://docs.microsoft.com/en-us/sql/data-quality-services/create-a-domain-rule.*

In the Domain Values tab of the Doman Management activity window, you add, import, edit or delete domain values. Values can be added manually or imported from Excel. You can also change the status of domain values as Correct, Invalid or Error and provide a replacement value for domain values with an Invalid or Error status.

Synonyms can also be defined in the Domain Values tab by selecting two or more values and selecting Set As Synonyms option from the right-click context menu or Set selected Domain ValuesAs Synonyms icon from the Domain Values menu options. You can set one of the synonym values as the Leading value. The leading value is used by DQS to replace synonym values found in the data during cleansing and matching activities.

In the Term-Based Relations tab of the Doman Management activity window, you add corrections to a term that is part of a domain value. Term-based relations are created by building a list of Value/Correct To pairs. The Value is searched within a domain value and replaced with the Correct To value if a match is found. For example, you can add a term-based relation that replaces the term Inc. to Incorporated. In this case, the domain value Contoso, Inc. will be changed to Conto, Incorporated.

The SupplierName is considered a single domain as it only relies on itself to represent a data field. Composite domains, rely on two or more single domains to represent data in a field satisfactorily. For example, a Geography domain may require multiple single domains including a City, State and Country domains.

To create a composite domain, such as the Geography domain, the single domains need to be created first, Once the single domains are created the composite domain can be defined by performing a Domain Management activity as describe in the following steps:

1. Click on the Create A Composite Domain icon from the Domain Management top menu bar.

2. In the Create a Composite Domain window, type **Geography** in the Composite Domain Name field.

3. Optionally, type a brief description in the Description field.

4. Select the Country, State and City domains from the Domains List and click on the right arrow to move the domains to the Domains in Composite Domain list. Reorder if necessary and click OK.

5. Figure 3-7 shows the Create a Composite Domain window for the Geography composite domain.

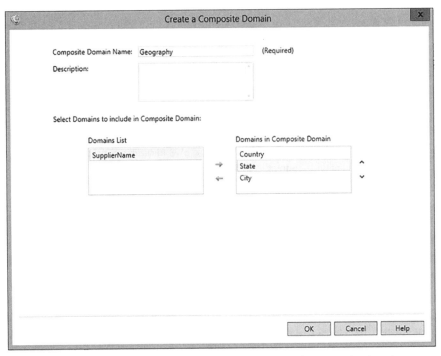

FIGURE 3-7 Create a Composite Domain window for the Geography composite domain

Perform knowledge discovery

The Data Quality knowledge base can be populated using interactive or computer-assisted processes. During the installation process of SQL Server 2016 Data Quality Services, you can choose to install the Data Quality Client to interactively create and maintain a DQS knowledge base. The DQS Client can be used to create data domains and add domain values manually or by importing them from an Excel spreadsheet or a data cleansing project.

In addition to interactively maintaining data through the DQS Client, you can maintain data by running a computer-assisted activity known as Knowledge Discovery. The Knowledge Discovery activity analyzes a sample of data that is used for data quality criteria. The algorithms built into DQS look for data inconsistencies and syntax errors and then propose changes to the data. You can then approve or reject the proposed changes or apply corrections manually.

To perform a Knowledge Discovery activity for the SuppliersName in the Suppliers Knowledge Base using an Excel data source, follow the steps below. For this example, you will need to download the SuppliersDomain.xlsx file from the book's companion website at: *https://www.microsoftpressstore.com/store/exam-ref-70-767-implementing-a-sql-data-warehouse-9781509306473*.

1. Open the Data Quality Services client and connect to the DQS instance.

2. Click on Open Knowledge Base button from the Knowledge Base Management section.

3. Select Suppliers from the Knowledge Base list.

4. Click on Knowledge Discovery under the Select Activity list, then click Next.

5. Select Excel File from the Data Source drop-down list.

6. Browse and select the SuppliersDomain.xlsx file.

7. Select SuppliersDomain.xlslx from the Worksheet drop-down list.

8. Under the Mappings section, select SupplierName (String) from the Source Column drop-down list, then select SupplierName from the Domain drop-down list in the corresponding row.

9. Click Next, then click the Start button.

10. Click Finish, then click Publish.

Figure 3-8 shows the results of the Knowledge Discovery from Supplier.

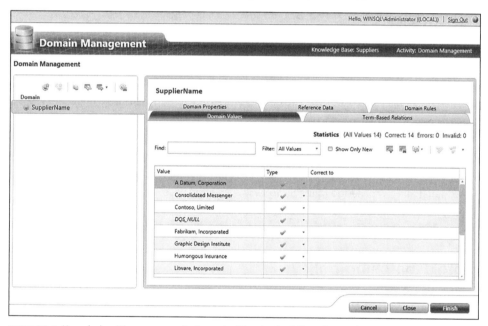

FIGURE 3-8 Knowledge Discovery results from the [Purchasing].[Suppliers] table

Skill 3.2 Maintain data quality by using DQS

We will now examine how to perform data quality activities such as matching and deduplication. In addition, we will cover data cleansing activities using both the DQS client and the SSIS DQS Cleansing Task.

> **This section covers how to:**
> - Add matching knowledge to a knowledge base
> - Create a matching policy
> - Prepare a DQS Knowledge Base for data deduplication
> - Clean data by using DQS knowledge
> - Clean data by using the SSIS DQS task

Add matching knowledge to a knowledge base

A matching knowledge can be useful when building and maintaining unique, unduplicated lists as Customers, Products, and Suppliers. You can use a DQS knowledge base to maintain unduplicated lists of Suppliers for example, by building a DQS knowledge base and setting up a DQS Matching Policy. During a matching activity, DQS evaluates the matching rules setup in the Matching Policy against the records being processed. It then provides a matching score for each record. If the matching score is greater than the minimum matching score configured then the two records are considered matches. You can set the minimum matching score under Administration>Configuration>General Settings section. The minimum score you can set is 50%.

To add matching knowledge to the Suppliers knowledge base, first we need to create a Matching Policy in the DQS Client. The Matching Policy is created by mapping source data fields to a domain, creating a matching rule, testing and revieing the results.

Create a matching policy

Follow the steps below to create a matching policy. For this example you will need to download the SuppliersDomain.xlsx file from the book's companion website at *https://www.microsoftpressstore.com/store/exam-ref-70-767-implementing-a-sql-data-warehouse-9781509306473*.

1. Open the Data Quality Services client and connect to the DQS instance.
2. Click on Open Knowledge Base button from the Knowledge Base Management section.
3. Select Suppliers from the Knowledge Base list.
4. Click on Matching Policy under the Select Activity list, then click Next.
5. Select Excel file from the Data Source drop-down list.

6. Browse and select the SuppliersDomain.xlsx file.

7. Select the SupplierforMatchingPolicy worksheet from the Worksheet drop-down list.

8. Under the Mappings section, select SupplierName (nvarchar) from the Source Column drop-down list, then select SupplierName from the Domain drop-down list in the corresponding row. Click Next.

9. Click the Create A Matching Rule icon on the menu bar.

10. Type a name and description for the Matching Rule.

11. Set the Min. matching score.

12. Under Rule Editor add SupplierName, then select Similarity from the Similarity drop-down list and set the Weight to 100%.

13. Click the Start button to preview the matching results.

14. Click Next, then click Finish.

Figure 3-9 displays the matching test results after processing the records in the Supplierfor-MatchingPolicy worksheet of the SuppliersDomain.xlsx file.

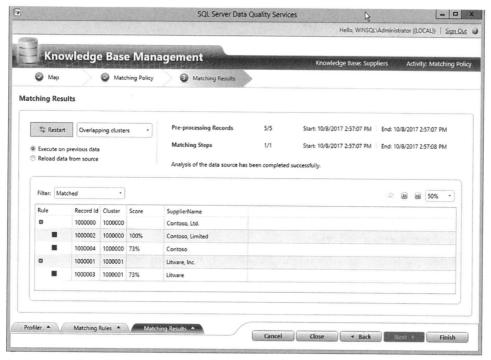

FIGURE 3-9 DQS matching results of the Matching Policy test

To add matching knowledge to a knowledge base, follow the steps below. For this example, you will need to download the SuppliersDomain.xlsx file from the book's companion website at *https://www.microsoftpressstore.com/store/exam-ref-70-767-implementing-a-sql-data-warehouse-9781509306473*.

1. Open the Data Quality Services client and connect to the DQS instance.

2. Click on New Data Quality Project button from the Data Quality Projects section.

3. Type a name and description for the Data Quality Project

4. Select Suppliers from the Use Knowledge Base drop-down list.

5. Click on Matching Policy under the Select Activity list, then click Next.

6. Select Excel File from the Data Source drop-down list.

7. Browse and select the SuppliersDomain.xlsx Excel file containing the list of Suppliers to be matched.

8. Select the worksheet containing the list of Suppliers to be matched from the Worksheet drop-down list.

9. Under the Mappings section, select SupplierName (nvarchar) from the Source Column drop-down list, then select SupplierName from the Domain drop-down list in the corresponding row.

10. Click Start to preview the matching results, then click Next.

11. Select Excel file from the Destination Type drop-down list.

12. Check the Survivorship Results check box, browse and select the Excel file to export.

13. Click Finish.

Prepare a DQS Knowledge Base for data deduplication

Before a data deduplication process is run using a Matching Activity, it is necessary to run a Data Cleansing Activity first on the dataset you wish to deduplicate. The Data Cleansing Activity will correct, standardize and flag invalid values. A cleansed dataset against valid values will yield more accurate matching results.

Data deduplication utilizes the weights and similarity thresholds setup in the Matching Policy. Misspelled, invalid and NULL values will lower the match score and reduce the number of matching records. It is important that these data quality issues are resolved initially before running a Matching Activity.

For example, during the Data Cleansing Activity for the Suppliers domain certain common misspellings or alternate spellings can be identified, corrected and standardized. Consider a scenario in which you are trying to deduplicate a list of suppliers from two different lists from a Purchasing application and Financial System. Suppose that the Purchasing application stores the name for the Contoso, Limited supplier as Contoso, Lmtd and a Financial application stores it as Contoso, Ltd. Notice the difference in spelling and abbreviation of the word Limited.

A Matching Activity run against these two records before being cleansed may produce a lower match score than what has been configured for the minimum score. During the Data Cleansing activity we have the opportunity to correct the supplier name to the more proper Contoso, Limited name using Terms-Based Relations and Synonyms. After the Data Cleansing activity cleanses these records, the Matching Activity will be able to match them with a higher score. In this case, the matching score would be 100% match.

Clean data by using DQS knowledge

The DQS Client allows you to run a Data Quality Project to perform a Data Cleansing Activity. During the Data Cleansing Activity, DQS detects new, invalid, and correct values based on existing valid values, Synonyms and Term-Based Relations. The interactive data cleansing allows you to accept or reject suggestions and corrections that the DQS cleansing activity identified. Once all records have been processed, you can export the data cleansing results data and cleansing info.

To cleanse data using DQS knowledge follow the steps below. For this example, you will need to download the SuppliersDomain.xlsx file from the book's companion website at: *https://www.microsoftpressstore.com/store/exam-ref-70-767-implementing-a-sql-data-warehouse-9781509306473*.

1. Open the Data Quality Services client and connect to the DQS instance.

2. Click on New Data Quality Project button from the Data Quality Projects section.

3. Type a name and description for the Data Quality Project

4. Select Suppliers from the Use Knowledge Base drop-down list.

5. Click on Cleansing under the Select Activity list, then click Next.

6. Select Excel File from the Data Source drop-down list.

7. Browse and select the SuppliersDomain.xlsx file.

8. Select the SuppliersforDataCleansing worksheet from the Worksheet drop-down list.

9. Under the Mappings section, select SupplierName (nvarchar) from the Source Column drop-down list, then select SupplierName from the Domain drop-down list in the corresponding row.

10. Click Next, then click Start to run the data cleansing analysis results. Upon completion click Next.

11. Review the results under the Corrected and Suggested values in the Profiler tab as shown in Figure 3-10, then click Next.

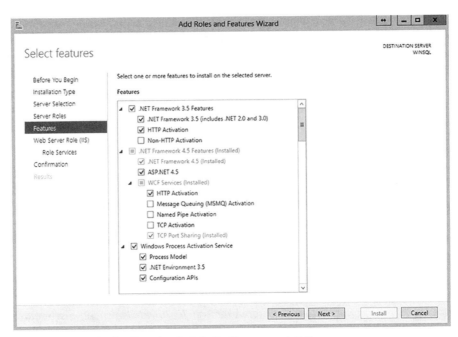

FIGURE 3-10 Data Quality Cleansing Activity Profiler source statistics

12. Review the records under each tab (Suggested, New, Invalid, Corrected, Correct). You can manage and review the data cleansing results. You can Approve or Reject the corrections or make your own corrections as seen in Figure 3-11. Click Next.

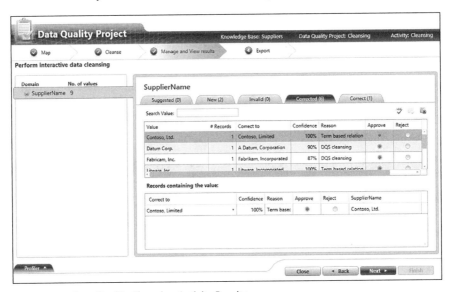

FIGURE 3-11 Data Quality Cleansing Activity Results

13. To Export the cleansing results, select the Destination Type, Database or filename and Output Format options and click on the Export button, then Click Finish.

Clean data by using the SSIS DQS task

SQL Server Integration Services (SSIS) includes a DQS Transformation to correct data from a connected data source. The DQS Transformation Output column is populated with one of five status as listed in Table 3-1 below. You can use a Conditional Split Transformation to separate out the output records based on its status. You can apply different business logic to each stream or insert them to a table of file destination for manual processing.

To clean data using the SSIS DQS task follow these steps:

1. Open a new SSIS package in Visual Studio.

2. Create a new Data Flow Task.

3. Add a Source Component to extract the data to be cleansed.

4. Add a DQS Cleansing transformation and connect it to the Source Component Output.

5. Edit the DQS Cleansing transformation and set the Data Quality connection manager and Data Quality Knowledge Base to use for the cleansing activity.

6. Click on the Mapping tab and map the Input Columns to the corresponding Knowledge Base Domain, then click OK.

7. Add a Conditional Split transformation and connect it to the DQs Cleansing Output.

8. Edit the Conditional Split transformation and add the following five outputs as shown in the Table 3-1.

TABLE 3-1 DQS Cleansing Conditional Split Outputs

Output Name	Condition
Correct	[Record Status] == "Correct"
Corrected	[Record Status] == "Corrected"
Invalid	[Record Status] == "Invalid"
Unknown	[Record Status] == "Unknown"
Suggestion	[Record Status] == "Suggestion"

Add a destination component to each of the outputs from the Conditional Split transformation.

9. Figure 3-12 shows the SSIS package and DQS task.

Skill 3.2 Maintain data quality by using DQS   CHAPTER 3   219

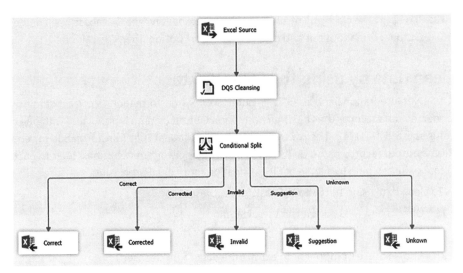

FIGURE 3-12 SSIS package and the DQS task

Skill 3.3 Implement a Master Data Services (MDS) model

In this section we detail how to install and configure SQL Server 2016 Master Data Services. We cover how to create and configure an MDS web application and MDS database using the MDS Configuration Manager. We also illustrate how to implement and deploy MDS objects including entities, attributes, and hierarchies, and finally show how to import and export data using MDS Manager and the Excel MDS add-in.

This section covers how to:

- Install MDS
- Use the Master Data Services Configuration Manager
- Create a Master Data Services database and web application
- Implement MDS
- Create models, entities, hierarchies, collections, and attributes
- Define security roles
- Import and export data
- Create and edit a subscription
- Implement entities, attributes, hierarchies, and business rules

Install MDS

Master Data Services is a web application that requires enabling the Web Server (IIS) Windows role, role services and features. In addition, it requires a dedicated database to store settings, database objects and data. MDS can be installed in a single server along with other SQL Server services or in a scale-out configuration to improve workload performance.

In a scale-out configuration, the MDS web application runs in a dedicated web server. The backend MDS database runs in a dedicated server running SQL Server Database Engine. Data stewards connect to the MDS web application from their workstation's web browser or through the Excel Add-in.

The installation of Master Data Services consists of three steps as follows:

1. Install required Windows roles and features

2. Install Master Data Services from the SQL Server installation media

3. Configure Master Data Services from the MDS Configuration Manager

Windows roles and features installation

To install the Windows roles and features required for MDS, you can use Windows Server Manager or through a PowerShell script. To start the Windows roles and features installation using Windows Server Manager follow these steps:

1. Open Server Manager and click on Manage on the menu bar, then click Add Roles and Features from the drop-down menu options to launch the Add Roles and Features Wizard.

2. On the Select installation type window, select the "Role-based or feature-based installation" option as shown in Figure 3-13 and click Next.

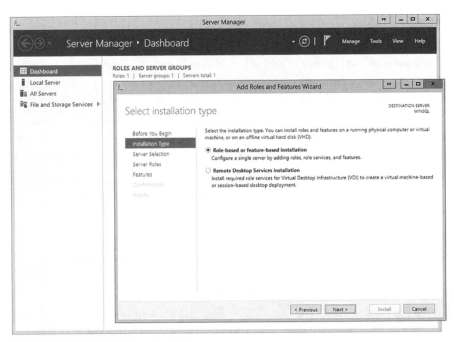

FIGURE 3-13 Roles and features installation type

3. On the Select destination server window, click the checkbox for the "Select a server from the server pool" option and select the server where MDS will be installed from the Server Pool list.

4. On the Select server roles window, select "Web Server (IIS)" and click on the Add Features button from the pop-up window as shown in Figure 3-14 and click Next.

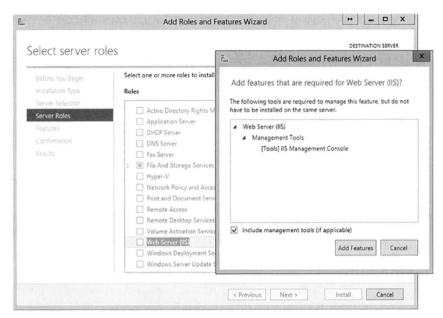

FIGURE 3-14 Web Server (IIS) role selection

5. On the Select features window, select the options as shown on Figure 3-15 and click Next.

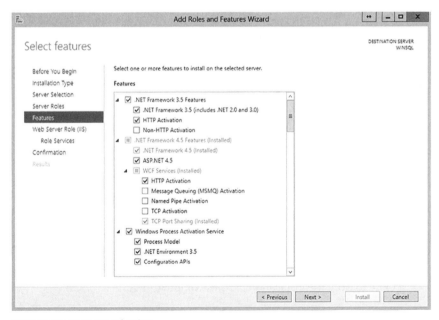

FIGURE 3-15 Features selection

6. On the Select role services window, select the options as shown in Figure 3-16 and click Next.

FIGURE 3-16 Web Server Role (IIS) Services selection.

7. On the Confirmation window, review changes and click Install to start the installation process. A restart may be required after the installation completes.

8. Click Close to close the Installation progress window.

Master Data Services installation

Master Data Services can be installed using the SQL Server Setup 2016 wizard or from the command prompt. To start the installation process using the SQL Server Setup 2016 Wizard, follow these steps:

1. Locate the SQL Server 2016 installation media and run Setup.exe. This will open the SQL Server 2016 Installation Center.

2. Click on Installation menu option and then click on New SQL Server Stand-Alone Installation Or Add Features To An Existing Installation to launch the SQL Server 2016 Setup wizard.

3. On the Microsoft Update window of the SQL Server 2016 Setup wizard, check the option box to enable Microsoft Updates and click Next.

4. On the next window, select the installation type option Perform A New Installation Of SQL Server 2016, if SQL Server 2016 services have not been installed or to install MDS on a new instance.

   If there is already an installation of SQL Server 2016 services and you would like to add MDS to the existing instance, then select Add Features To An Existing Instance Of SQL Server 2016. In this case, you will need to select the instance to which you will be adding MDS to.

5. Once you have selected the installation type, click Next. On the Feature Selection window, select Master Data Services from the list as shown in Figure 3-17 and click Next.

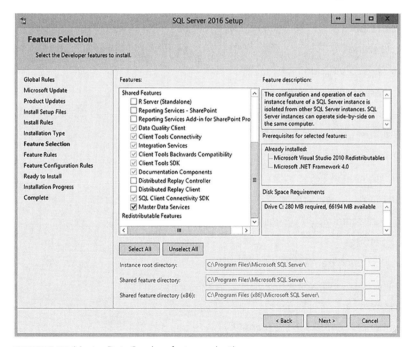

FIGURE 3-17 Master Data Services feature selection

6. If installing a new instance of SQL Server, complete the setup process to configure the new instance name, instance id, users and default data directories.

7. On the Ready to Install window, verify the SQL Server features to be installed and click Install to start the installation process.

8. Once installation completes, click Close to exit the SQL Server setup wizard.

Use the Master Data Services Configuration Manager

The Master Data Services Configuration Manager can be launched from the shortcut located at the Start>Programs>Microsoft SQL Server 2016>Master Data Services folder or directly from "C:\Program Files\Microsoft SQL Server\130\Master Data Services\Configuration\MDSConfig-Tool.exe".

The Master Data Services Configuration Manager can be used to do the initial setup and configuration of the MDS database and web application. The MDS Configuration Manager can be also used to upgrade the MDS database after a new SQL Server update has been installed or to repair the MDS database in case of corruption or configuration mismatch after a database has been restored from a backup.

The Master Data Services Configuration Manager can also be used in migration scenarios, for example, when the MDS database needs to be moved to a different SQL Server instance or when to associate a different web application with an existing MDS database.

In addition, the Master Data Services Configuration Manager is used to specify a series of system settings related to database and web application services. The main settings and setting categories include:

- General Settings
    - Database connection time-out
    - Database command time-out
    - Web service time-out
    - Client time-out
    - Number of rows per batch
    - Log retention in Days
- Version Management Settings
    - Copy only committed versions
- Staging Settings
    - Log all staging transactions
    - Staging batch interval
- Explorer Settings
    - Number of members in the hierarchy by default
    - Show names in hierarchy by default

- Number of domain-based attributes in list
- Add-in for Excel Settings
  - Show Add-in for Excel text on website home page
  - Add-in for Excel install path on website home page
- Business Rule Settings
  - Number to increment new business rules by
  - Number of members to apply business rules to
  - Notification Settings
  - Master Data Manager URL for notifications
  - Notification email interval
  - Number of notifications in a single email
  - Default email format
  - Regular expression for email address
  - Database Mail account
  - Database Mail profile

For a detail list and descriptions for each of these settings please visit: *https://docs.microsoft.com/en-us/sql/master-data-services/system-settings-master-data-services*.

Create a Master Data Services database and web application

Once all required Windows roles, services and features are installed along with Master Data Services you can proceed to configure MDS using the MDS Configuration Manager. The configurations required to get MDS up and running include the following:

- Create the MDS database and
- Set the MDS Administrator (Super User) account
- Configure the MDS web application

To start the MDS configuration follow these steps:

1. Launch Master Data Services Configuration Manager and verify that the Internet Information Services (IIS) prerequisites pass validation as shown in Figure 3-18.

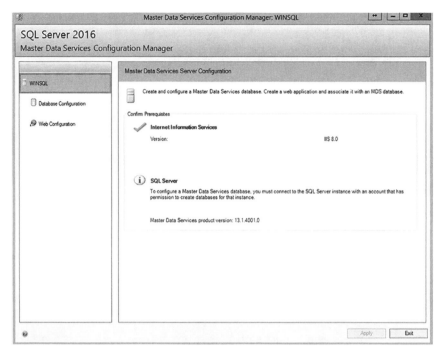

FIGURE 3-18 Master Data Services Configuration Manager prerequisites validation

If prerequisites have not been met, revisit the Windows roles and features installation section to ensure all required roles and features have been installed. In addition, refer to the Web Application Requirements (Master Data Services) documentation at: *http://go.microsoft.com/fwlink/?LinkId=506677.*

Once all prerequisites have been met, we create the MDS database and set the MDS Administrator account by following these steps.

1. Click on Database Configuration on the left section of the MDS Configuration Manager, then click on Create Database to launch the Create Database Wizard and then click Next.

2. Type the name of the SQL Server instance where the MDS database will be created, then choose the authentication type, test connection and then click Next as shown in Figure 3-19.

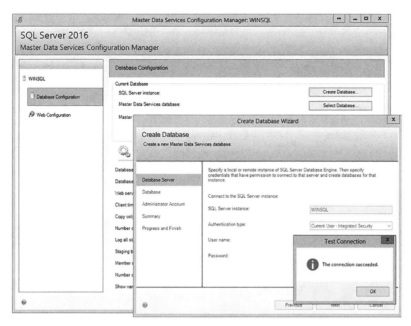

FIGURE 3-19 MDS Create Database Wizard SQL Server instance connection test.

3. Type the database name and select the database collation to use and then click Next.

4. Type the Windows account that will be used as the MDS Administrator (Super User) account and then click Next.

5. Verify that all information is correct in the Summary screen and then click Next.

6. After the MDS database is created and configured successfully click Finish.

   Next, we configure the MDS web application by following these steps:

1. Click on Web Configuration on the left section of the MDS Configuration Manager.

2. Under the Website section, choose an existing website or create a new website for the MDS application. For this example, we will create the MDS application using the Default Web Site.

3. Click Create to configure the MDS application.

4. Type an alias or accept the default MDS alias.

5. Type a name or accept the default name for the new application pool that will be created.

6. Type the credentials of the account that will be used as the application pool's identity and then click OK.

7. Under Associate Application with Database section, click Select to associate the web application with the MDS database created in the previous steps as shown in Figure 3-20.

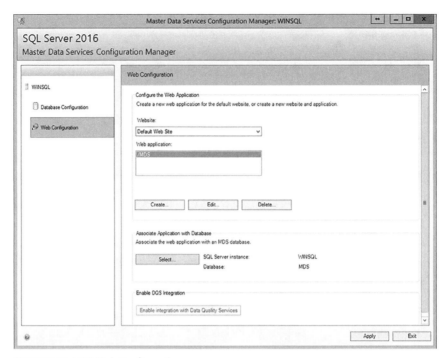

FIGURE 3-20 MDS Web Configuration

8. Click Apply to create and configure the MDS Web Application.

9. Click OK on the pop-up window to launch the MDS Web Application. The "Getting Started with SQL Server 2016 Master Data Services" page launches.

10. Click on the "Open the Master Data Services home page" link to open the main MDS application site or navigate to *http://localhost/MDS*.

MDS installation and configuration is now complete.

Implement MDS

Master Data Services allows organizations to manage their master data in a centralized repository with easy to use interfaces. The implementation of Master Data Services is part of an organization's Master Data Management (MDM) solution. An MDM solution involves business and technology process alignment and is often managed by a data governance committee made up of functional business stakeholders, subject matter experts and data stewards.

MDS was designed with business users in mind. It allows non-technical users to create and manage data models, entities, attributes, hierarchies, attribute collections and apply business rules to the master data. Business users can use the intuitive web-based user interface or through the MDS Excel add-in, which provides a more familiarized experience in Excel.

MDS provides technical users the ability to programmatically create and manage master data using backend database objects or through the Master Data Manager Web Service. For example, ETL developers can import, update or delete master data using stored-procedures and staging tables that get automatically created for each entity. MDS is typically implemented in data warehouse projects in which master data needs to be validated by data stewards after each ETL load. For more information review the Master Data Services Database documentation which can be found at *https://docs.microsoft.com/en-us/sql/master-data-services/master-data-services-database*.

The Master Data Manager Web Services is a Windows Communication Foundation (WCF) service that can be used by developers to control MDS features through custom coding, incorporate MDS features into applications, perform repetitive or complex actions not available through user interface or create custom workflows in response to business rules. For more information about the Master Data Manager Web Service review the Master Data Services Developer Documentation which can be found at *https://docs.microsoft.com/en-us/sql/master-data-services/develop/master-data-services-developer-documentation*.

Create models, entities, hierarchies, collections, and attributes

Master Data Services provides the ability to define logical and physical structures of your master data. The highest-level container in the structure of your master data is the model. A model contains one or more entities and entities contain data records known as members. A good analogy is to compare MDS structures to SQL Server objects. For example, a model can be comparable to a database, an entity can be comparable to a table, and attributes can be comparable to columns and members to rows in a table.

MDS structures can be created using the Master Data Manager or through the Excel add-in. In this section, we will use the Master Data Manager to create MDS structures. The same steps will be covered using the Excel add-in in the following section.

The first step is to create a new model. In this case, we will create an MDS model to create and maintain master records for suppliers from the World Wide Importers sample database.

Create a new model

To create a new model, follow these steps:

1. Open the Master Data Manager and click on System Administration.
2. Click on Manage in the menu option, then select Models from the drop-down list.
3. Click on the Add button and fill out the Add Model form as follows:
   - Name: Suppliers
   - Description: Master list of suppliers.
   - Log Retention: Yes
   - Days: 30

4. Check the option Create Entity With Same Name As Model and press Save. Figure 3-21 shows the Add Model window and information supplied.

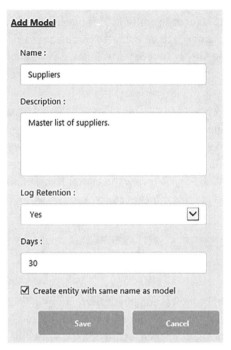

FIGURE 3-21 Add Model window for the Suppliers model

There are two important settings in the Add Model window, Log Retention and Create Entity With Same Name As Model. The Log Retention setting specifies how many days transaction log data is retained for the model. This setting determines the history of transactions available in the Version Management functional area. Transactions older than the number of days specified in this setting are deleted by the SQL Server Agent job, MDS_MDM_Sample_Log_Maintenance. This job is added automatically during the MDS installation and is scheduled to run nightly.

The three options for the Log Retention option include (see Table 3-2).

TABLE 3-2 Log Retention options

Log Retention	Description
Yes	Logs will be retained for the number of days specified under the Days textbox. If the value is 0, only logs for the current day are kept. Previous day records are truncated.
No	Logs will not be cleaned.
System Setting	Logs will be retained according to the system setting in the MDS Configuration Manager, specified in the Database Configuration section, under Log retention in Days setting.

Please note that only transactions for data inserted, modified or deleted through the Master Data Manager web interface or the Excel add-in are logged by default. Transaction record logging using the staging tables is turned off by default. This setting can be modified using the MDS Configuration Manager in the Database Configuration section under Log All Staging Transactions setting.

The Create Entity With Same Name As Model option, as the name implies, creates an entity in the model with the same name as the model. In this case, it will create a Supplier entity in our Supplier model. Typically, every model has an entity named after itself. For example, a Customer model will contain a Customer entity and a Product model will contain a Product entity. This option can be disabled if you do not plan to use an entity with the same name as the model or if you want to create one yourself after the model has been created.

When a new model is created, an initial *VERSION_1* is assigned with a status set to Open for editing. You can lock or unlock a model to prevent future modifications. Once a model is validated, it can be committed. You can create copies of a committed model to create a new version of the model. Only uncommitted versions can be updated.

Create a new entity

To create a new entity, follow these steps:

1. Open the Master Data Manager and click on System Administration.
2. Click on Manage in the menu option, then select Entities from the drop-down list.
3. Select Suppliers from the Model drop-down list.

   Note: If the Suppliers model does not appear in the drop-down list, go back to the Master Data Manager home page by clicking on the Home link in the bread-crump, then scroll down and click on the Refresh Cached Information link at the bottom of the home page.

4. Click on the Add button and fill out the Add Entity form as follows:

   ■ Name: DeliveryMethod

   ■ Description: Delivery methods available for WWI suppliers.

   ■ Name for staging tables (optional): <blank>

   ■ Transaction Log Type: Member

5. Check the option Create code values automatically.
6. Check the option Enable data compression.
7. Uncheck Approval Required as shown in Figure 3-22 shows the Add Entity window and information supplied. Click Save.

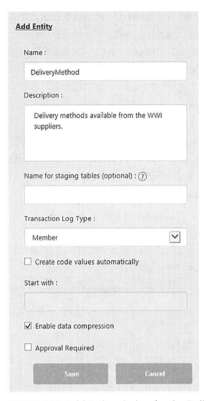

FIGURE 3-22 Add Entity window for the DeliveryMethod entity

Each time you create a new entity, a dedicated staging table and stored procedure with similar name are created automatically in the MDS database under the *stg* schema. These objects are used as part of the staging process to insert, update or delete master data from the entity. You can choose to provide a different name for the staging table and stored procedure.

The Transaction Log Type option allows you to set transaction log type of an entity, to one of the following, shown in Table 3-3.

TABLE 3-3 Entity Transaction Log Type options

Log Type	Description
Attribute	Only changes to attributes are logged.
Member	Both attribute and member data (records) are logged.
None	No logs are kept for changes to attributes or members.

The Enable Data Compression, option, specifies that the data will be compressed in the MDS database. MDS leverage on SQL Server row compression technology. Row compression reduces the size of the data stored in the MDS tables and reduces I/O requirements when retrieving data. Please note that data compression and decompression is CPU intensive. It is recommended to test the performance benefit of enabling row compression.

The last option in the Add Entity window is the Approval Required option. If enabled, all changes to the entity will require approval by an entity administrator.

Create a new attribute

Attributes are the objects contained in an entity. Attribute values describe the members of an entity. There are two required attributes in every entity, Code and Name. They are automatically created each time you create a new entity. These two attributes cannot be renamed or deleted. Table 3-4 describes these two required attributes.

TABLE 3-4 Entity Transaction Log Type options

Attribute	Required	Unique	Description
Code	Yes	Yes	Uniquely identifies a member in an entity. It can be defined to create code values automatically or as a manually entered value.
Name	Yes	No	Name values do not have to be unique in an entity. The Name attribute is required to exist in every entity, but a value is not required.

In addition to Code and Name, additional attributes can be defined as one of three types as described in Table 3-5.

TABLE 3-5 Entity Transaction Log Type options

Attribute Type	Description
Free-form	Allows input of values of type text, numeric, datetime or link.
Domain-based	Allows selection of a member from another entity.
File	Allows upload of files, documents or images.

To create a new domain-based attribute, follow these steps:

1. Open the Master Data Manager and click on System Administration.
2. Click on Manage in the menu option, then select Attributes from the drop-down list.
3. Select Suppliers from the Model drop-down list.
4. Select Suppliers from the Entity drop-down list.

    Note: If Suppliers does not appear in the Model or Entity drop-down lists, go back to the Master Data Manager home page by clicking on the Home link in the bread-crump, then scroll down and click on the Refresh Cached Information link at the bottom of the home page.

5. Select Leaf from the Member Type drop-down list.
6. Click on the Add button and fill out the Add Attribute form as follows:
   - Name: DeliveryMethod
   - Display Name: Delivery Method

- Description: Delivery method for the WWI supplier.
- Display Width (Pixel): 100
- Attribute Type: Domain-based
- Domain Entity: DeliveryMethod

7. Uncheck Enable Change Tracking as shown in Figure 3-23 shows the Add Attribute window and information supplied.

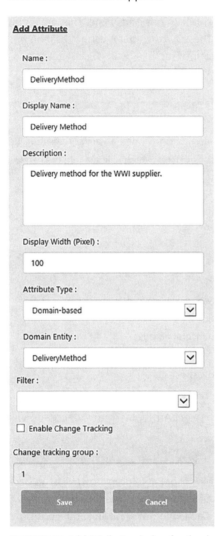

FIGURE 3-23 Add Attribute window for the domain-based attribute DeliveryMethod

The domain-based attribute added to the Suppliers entity, will be based on values from the DeliveryMethod entity. When adding a new member to the Suppliers entity, the values for DeliveryMethod entity will be available as a pick-list. As you can see, domain-based attributes are a great way to control the values of a particular attribute. Common domain-based attributes include Yes/No or True/False values list.

Define security roles

Master Data Services allows you to control access to the master data and functional areas. MDS security is defined using Active Directory users and groups and is managed in the *User and Group Permissions* functional area in Master Data Manager. Although, roles cannot be explicitly created in MDS, security roles can be derived based on the permissions assigned to each user or group. Permissions can be logically grouped based on the type of tasks users can accomplish such as data tasks or administrative tasks. Data tasks include the ability to read, create, update, and delete master data. Data tasks are typically carried out by data stewards, which are often the subject matter experts in a business area.

Administrative tasks include the ability to create, update and delete MDS objects such as models, entities and attributes. Other administrative tasks include managing security, subscription views, flags, versions and indexes. Administrative tasks are typically carried out by data custodians. In some organizations, certain tasks such as creating and updating entities and attributes are often shared with data stewards. The duties and responsibilities in an MDM project are established by the data governance framework adopted by the organization.

In Master Data Services, security can be defined at various levels of granularity, from top-level administrators to very finite leaf attribute level permissions. Top level administrators also known as superusers are users assigned to the Super User functional area in MDS. A user with permissions to the Super User functional area is effectively an administrator on all models and has permissions to all administrative functional areas in MDS. A default super user is specified for the Administrator Account when the MDS database is initially created using the Master Data Services Configuration Manager.

There are four types of administrators as described in Table 3-6.

TABLE 3-6 Administrator role types in MDS

Administrator Type	Description
System (default super user)	Assigned when MDS database is initially created. Can be assigned to only one user account. Can only be changed by updating UserId = 0. Has access to all functional areas. Is an administrator on all models.
Super User	Has access to all functional areas. Is an administrator on all models.
Model	If the user has access to the *Explorer* functional area, the user can create, update and delete master data for the model. If the user has access to administrative functional areas, the user can perform all administrative tasks for the models it is an administrator of.
Entity	If the user has access to the *Explorer* functional area, the user can create, update and delete master data for the entity. If an entity is defined as Approval Required, all changes to the master data in the entity must be approved or rejected by the entity administrator.

In addition to administrator roles, users can be granted or denied granular permissions to the master data. These permissions can be a mix of the following five permissions as described in Table 3-7.

TABLE 3-7   Five permissions

Permission	Description
Deny	Object or members will not be displayed.
Read	Object or members will be displayed. No ability to create, update or delete members.
Create	Only ability to create new members. No ability to update or delete existing members. Read permission automatically assigned.
Update	Only ability to update existing members. No ability to create or delete members. Read permission automatically assigned.
Delete	Only ability to delete existing members. No ability to create or update existing members. Read permission automatically assigned.

You can use the All permission shortcut to assign Read+Create+Update+Delete permissions.

For illustration purposes, let's assume we are tasked with providing a new user permission to create and update members of the CreditTerms entity on the Customer model using Master Data Manager. To achieve this task using Master Data Manager follow these steps.

1. Open the Master Data Manager and click on Users and Group Permissions.

2. Click on the Add Users icon

3. Type the new user's username. Use domain\username for AD users or computername\username for local users, then click OK.

4. On the users list, select the user that was just added and click on the Edit Selected User icon.

5. Click on the Functions tab, then click the Edit icon.

6. Select the Explorer function from the list and click on the Add (arrow) icon to add the Explorer functional area to the list of assigned functions, then click Save.

7. Click on the Models tab, then select the Customer model from the Model drop-down list.

8. Click the Edit icon, expand Customer. Expand Entities.

9. Click on the CreditTerms entity, hover over Grant Access, then select Create.

10. Click on the CreditTerms entity, hover over Grant Access, then select Update.

11. Click on the Save icon.

Figure 3-24 shows the Model Permission Summary section after the above permissions have been applied. Notice that the Read permission was automatically added along with the create and update permissions.

FIGURE 3-24 Model Permission summary section.

With these set of permissions, you could define roles using Active Directory groups. For example, you could define a read-only Active Directory group and assign users to this group who should be able to view the master data but not create, update or delete master data. You can also create separate Active Directory groups to create, update and delete members. You can then assign users to the specific Active Directory groups corresponding to the permissions they should have. Each Active Directory group would align with a specific MDS permission. This approach can be used in place for MDS roles.

Import and export data

Master Data Services provide several mechanisms to import data. This includes importing data through Excel add-in, web services and through the staging process. The Excel add-in and web services are great for loading a few hundred to several thousand rows. To load larger volumes of master data, the staging process is recommended.

In addition to the ability to import data through backend SQL Server tables, data can be exported from the MDS database using SQL Server views known as Subscription views. These views can be used by subscribing services to consume the master data. Subscription views are created in the Master Data Manager under the Integration Management functional area.

In the next sections we cover, how to stage and load data and how to create and edit a subscription view.

Stage and load data

The staging process involves staging entity data in entity-specific leaf member staging tables and stored procedures. The leaf member staging tables are used to create, update, deactivate, and delete leaf members and update attribute values for leaf members.

When Suppliers and DeliveryMethod entities were created, a set of staging tables and stored procedures were automatically created in the *stg* schema. The naming convention of the staging tables and stored procedures follow the name of the entity or the name provided for the staging table in the Add Entity window as shown in Table 3-8.

TABLE 3-8 Leaf member staging table and stored procedure name format

Object Type	Object Name Format
Staging Table	stg.<EntityName>_Leaf
Stored Procedure	stg.udp_<EntityName>_Leaf

The leaf member staging tables include the following fields as described in the Microsoft Documentation (Figure 3-9)found at *https://docs.microsoft.com/en-us/sql/master-data-services/leaf-member-staging-table-master-data-services*.

TABLE 3-9 Leaf member staging table fields.

Column Name	Required	Description
ID	No	Auto-incremental integer value. This column should not be populated. If the batch has not been processed, this field is blank.
ImportType	Yes	Determines how matching members are processed. Values: 0: Create new members. Replace existing MDS data with staged data, but only if the staged data is not NULL. NULL values are ignored. To change a string attribute value to NULL, set it ~NULL~. To change a number attribute value to NULL, set it to -98765432101234567890. To change a datetime attribute value to NULL, set it to 5555-11-22T12:34:56. 1: Create new members only. Any updates to existing MDS data fail. 2: Create new members. Replace existing MDS data with staged data. If you import NULL values, they will overwrite existing MDS values. 3: Deactivate the member, based on the Code value. All attributes, hierarchy and collection memberships, and transactions are maintained but no longer available in the UI. If the member is used as a domain-based attribute value of another member, the deactivation will fail. See ImportType5 for an alternative. 4: Permanently delete the member, based on the Code value. All attributes, hierarchy and collection memberships, and transactions are permanently deleted. If the member is used as a domain-based attribute value of another member, the deletion will fail. See ImportType6 for an alternative. 5: Deactivate the member, based on the Code value. All attributes, hierarchy and collection memberships, and transactions are maintained but no longer available in the UI. If the member is used as a domain-based attribute value of other members, the related values will be set to NULL. ImportType 5 is for leaf members only. 6: Permanently delete the member, based on the Code value. All attributes, hierarchy and collection memberships, and transactions are permanently deleted. If the member is used as a domain-based attribute value of other members, the related values will be set to NULL. ImportType 6 is for leaf members only.
ImportStatusID	Yes	Indicates the status of the import process. 0, which you specify to indicate that the record is ready for staging. 1, which is automatically assigned and indicates that the staging process for the record has succeeded. 2, which is automatically assigned and indicates that the staging process for the record has failed.
Batch_ID	No	Automatically assigned batch identifier. If the record has not been processed it will be blank. Required by the web service only.
BatchTag	Yes	Unique name for the batch. Required except by the web service. Can be left blank.
ErrorCode	No	Display an error code with a ImportStatusID of 2.
Code	Yes	Unique code value for the member required except when codes are generated automatically for ImportType 1 or 2.
Name	No	A name for the member. Does not need to be unique.
NewCode	Yes	Used when changing the member code.

In addition to these fields, columns for each attribute defined in the entity will also be defined in the leaf member staging table. These attributes are added or updated using ImportType 0 or 2. For free form attributes specify the text or string value. For domain-based attributes specify the code for the member of the referenced entity. File attributes cannot be uploaded using the staging process.

The leaf member staging tables are typically populated using an ETL tool such as SQL Server Integration Services during a data warehouse load process. Once data is staged in the leaf member staging tables, the staging stored procedure is executed to load the data into the internal MDS entity tables. The parameters used in the staging stored procedures are listed in Table 3-10.

TABLE 3-10   Leaf member store procedure parameters

Parameter	Required	Description
VersionName	Yes	Version name of the model.
LogFlag	No	Determine where transactions are logged during the staging process. 0, Do not log transactions (default). 1, Log transactions.
BatchTag	No	The BatchTag value as specified for the records in the staging table.
Batch_ID	No	The Batch_ID value as specified for the records in the staging table.
UserName	No	Optional parameter to identify staging system's service account.
User_ID	No	Optional parameter to identify staging system's service account.
Debug	No	Optional parameter to display execution metadata.

The general syntax to execute the staging stored procedure for the Suppliers entity created previously is as follows:

Example of the execution of the Suppliers entity staging stored procedure

```
DECLARE @VersionName nvarchar(50)
DECLARE @LogFlag int
DECLARE @BatchTag nvarchar(50)
DECLARE @Batch_ID int
DECLARE @UserName nvarchar(100)
DECLARE @User_ID int
DECLARE @Debug bit

SET @VersionName = N'VERSION_1'
SET @LogFlag = 1

EXECUTE [stg].[udp_Suppliers_Leaf]
  @VersionName
, @LogFlag
```

Create and edit a subscription

To create a subscription for the Suppliers entity in Maser Data Services follow these steps:

1. Open the Master Data Manager and click on Integration Management.

2. Click on Create Views from the menu option.

3. Click the Add button and fill out the Add Subscription View window as follows:

    ■ Name: Suppliers_LeafMembers

    ■ Model: Suppliers

    ■ Version Option: Version

    ■ Version: VERSION_1

    ■ Data Source: Entity

    ■ Entity: Suppliers

    ■ Format: Leaf members

    Figure 3-25 shows the Add Subscription view window and information supplied.

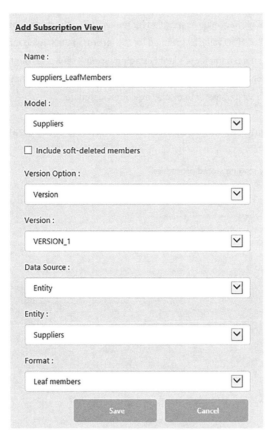

FIGURE 3-25 Add Subscription View window for the Suppliers entity leaf members

If enabled, the Include Soft-Deleted Members option will also include members that have been flagged for deletion but have not been purged from the MDS table. In this case, the subscription view will include a State field with a value of Active for non-deleted member or Inactive for soft-deleted members. Once soft-deleted members are purged, only Active members will show in the subscription view.

To edit a subscription view, follow these steps:

1. Open the Master Data Manager and click on Integration Management.

2. Click on Create Views from the menu option.

3. Select the subscription view from the list, then click the Edit button.

4. Modify the view definition, then click Save.

Implement entities, attributes, hierarchies, and business rules

Typically, Master Data Management (MDM) projects are based on data domains from disparate transactional systems. MDM projects aim to create references or crosswalks between different systems. For example, a company with many divisions may have different transactional systems in which customer information is captured and stored. Some customers may have multiple records across each of these transaction systems An MDM project may be put in place to create a master record, often referred to as the "golden" record for each of their customers.

In this case, Master Data Services can be used as part of the MDM project to store, validate, manage, and qualify master customer records. As part of the MDM implementation, a customer entity along with customer attributes will be required. Each customer record is identified with a unique customer code. This code can be generated in the MDS entity or it can be populated using the transactional system's customer identifier. It is recommended to generate a unique code in MDS to avoid code value collisions across transactional systems.

If customer records are matched from multiple transactional systems, attributes can be added to the customer entity to store each of the transactional system's customer identifier either as free-text or a domain-based attribute. Another approach would be to create crosswalk entities to relate a source system, a customer identifier and an MDS master customer record.

The MDS implementation of the customer entity may also include additional attributes maintained in non-transactional systems such as customer classifications or sales territory assignments. These attributes can be used to create hierarchy structures that can be used for drill-downs or as filters for customer records. MDS allows the ability to define derived hierarchies based on attribute relationships of an entity. Some examples of derived hierarchies for the customer entity include CustomerType and a CustomerGeography hierarchy.

To create a CustomerGeography derived hierarchy using the Customer sample model follow these steps:

1. Open the Master Data Manager and click on System Administration.

2. Click on Manage in the menu option, then select Derived Hierarchies.

3. Select Customer from the Model drop-down list.

4. Click the Add button.

5. Type CustomerGeography as the derived hierarchy name, then click on the Save icon.

6. Drag Customer from the list of Available Entities and Hierarchies list and drop it in the Drop Parent Here section under Current Levels.

7. Drag StateProvince from the list of Available Entities and Hierarchies list and drop it in the Drop Parent Here section under Current Levels.

8. Drag Country from the list of Available Entities and Hierarchies list and drop it in the Drop Parent Here section under Current Levels.

Figure 3-26 shows the CustomerGeography edit screen.

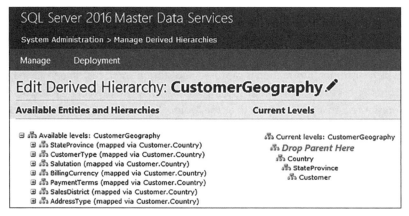

FIGURE 3-26 Derived hierarchy edit screen

Another important functionality of MDS is the ability to specify business rules for attribute values. MDS business rules enforce rules to ensure the quality and accuracy of the master data. Business rules follow an If-Then-Else logic. For example, if an attribute value meets a specific condition then an action is taken otherwise an else action is taken.

Business rules can be based on the following

- Value of an attribute
- Change to a value of an attribute
- User-defined script

Generally, a business rule is applied when the *If* portion of the condition is met. For example, for the Customer entity, if the value of the Country attribute is equal to *US* (United States), then the PostalCode should be a 5-digit code. Another business rule example would be when the CreditLineLimit of a Customer changes, an external action such as start workflow can be triggered. A loan underwriter may be part of the workflow to approve changes to credit line amounts.

More complex logic may be required to evaluate a condition. For this type of scenario, a user-defined script can be used to return a True or False result. In addition, a business rule can be implemented with no *If* condition. In this case, the business rule will apply to all attribute values regardless of any condition. This is particularly helpful to enforce required values.

Business rules are applied to existing data. Data can still be inserted even if it does not pass business rule validation. Data that does not pass validation is flagged so that it can be reviewed and corrected. An MDS model cannot be committed unless all attribute values pass business rule validations.

To create a business rule that enforces that US based Customers must have a 5-digit Post-alCode, follow these steps:

1. Open the Master Data Manager and click on System Administration.

2. Click on Manage in the menu option, then select Business Rules.

3. Select Customer from the Model drop-down list.

4. Select Customer from the Entity drop-down list.

5. Select Leaf from the Member Type drop-down list.

6. Click the Add button and fill out the Add Business Rule window as follows

   - Name: Valid US ZIP or ZIP+4 format

   - Description: Check that US Postal Code format is ZIP or ZIP+4

7. Click Add under the If section and fill out the Create Condition window as follows:

   - Attribute: Country

   - Operator: is equal to

   - Is equal to: Attribute value

   - Attribute value: US

8. Click the Save button on the Create Condition window

9. Click Add under the Then section and fill out the Create Action window as follows:

   - Attribute: Postal Code

   - Operator: must contain the pattern

   - Must contain the pattern: Attribute value

   - Attribute value: ^[0-9]{5}(?:-[0-9]{4})?$

10. Click the Save button on the Create Action window.

11. Click the Save button on the Add Business Rule window.

    Figure 3-27 shows the Add Business Rule window and information supplied.

FIGURE 3-27 Add Business Rule window for US Postal Code ZIP and ZIP+4 format validation

Skill 3.4 Manage data by using MDS

In this section you will learn how to use MDS tools. You will see how to take advantage of the Master Data Services Add-in for Excel, and how to create a Master Data Management hub.

> **This section covers how to:**
> - Use MDS tools
> - Deploy a sample model using MDSModelDeploy.exe
> - Use the Master Data Services web application
> - Use the Master Data Services Add-in for Excel
> - Create a Master Data Manager database and web application
> - Create a Master Data Management hub

Use MDS tools

Master Data Services includes several components and tools that can be used to manage master data. These tools include:

- Master Data Services Configuration Manager, a tool you use to create and configure Master Data Services databases and web applications.

- Master Data Manager, a web application you use to perform administrative tasks (like creating a model or business rule), and that users access to update data.

- MDSModelDeploy.exe, a tool you use to create packages of your model objects and data so you can deploy them to other environments.

- Master Data Services web service, which developers can use to extend or develop custom solutions for Master Data Services.

- Master Data Services Add-in for Excel, which you use to manage data and create new entities and attributes.

Deploy a sample model using MDSModelDeploy.exe

The installation of Master Data Services includes a command line deployment tool called MDSModelDeploy to deploy MDS models and data. The default installation of MDS places the executable file MDSModelDeploy.exe at C:\Program Files\Microsoft SQL Server\130\Master Data Services\Configuration.

The unit of deployment is known as a package. A package may contain MDS model objects only or both model objects and data. Please note that you can also deploy MDS model objects using the Model Deployment Wizard from the MDS web application but is limited to model objects only with no data. The MDSModelDeploy tool allows you to deploy both model objects and their corresponding data.

In addition to the MDSModelDeploy tool, the Master Data Services installation places three sample packages that can be deployed for learning purposes. The default installation of MDS places the sample packages at C:\Program Files\Microsoft SQL Server\130\Master Data Services\Samples\Packages. The sample packages included are as follows:

- charofaccounts_en.pkg:

- customer_en.pkg

- product_en.pkg

To deploy the sample packages, follow these steps:

1. Open a Command Prompt window as Administrator.

2. Navigate to C:\Program Files\Microsoft SQL Server\130\Master Data Services\Configuration.

3. Type **MDSModelDeploy listservices** to list all MDS web application services running on the server. The result of this command returns the MDS Service Name, Web Site and

Web Application Alias Name. In this case, the MDS Service Name shown in Figure 3-28 is MDS1.

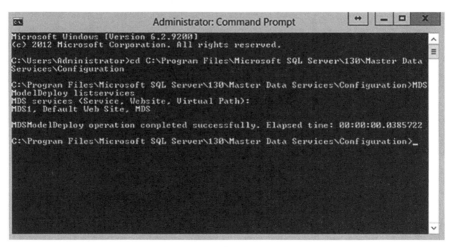

FIGURE 3-28 MDSModelDeploy listservices results

4. Type the commands below in the Command Prompt window to deploy each of the sample packages to the MDS1 instance as follows:

   chartofaccounts_en.pkg

   ```
   MDSModelDeploy deploynew -package "C:\Program Files\Microsoft SQL
   Server\130\Master Data Services\Samples\Packages\chartofaccounts_en.pkg" -model
   ChartofAccounts -service MDS1
   ```

   customer_en.pkg

   ```
   MDSModelDeploy deploynew -package "C:\Program Files\Microsoft SQL
   Server\130\Master Data Services\Samples\Packages\customer_en.pkg" -model Customer
   -service MDS1
   ```

   product_en.pkg

   ```
   MDSModelDeploy deploynew -package "C:\Program Files\Microsoft SQL
   Server\130\Master Data Services\Samples\Packages\product_en.pkg" -model Product
   -service MDS1
   ```

5. Type **exit** to close the Command Prompt window.

   Now that the sample packages have been deployed you can explore them in the MDS web application. If the sample package models are not listed in the Model drop-down list, click on the "Refresh cached information" link on the bottom-left corner of the MDS web application home page. You may need to download and install the Silverlight plug-in to explore the data in the sample packages.

Notice that in the commands we above we specified `deploynew` for our deployment option. The `deploynew` option creates a new model with the name specified after the `-model` switch. The other two options to deploy packages include `deployclone` and `deployupdate`. Table 3-11 lists and describes each deployment option.

TABLE 3-11 The deployment options

Deployment Option	Description
deploynew	Creates a new model with a unique identifier. Updates to the model objects and data is not possible using model deployment tools.
deployclone	Creates a new model with the same unique identifiers as the original model in the package. Updates to model objects and data is possible using model deployment tools.
deployupdate	Updates an existing model that was previously cloned with the contents of the model in the package.

Use the Master Data Services web application

The Master Data Services web application, also known as the Master Data Manager, allows users to perform both administrative and data tasks. The MDS web application has several functional areas that can be restricted to specific users and groups. By default, the MDS Administrator account, also known as the Super User account, has access to all functional areas of the Master Data Services web application.

The functional areas of the MDS web application are listed and described in Table 3-12.

TABLE 3-12 Functional MDS web app areas

Task Type	Functional Area	Description
Data Tasks		
	Explorer	View and edit master data and hierarchy relationships.
	Install MDS in Excel	Link to download the MDS Add-in for Excel.
Administrative Tasks		
	System Administration	Build the model structure, create a business rules, and deploy model packages.
	Integration Management	Import data into MDS and create SQL views for use by subscriptions systems.
	Version Management	Create versions of master data.
	User and Group Permissions	Assign permissions to master data.

Use the Master Data Services Add-in for Excel

The Master Data Services add-in for Excel allows users (data stewards) to add, update and delete master data stored in a Master Data Services model within Excel. It also allows model administrators to create, edit and delete entities and attributes.

The Master Data Services Add-in for Excel can be downloaded at: *https://www.microsoft.com/en-us/download/details.aspx?id=54269*. As part of its requirements, Visual Studio 2010 Tools for Office Runtime may need to be downloaded and installed from *https://www.microsoft.com/en-us/download/details.aspx?id=48217* as well.

Once you successfully install the Master Data Services add-in for Excel, a new toolbar named Master Data will display in the Excel ribbon as show in Figure 3-29.

FIGURE 3-29 Master Data Services Add-in for Excel

To use the MDS Add-in for Excel, first create a connection to the Master Data Services instance by following these steps:

1. Click on the Connect icon in the Master Data toolbar to open the Manage Connections window.

2. Click on Create New Connection or on the New button.

3. Type a Description of the MDS instance. For example: MDS1 Dev.

4. Type the MDS server address. For example: *http://localhost/MDS*.

   Click Test to verify the connection as shown in Figure 3-30.

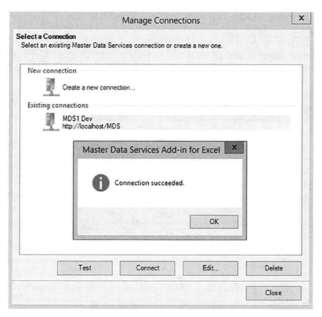

FIGURE 3-30 MDS Add-in for Excel connection test

5. Click Connect. The Master Data Explorer pane opens.

6. Click on the Model drop-down list to select one of the sample models deployed previously. For example: Customer.

7. Double-click on one of the entities in the Entity list section. For example: Customer. The Customer entity master data displays on the worksheet section.

Adding new records using the MDS Add-in for Excel

To add a new record to the Customer entity using the MDS Add-in for Excel follow these steps:

1. Navigate to the first empty row and click on the first cell to start editing. The first cell of the row will correspond to the Name attribute of the Customer entity.

2. Type **XYZ Bike Store** for the Name attribute and then press TAB. Notice that after you edit the cell's content the entire row changes color to indicate that a new row is being added to the entity.

3. Type **999** for the Code attribute and then press TAB.

4. Type **123 Main Street** for the AddressLine1 attribute and then press TAB until you reach the Country attribute.

5. Click on the drop-down arrow and select US {United States} from the drop-down list for the Country attribute.

6. Press Shift-TAB or click the cell for StateProvince. Click on the drop-down arrow and select FL {Florida} from the drop-down list.

7. Click on the Publish icon in the Master Data toolbar to upload the new record to MDS. The Publish and Annotate window opens.

8. Type a brief description of the changes performed and click Publish as shown in Figure 3-31.

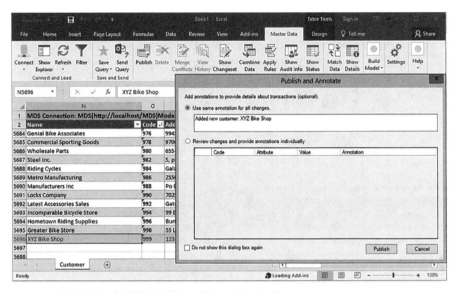

FIGURE 3-31 MDS Excel Add-in Publish and Annotate window.

The new customer record has now been published to the MDS instance. You can confirm that the record has been published successfully by clicking on the Refresh button on the Excel ribbon. You can also view the record in the MDS web application by selecting the Customer model and opening data explorer to view the Customer entity records.

Combining data using the MDS add-in for Excel

Entity data in MDS can be combined from an existing Excel worksheet using the Combine Data menu option in the Master Data Tab. To combine data using the MDS add-in for Excel follow these steps:

1. Open Excel and click on the Master Data tab.

2. Click on the Connect menu option and select the MDS instance to connect to.

3. On the Master Data Explorer window select the Suppliers model, then double-click on the Suppliers entity.

4. Click on the Combine Data menu option.

5. On the Combine Data window, select the cell range from the worksheet where the new data to appended is located. Include the headers in the cell range.

6. Map the header names to the corresponding Suppliers entity attributes as shown in Figure 3-32.

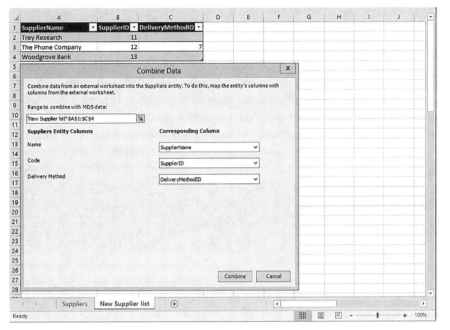

FIGURE 3-32 MDS Excel Add-in Combine Data window

7. Click Combine, then click on the Publish menu option of the Master Data tab.

Deleting master data using the MDS add-in for Excel

The MDS add-in for Excel provides a quick and straightforward way to delete master data. To delete one or more members from an entity, follow these steps:

1. Open Excel and click on the Master Data tab.

2. Click on the Connect menu option and select the MDS instance to connect to.

3. On the Master Data Explorer window select the Suppliers model, then double-click on the Suppliers entity.

4. Select the rows you want to delete, then click on the Delete menu option in the Master Data tab.

5. Click Yes on the row deletion confirmation dialog box.

Create a Master Data Management hub

Master Data Services can be implemented as part of any MDM solution. Most common MDM solution architectures follow the hub and spoke pattern, commonly referred to as a data hub. In a data hub, data flows in to a centralized location from one or more sources and data flows out to one or more destinations. This type of architecture provides a complete, consolidated and synchronized view of the organization's master data.

The two most common implementation approaches of a Master Data Management hub architecture are the *Repository* and *Registry* approach. In a Repository approach, the master data hub serves both as the System of Entry (SOE) and System of Record (SOR). New master data is created and stored in the master data hub and then published for other applications to consume. In this approach, when customer information is needed in an order entry application for example, the order entry application sends a customer lookup request to the master data hub. If the customer exists, the master data hub sends back the requested information to the order entry application. If the customer does not exist, a process will be triggered to create a new customer record and synchronized between the master data hub and the order entry application.

In the Registry approach, also known as the Centralized approach, a master customer entity is maintained in the master data hub and published for other applications to consume. In some cases, line of business applications is modified to use master data tables directly. The advantages of using the master data hub tables directly include avoiding duplication of data and conflicts arising from data synchronization.

In the Registry approach, also known as the Federated approach, the line of business applications create and store their own records. The master data hub is used to store relationships between the records of the line of business applications. These relationships are then used by line of business applications as lookups for data stored in other applications.

In this approach, the order entry system from our previous example would create and maintain its own customer information. The customer information will then be pushed or pulled into the master data hub along with customer data from other line of business applications such as a Customer Relationship Management (CRM) application. As part of the MDM solution, these customer records are then being matched and entities are created in the master data hub that serve as a crosswalk between the various sources. Only the key columns needed to uniquely identify a customer record such as the customer ID, GUID, or Code are stored in these relationship entities.

In some MDM implementations, a third Hybrid approach is used. In this approach, just like the Registry approach, master records are created and maintained in the line of business applications and the master data hub keeps the key relationships between the source systems. In addition, in the Hybrid approach, the master data hub replicates additional non-key attributes that are commonly used by other applications.

An example where a Hybrid approach is particularly useful is for maintaining customer billing information. In many cases, people and businesses use alias names that do not match their legal or trade name. For example, an order entry application may capture the name of a business as Contoso, Ltd., while a CRM application may have captured it as Contoso of Seattle. Matching and survivorship rules in the master data hub, may store the correct legal name as Contoso, Ltd. The correct legal name can now be used by other applications when referencing the same customer.

In addition to an architectural approach, there are several other considerations when implementing a Master Data Management hub. Some of these considerations include:

- Data Integration
- Hierarchical relationships
- Data Quality
- Data Synchronization
- Metadata
- Data Stewardship and Governance

Data integration is the process through which data from multiple data sources are extracted and loaded into a combined data model in the master data hub. Data integration often involves transforming the data and applying additional rules to match and relate data from often heterogeneous sources into more homogeneous structures.

A key feature in a Master Data Management hub is the ability to represent the data in hierarchical fashion. These hierarchies are either a physical or logical representation of the relationships in the data itself. For example, customers can be represented in a geography hierarchy based on their home address zip code, city and country. At the same time, customers can be represented in a hierarchy based on customer attributes such as gender, race or income ranges.

The quality of the data plays one of the most crucial factors in the success of any data-driven solution. The Master Data Management hub is the perfect opportunity to validate, cleanse, standardize, complete and match master data. Historically, line of business applications has been developed with one primary goal, to capture transactions as fast and efficient as possible. This means that they often require minimal data to process a transaction with loose data validation rules. For example, a customer may be entered using the alias of Bob with no zip code for his home address. In the Master Data Management hub, business rules can be created and triggered to modify common alias names such as Bob to the proper name form Robert. In addition, incomplete addresses can be geocoded to fill in missing pieces of information such as the corresponding zip code.

Synchronizing data across multiple systems can be a challenge in large organizations with large volumes of data and heterogeneous line of business applications. Replicating changes to the master data between these applications may not be a simple task and may require complex processes to handle errors and conflicts with the data.

An effective Master Data Management hub should provide information about the data, also known as metadata. Metadata is more than a data dictionary which provides valuable information about data types and how data is structured. An effective metadata framework provides information about the what, how, where and when of the data. It should provide a description of the data sources, destinations, timeliness of the data, what transformations and other business rules are applied to the source data, how is data filtered, completed and validated.

Automation of the processes that handle the integration, quality and synchronization of the data can be achieved to a certain degree of success. In most cases, a Master Data Management hub needs to be constantly reviewed and corrected by the subject matter experts that know and understand the data. Constant evaluation of the business rules applied to the data is necessary to ensure continuous and consistent data quality. Data stewards are essential to the process of good master data management practices.

Thought exercise

In this thought exercise, demonstrate your skills and knowledge of the topics covered in this chapter. You can find the answer to this thought experiment in the next section.

The World Wide Importers company wants to establish a process in which loan officers are alerted of any credit line amount changes to their customers records to review and approve or reject such changes. What solution can be put in place to satisfy this requirement?

Thought exercise answer

This section provides the solution for the thought experiment.

An MDS business rule can easily support this requirement by triggering a workflow. The workflow can be configured to email one or more loan officers and require approval of the attribute change. Once the change has been approved by a loan officer the change will be applied. If the change is rejected, the change will be reverted to its original value.

The business rule can be created on a column in the Customer record called CreditLimit. The business rule would look as follows: **If** CreditLimit has changed **Then** start workflow

Chapter summary

- Step-by-step instructions were provided to install and configure Data Quality Services, create a Data Quality Knowledge Base, a domain based on the WWI Supplier table along with matching and cleansing operations with DQS.

- Incorrect or "bad" data is often a symptom of weak or lack of data validation rules during data entry or simply because of data integration processes and data corruption and that the main use cases for a DQS Knowledge Base involves the need to create, maintain and execute data quality operations resulting from data incompleteness, inconsistency, inaccuracy, invalidity, duplication and non-conformity

- Step-by-step instructions were provided to install and configure Master Data Services, how to create a model, entity, attribute, hierarchy and subscription view.

- Master data and functional areas are secured in MDS and the different administrator types.

- Master data can be maintained using the MDS Excel add-in and the Master Data Manager.

- Data can be imported using the staging tables and stored procedures created for each entity.

Index

A

additive measures 21
administrative tasks 237
administrator role types 237
Advanced Editor 180–181
alternate key columns 5, 6
asynchronous transforms 140–143
attributes
    business rules for 244–245
    changing 127
    changing values of 10–11
    columns 5–7
    creating 235–237
    dimension tables, determining 2–4
    fixed 127
    grouping related 4
    implementing 243
auditing 16–17
audit logging 160
Audit transform 137–139

B

backup files 46, 47
Balanced Tree (B-Tree) structure 25
blocking transforms 140
breakpoints 171–174
built-in connectors 79
business rules 244–246, 256

C

cache limitations 145
calendar hierarchy 8
CDC. *See* Change Data Capture

Centralized approach 254
Change Data Capture (CDC) 83, 146, 147–148
    components of 155–156
    control task 155–156
    in SSIS 155–159
    source 156–158
    splitter 158–159
    Transact-SQL 151–155
changing attributes 127–128
CHECK constraint 55
checkpoints 109
CLR. *See* Common Language Runtime (CLR)
clustered indexes 40, 146
    columnstore 38–39, 40
    converting rowstore to columnstore 38
    implementing 36–38
    rowstore 25, 28–30
columns
    dimension 5–7
    in fact tables 19
    mapping 143–144, 181–183
    partition 48
    truncation 180–181
columnstore indexes 25–28, 33
    clustered 38–39, 40
composite domains 211–212
composite keys
    creating 19–20
    primary 6
concurrent users 42–43
confirmed dimensions 7
Connection Manager 90–93, 160, 167–168, 189–190
connectivity 167–168
connectors
    built-in 79

Q

R

S

About the authors

 JOSE CHINCHILLA is Microsoft Certified Professional with dual MCITP certifications on SQL Server Database Administration and Business Intelligence Development. His career focus for the last 15+ years has been in Database Modeling, Data Warehouse and ETL Architecture, OLAP Cube Analysis, Master Data Management, Data Quality Frameworks and Big Data solutions. Jose has extensive experience in the architecture, development and implementation of both on-premise and Microsoft Azure cloud based Data Analytics solutions in several Fortune 500 companies. Jose has spoken at national and regional technical conferences such as PASS Summit, SQL Saturday, 24 Hours of PASS and other events such as Code Camps. He is the founder and CEO of Agile Bay, Inc and serves as President of the Tampa Bay Business Analytics User Group. Jose enjoys boating with his family and working on classic muscle cars.

 RAJ UCHHANA is an enterprise data architect specializing in business intelligence, enterprise data warehousing, and Microsoft's Power BI. He's also an author, innovator and entrepreneur with more than 25 years of experience. He has also worked on Massively Parallel Processing (MPP) systems such as Analytics Platform System (formerly Parallel Data Warehouse), on which he built a 50TB data warehouse using hybrid and Kimball methodologies. Raj can be reached at Raj@BusinessIntelligenceNow.com or at *http://BusinessIntelligenceNow.com*.

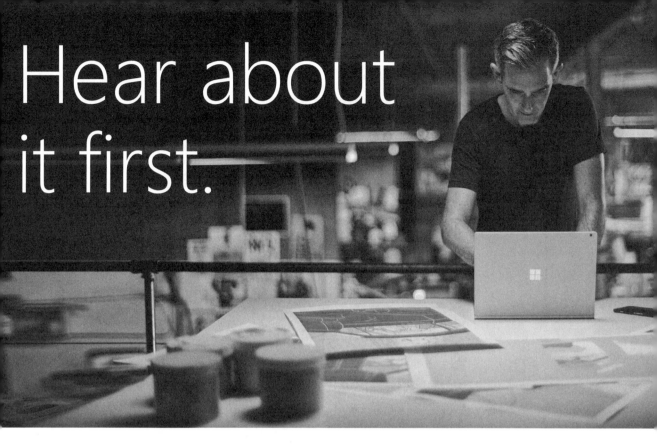

Hear about it first.

Get the latest news from Microsoft Press sent to your inbox.

- New and upcoming books
- Special offers
- Free eBooks
- How-to articles

Sign up today at MicrosoftPressStore.com/Newsletters

 Microsoft

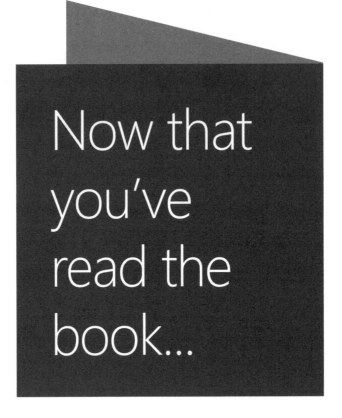

Now that you've read the book...

Tell us what you think!

Was it useful?
Did it teach you what you wanted to learn?
Was there room for improvement?

Let us know at https://aka.ms/tellpress

Your feedback goes directly to the staff at Microsoft Press,
and we read every one of your responses. Thanks in advance!